CURRICULUM LEADERSHIP
RETHINKING SCHOOLS FOR THE 21ST CENTURY

Edited by

Regis Bernhardt
Carolyn N. Hedley
Gerald Cattaro
Vasilios Svolopoulos

Fordham University

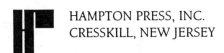

HAMPTON PRESS, INC.
CRESSKILL, NEW JERSEY

Printed in the United States of America

Library of Congress Cataloging-in-Publication Data

Curriculum leadership : rethinking schools for the 21st century /
    edited by Regis Bernhardt ... [et al.].
      p. cm.
    Includes bibliographic references and indexes.
    ISBN 1-57273-149-9 (cloth). -- ISBN 1-57273-150-8 (pbk.)
    1. Curriculum planning--United States. 2. Teacher participation
in curriculum planning--United States. 3. Constructivism
(Education)--United States. I. Bernhardt, Regis.
    LB2806.15.C862 1998
    375'.001--dc21   97-52261
                                             CIP

Hampton Press, Inc.
23 Broadway
Cresskill, NJ 07626

CONTENTS

CONTRIBUTORS

PATRICIA ANTONACCI is a professor at Fordham University Graduate School of Education. Formerly, she was a reading specialist in Yonkers Public Schools. She has edited many books, including *Home and School: Early Reading and Writing* and *Thinking and Literacy.*

REGIS BERNHARDT is Dean of the Fordham University Graduate School of Education. As a faculty member and dean of the school, he has worked to build partnerships with schools and to implement the concepts and practices of the Professional Development School.

CATHY COLLINS BLOCK, Professor, Texas Christian University has written extensively on teaching thinking and has a program out by that name. The program, *Teaching Thinking*, and her book with the same title have been used to conduct the research that she describes in her chapter. Her works include over 10 books in the area of teaching thinking. Additionally, she has edited several reading series.

THERESA BOLOGNA, a Professor at Fordham University Graduate School of Education, is Head of the Early Childhood Program in the Division of Curriculum and Teaching. Her research interests include concerns for the early detection of learning difficulties and concepts for inclusion for the early learner.

ANGELA CARRASQUILLO, Professor and Head of the Language, Literacy, and Learning Program at Fordham University, is currently Chair of the Division of Curriculum and Teaching. Dr. Carrasquillo has been President of ENLACE, past president of NYSABE, and a board member of NABE. She has authored many books, including *Teaching English to Speakers of Other Languages, Language Minority Students in the Majority Classroom,* and *Hispanic Children and Youth in the United States.*

GERALD CATTARO is Head of the Nonpublic Schools Program at Fordham University. He has been an effective Curriculum Leader as a principal and administrator of Catholic Schools in New York City.

CATHLEEN CAVANAUGH, Teaching Associate, Starpoint School, Texas Christian University, is a colleague who works closely with Dr. Cathy Collins Block on her research on teaching thinking. She teaches in the Teaching Thinking Program at Starpoint School.

TERRY CICCHELLI, Professor and Vice Chair of the Division of Curriculum and Teaching, has written in the areas of creative concepts of leadership and notions of inclusion. Currently, she is heading a grant for the Superintendent's Network for New York City Schools Administrators and Superintendents. Her publications include *Staying in School: School University Partnerships for Learning and Teaching* and *Exceptional Children in the Regular Classroom.*

LINDA DARLING-HAMMOND is Co-director of the National Center for Restructuring Education, Schools, and Teaching (NCREST) at Teachers College, Columbia University. She is a leader in the Professional Development Schools movement, fostering collaboration among the various learning communities of schools, communities, and universities. Her publications include *Professional Development Schools: Schools for Developing a Profession.*

DANIEL DUKE, Professor, University of Virginia, has been Chair of the Department of Educational Leadership and Policy Studies at the Curry School of Education. He is president of the Council for Education Administration and Director of the Thomas Jefferson Center for Educational Design and Planning. His publications include books on decision making and school policy, among which are *The Case for Commitment to Teacher Growth: Research on Teacher Evaluation* and *School Leadership and Instructional Improvement.*

BRUCE GANSNEDER is a professor in the Educational Leadership, Foundations, and Policy Department at the University of Virginia. His research projects include the Phi Delta Kappa Grant Award for *Teacher Involvement in School Decision-Making.*

ANNE GARGAN, currently a Professor at Fordham University, has been a principal and district director in the New York City Schools, where she was able to carry out collaborative approaches in the administration of schools. She is concerned with collaborative teaching and learning, higher order thinking, interdisciplinary instruction, and new models for cooperative supervision. She has been active in the development of a new program in school administration, the VIA program.

RITA GUARE is a professor at Fordham University, where she works in the recently restructured doctoral program in Administration, Policy, and Urban Education—the VIA program.

CAROLYN HEDLEY is Professor Emeritus at Fordham University Graduate School of Education. She currently teaches at the University of South Florida She has edited many books, the most recent of which is *Thinking and Literacy,* coedited with Pat Antonacci and Mitch Rabinowitz. She has run many institutes and conferences in curriculum leadership and in language, literacy, and learning.

THOMAS HOERR, Director of the New City School, St. Louis, for 15 years was one of the first school administrators to implement concepts developed by Harold Gardner using his theory of multiple intelligence. He is a prolific writer; with his teachers and staff, he has developed a book regarding the New City MI project, *Celebrating Multiple Intelligences: Teaching for Success*, and is currently working with Phi Delta Kappa on the books *Implementing Multiple Intelligences* and *Collegiality: A New Way to Define Instructional Leadership.*

WILLIAM PENUEL is with the Metropolitan Nashville Public Schools. He develops his research as part of his work in after-school and summer session workshops. The youth empowerment concepts he uses are developed from theory based on Vygotsky's and Bakhtin's work. He often co-authors with J. Wertsch; recently they published *Vygotsky and Identity Formation: Toward a Sociocultural Approach.*

BRIAN ROWAN is a professor and Dean of Research in the School of Education at the University of Michigan. He conducts research in educational administration and policy analysis. Prior to his tenure at the University of Michigan, he worked at the Far West Laboratory for Research and development. Recent titles of his work include *Institutional Study of Organizations* and *The Organizational Design of Schools.*

WILLIAM STEPIEN is the Director of the Center for Problem Based Learning, Illinois Mathematics and Science Academy in Aurora, Illinois, where he conducts research in problem-based learning using authentic real-world problems as the basis for curriculum development. His most recent work is titled *Problem Based Learning for Traditional and Interdisciplinary Classrooms*.

MARTHA STONE WISKE is Co-director of the Educational Technology Center, Harvard Graduate School of Education. She was active in the development of the national Professional Standards for Teaching Mathematics, spearheading the National Standards movement. Her latest publications include *How Teaching for Understanding Changes the Rules in the Classroom* and *How Teachers Are Implementing the NCTM Standards*.

BARRY ZIMMERMAN, Professor of Educational Psychology, Graduate School of the City University of New York, has long been an advocate of social learning theory. He has worked and done much of his writing with Albert Bandura. His recent work with D. H. Shunk includes *Self-regulation of Learning and Performance: Issues and Educational Applications*.

INTRODUCTION

━━━━━━━━━━━━━━━━━━━━━━━━━━━━━━━━━

Schools have always been concerned with performance: the performance of students in terms of achievement and the performance of teachers and administrators who bring about student learning. With the introduction of the Professional Development School at the university, performance demands combine with collegial interaction to benefit schools, communities, and universities alike. To quote a recent issue of *Educational Leadership*:

> Educators who wanted to reform assessment soon found themselves dealing with other aspects of schooling: record keeping, reporting, curriculum and instruction. They found what the basketball coach and the choir director knew all along: a performance orientation changes not only the way you assess learning, but the way you teach for it. . . . Some of the factors that brought attention to student performance led also to concern over the performance of educators. (Brandt, 1996, p. 3)

The implication of the development of a performance-based curriculum that fosters and depends on collegiality is that teachers and principals will have a great deal of control over the schooling that occurs; both are managers and instructional leaders. In collegial curriculum development, administrators, teachers, and students want to achieve at their respective levels of endeavor and to feel that they are part of a learning community. Learning must be positive, rich, coherent, and involving. Concerns of performance and achievement will probably bring about national standards, or at least standards set by the various national professional organizations. These standards must provide opportunities for learning for all students. Incentives for good program design, for educational innovation, and for effective curriculum implementation with clear designations for responsibility should be provided and rewarded. These programs most probably will be run by state and local government, but with oversight and some summative assessment provided through national goals and national assessment. These directions for curriculum leadership are among the concerns of this book.

In some ways, the university as a part of the professional development of the learning community has yet to find its way as a contributor to the rethinking of educational excellence. If the local schools and the unions are taking over a greater role with a greater mandate for teachers rethinking their practice, does the university take its cues from these forces and simply try to fit in? A thoughtful educator would say, "No!" Collaboration, dedication, and ingenuity are needed from the Professional Development School. A great deal of positive dialogue is already occurring in program development between schools and the university in such areas as assessment, ethnographic research, peer coaching and collaboration, field-based teacher preparation, reflective techniques, case studies of schooling, increased use of observation, development of technological literacy, performance-based standards, and performance-based assessment. We at the Fordham Graduate School of Education have been working on the kinds of programs and collaborative collegiality described here. We decided to address these concerns in a focused way by conducting an institute where we brought experts, some from our own staff, in order to continue to rethink our role and relationship to communities and schools. The Institute on Curriculum Leadership: Rethinking Schools in the 21st Century was developed by the Division of Curriculum and Teaching and the Division of Administration, Policy, and Urban Education (a unique collaboration in itself). We invited experts and gave each one a topic to present and collaborate with over 100 participants; following their contribution, each speaker/mediator agreed to write a chapter for this work.

The invited curriculum leaders spoke within their topical area to such issues as educational excellence, student achievement and performance, advances in assessment, knowledge bases and procedures for implementing a constructivist and collaborative curriculum, classroom climates for learning, delivery systems and methods for learning, conceptual development across the disciplines, and the use of technology. Dimensions of multiculturalism, inclusion, justice, and fair play were regarded as curriculum concerns. Models and methods for learning were part of the applicational presentation of each of the contributors. From these presentations, this book was created.

The one exception regarding our criteria for including chapters from conference presenters was Chapter 1 contributed by Linda Darling-Hammond. Her work on rethinking teacher development targeted the major themes of the book—changing educational policies, school regulations, and management structures. It follows that there must be much more intensive training of teachers for developing "a reflective problem-solving orientation by engaging them in teacher research and inquiry" (Darling-Hammond, Chapter 1). Darling-Hammond endorses the Professional Development School, with structures for collaborative inquiry and standard setting providing an overview of what is to come in this volume.

Part I: Policies for Collaborative Leadership of Constructivist Curricula begins with Linda Darling-Hammond's chapter on teacher education. Not only is the teacher expected to know curriculum content, he or she must understand the nature of cognition and learning. Dr. Darling-Hammond makes the case for increased and ongoing professional development to foster the advanced knowledge now expected of teachers. She supports stiffer initial teacher education programs, advocating teacher networks, enriched professional roles, and collaborative working conditions. In Chapter 2, her concerns are operationalized by Anne Gargan and Rita Guare with their description of innovative administrative programs for teacher leaders. A model doctoral program for teacher leaders, the VIA program, is presented as an example of how to be integrative and collaborative in positions of leadership. In Chapter 3, Brian Rowan reports his research on the task characteristics of teaching. According to him, the majority of teachers in his study view teaching as routine, much like a salesperson or a clerk. This standardized view of the school and the hierarchical view of learning seemingly shared by many teachers has implications for the school structuring and the professionalism movement. He asks whether teachers are willing to commit themselves to a greater professionalism. Pat Antonacci and Regis Bernhardt present a positive case study of one school involved in the transition to greater professionalism. Their view of how change occurs in education gives a more heartening perspective of what can happen in real-world schools.

Catholic schools are being looked at as a befitting model of good schooling for nonachieving students. Dr. Jerry Cattaro, who has worked consistently in Catholic, nonpublic school settings, makes the case for an organizational structure in schools that is capable of delivering change primarily because it includes community in a more complete and systematic way than many public schools. In another study of collaborative involvement, Dan Duke and Bruce Gansneder find that staff development occurs best when individual teachers monitor specific nonachieving students and provide task-specific assistance to targeted students. Their study reports stunning results when this method of staff development is applied to at-risk students. Part I culminates with performance concerns. Stone Wiske presents a first attempt at developing national standards by a professional organization—the National Council of Teachers of Mathematics (NCTM)—in one discipline, mathematics. She not only endorses the notion of national standards, a worry for some educators, but demonstrates how helpful national standards can be if they promote goals that are consonant with those in the most enlightened and successful schools. She advocates constructions for understanding for students; greater development of teachers' knowledge; transformation of students' knowledge, skills, and dispositions; alterations in curriculum materials and policies; the use of technology; better assessment techniques, and changes in learning organizations.

Part II: Theoretical Perspectives for Collaborative, Constructivist Curricula provides theory from several areas: social learning theory as developed by Barry Zimmerman and Albert Bandura and the constructivist theories of Lev Vygotsky and Mikhail Bakhtin. The theories of these thinkers seem to complement one another as they were presented here. Barry Zimmerman's chapter on the acquisition of student self-regulatory skills, so clearly tied to achievement and performance, is the opening work in Part II. Techniques and models for self-regulation, including goal setting and strategic planning, are provided. The results of research using these models and techniques have shown them to be highly promising in achieving higher student performance. Bill Penuel examines the sociocultural concepts of Vygotsky and Bakhtin regarding speech and identity in a youth empowerment, peer-leader program. He examines the three basic themes of Vygotsky: "the use of genetic analysis to study individual functioning, the claim that individual mental functioning has sociocultural origins; and the claim that human action is mediated by cultural tools and signs" (Penuel, Chapter 9).

Angela Carrasquillo examines the community of linguistically and culturally diverse students, using demographics from census data. She examines issues of achievement, poverty, violence, conflicts among cultural values, language differences, and their impact. She develops roles for leaders of this diverse community and suggests a curriculum for a diverse community that must be developed in collaboration with that community. Consonant with these concerns, Terri Bologna presents the challenges of curriculum planning for inclusion with the needs of the young learner particularly addressed. She is cautious about the way inclusion should occur. Terry Cicchelli fosters the notion of inclusion by a rigorous plan for staff development, so that administrators, teacher leaders, teachers, and students alike feel comfortable with new schemes for inclusion in an era of decreased resources for education.

Part III: Contexts and Strategies for Learning—The How To for Constructivist Curricula begins with a provocative chapter on teaching thinking by Cathy Collins Block and Cathleen Cavanaugh and offers a program that is flexible and palatable for doing just that—promoting higher level thought across the curriculum through techniques that are portable and researchable. She reports on her research that indicates teaching thinking increases the learner's thinking repertoires, helps students gain greater control over their lives, and enables them to meet challenges more effectively.

In a closely related area, Tom Hoerr, Director of the New City School in St. Louis, implemented Howard Gardner's theories of multiple intelligences (MI) as the most suitable philosophy for his school. After thoroughly developing Gardner's theory, Hoerr states that it is a theory of intelligence, not an educational theory, and therefore can be interpreted variously by educators. He describes the fascinating journey and the dynamics that he and his teachers, staff, and students went through to arrive at an implementation of Gardner's work. Implementing theories of multiple intelligence must necessarily be an ongoing, reflective process.

On the same day that Hoerr presented his work, Bill Stepien spoke about authentic real-world, problem-based learning. The mesh of these two men's work was remarkable. Stepien described how to design problem-based learning units. Beginning with an ill-structured problem, he suggests ways for meeting or defining the problem, conducting inquiry and investigation, building solutions, and debriefing the unit. He defines and develops problem-based concepts using examples from his research for each of the phases that occur, making apprenticeship-like replication possible.

We hope the dialogue regarding curriculum leadership is enhanced by this work. Other books may be found that deal with the concerns of these chapters as separate topics, but this volume unifies much of the current thinking in curriculum leadership and development. The themes of the book form a coherent and consistent view for managing resources in education, a project we hope to accomplish as a School of Education for our own direction and development. In accomplishing the task of setting our own themes, goals, and priorities for the educational enterprise, we are fostering the continued dialogue regarding schooling and excellence.

REFERENCE

Brandt, M. (1996). Coaching and collegiality. *Educational Leadership*, 53(6), 3.

PART

I

POLICIES FOR COLLABORATIVE LEADERSHIP OF CONSTRUCTIVIST CURRICULA

1 THE QUIET REVOLUTION: RETHINKING TEACHER DEVELOPMENT*

Linda Darling-Hammond

La Trobe University, Bendigo

Reforms that invest time in teacher learning and give teachers greater autonomy are our best hope for improving America's schools. (Darling-Hammond, 1996, p. 4)

Over the last decade, a quiet revolution in teaching has been underway. The profession has begun to engage in a serious standard setting that reflects a growing knowledge base and consensus about what teachers should know and be able to do to help students learn according to challenging new standards. Most states have launched efforts to restructure schools and to invest in greater teacher knowledge.

Changes are also taking place in teacher preparation programs across the country; performance-based approaches to licensing and accreditation are being reconsidered, and a new National Board for Professional Teaching Standards has created assessments for certifying accomplished teachers. School districts and grassroots networks are creating partnerships to support teacher development and to rethink schools.

*This chapter originally appeared as: Darling-Hammond, L. (March 1996). The Quiet Revolution: Rethinking Teacher Development. *Educational Leadership, 53*(6), 4-10. Reprinted with permission.

These initiatives are partly a response to major changes affecting our society and schools. Because rapid social and economic transformations require greater learning from all students, society is reshaping the mission of education. Schools are now expected not only to offer education, but to ensure learning. Teachers are expected not only to "cover the curriculum," but to create a bridge between the needs of each learner and the attainment of challenging learning goals.

These objectives—a radical departure from education's mission during the past century—demand that teachers understand learners and their learning as deeply as they comprehend their subjects, and that schools structure themselves to support deeper forms of student and teacher learning than they currently permit. The invention of 21st-century schools that can educate all children well rests, first and foremost, on the development of a highly qualified and committed teaching force.

As recently as 10 years ago, the idea that teacher knowledge was critical for educational improvement had little currency. Continuing a tradition begun at the turn of the 20th century, policymakers searched for the right set of test prescriptions, textbook adoptions, and curriculum directives to be packaged and mandated to guide practice. Educational reform was "teacher proofed" with hundreds of pieces of legislation and thousands of discrete regulations prescribing what educators should do.

More recent efforts differ from past strategies that did not consider how ideas would make it from the statehouse to the schoolhouse. New initiatives are investing in the front lines of education. Policymakers increasingly realize that regulations cannot transform schools; only teachers, in collaboration with parents and administrators, can do that.

Indeed, solutions to all the problems that educational critics cite are constrained by the availability of knowledgeable, skillful teachers and school conditions that define how that knowledge can be used. Raising graduation requirements in mathematics, science, and foreign language, for example, is of little use if there are not enough teachers prepared to teach those subjects well. Concerns about at-risk children cannot be addressed without teachers prepared to meet the diverse needs of students with varying learning styles, family situations, and beliefs about what school means for them.

In policy terms, betting on teaching as a key strategy for reform means investing in stronger preparation and professional development while granting teachers greater autonomy. It also means spending more on teacher development and less on bureaucracies and special programs created to address the problems created by poor teaching. Finally, we must put greater knowledge directly in the hands of teachers and seek accountability that will focus attention on "doing the right things" rather than on "doing things right." Such reforms demand changes in much existing educational policy, current school regulations, and in management structures.

POSSIBILITIES FOR TRANSFORMING TEACHING

Several current efforts hold great promise to transform teaching: redesigning initial teacher preparation, rethinking professional development, and involving teachers in research, collaborative inquiry, and standard setting in the profession. Given the fact that fully half of the teachers who will be teaching in the year 2005 will be hired over the next decade (and large-scale hiring will continue into the decade thereafter), this is a critical time to transform the quality of teacher preparation.

New Ideas About Teacher Preparation

Over the past decade, many schools of education have made great strides in incorporating new understandings of teaching and learning into their programs for prospective teachers. More attention to learning and cognition has accompanied a deepening appreciation for content pedagogy and constructivist teaching. In addition, teacher preparation and induction programs are increasingly helping prospective teachers and interns develop a reflective, problem-solving orientation by engaging them in teacher research, school-based inquiry, and inquiry into students' experiences. These approaches help teachers build an empirical understanding of learners and a capacity to analyze what occurs in their classrooms and in the lives of their students.

Efforts to develop teachers as managers of their own inquiry stand in contrast to earlier assumptions of teachers and about teaching generally: Beginning teachers need to focus only on the most rudimentary tasks of teaching with basic precepts and cookbook rules to guide them, and more seasoned teachers should be the recipients, not the generators, of knowledge. Teacher preparation is now seeking to empower teachers to use and develop knowledge about teaching and learning as sophisticated and powerful as the demands of their work require.

Professional Development Schools

A growing number of education schools are working with school systems to create professional development schools that will prepare teachers for what schools must become, not only for schools as they are. Too often there is a disparity between the conceptions of good practice that beginning teachers are taught and those they encounter when they begin teaching.

Professional development schools, which now number several hundred across the country, prepare beginning teachers in settings that support state-of-the-art practice and provide needed coaching and collaboration. Where districts and schools of education are creating professional development school partnerships, they are finding ways to marry state-of-the-art practice for students and state-of-the-art preparation and induction for teachers (Darling-Hammond, 1994).

Teacher education reformers are beginning to recognize that prospective teachers, like their students, learn by doing. As teacher educators, beginning teachers, and experienced teachers work together on real problems of practice in learner-centered settings, they can begin to develop a collective knowledge base and a common set of understandings about practice.

Collaborative Inquiry and Standard Setting

In addition to these reforms, important initiatives are underway to develop more meaningful standards for teaching, including performance-based standards for teacher licensing; more sophisticated and authentic assessments for teachers; and national standards for teacher education, licensing, and certification. These national efforts are being led by the National Board for Professional Teaching Standards (NBPTS), Interstate New Teacher Assessment and Support Consortium (INTASC), and National Council for Accreditation of Teacher Education (NCATE).

The new standards and assessments take into explicit account the multicultural, multilingual nature of a student body that possesses multiple intelligences and approaches to learning. The standards reflect the view of teaching as collegial work and as an intellectual activity. In many restructuring schools and schools of education, prospective, new, and veteran teachers are conducting school-based inquiry, evaluating programs, and studying their own practices—with one another and with university-based colleagues.

In many restructured schools, teachers are developing local standards, curriculum, and authentic student assessment. Those who develop assessments of their own teaching—for example, through the certification process of the National Board for Professional Teaching Standards—also discover that careful reflection about standards of practice stimulates an ongoing learning process.

ISSUES IN TEACHER PREPARATION

If we are to sustain these promising new initiatives, however, we must confront deeply entrenched barriers. As an occupation, teaching has historically been underpaid and micromanaged, with few investments in teachers' learning and few supports for teachers' work. By contrast, European and Asian countries hire a greater number of teachers who are better prepared, better paid, better supported, and vested with more decision-making responsibility. The conditions that enable these countries to provide much greater time and learning opportunity for teachers suggest that rethinking school staffing and scheduling must go hand in hand with redesigning teacher development.

Compared to the standards of other professions and of teacher preparation and other countries, United States teacher education has been thin, uneven in quality, and underresourced. Although a growing number of teachers participate in rigorous courses of study, including intensive internships (increasingly, five- or six-year programs), many still attend underfunded, undergraduate programs that their universities treat as "cash cows." These programs, typically less well funded than any other department or professional school on campus, produce greater revenues for educating future businessmen, lawyers, and accountants than they spend on educating the future teachers they serve (Ebmeier, Twombly, & Teeter, 1990; Sykes, 1985).

In addition to the tradition of emergency certification that continues in more than 40 states, some newly launched alternative certification programs provide only a few weeks of training for entering teachers, skipping such fundamentals as learning theory, child development, and subject matter pedagogy, and placing recruits in classrooms without previous supervised experience. Each year about 20,000 individuals enter teaching without a license, whereas another 30,000 enter with substandard credentials.

In addition to a lack of support for beginning teacher preparation, districts spend less than one half of 1% of their resources on staff development. Most corporations and schools in other countries spend many times that amount. Staff development in the United States is still characterized by one-shot workshops rather than more effective, problem-based approaches that are built into teachers' ongoing work with colleagues. As a result, most teachers have few opportunities to enhance their knowledge and skills over the course of their careers. The lack of investment in teacher knowledge is a function of the factory model approach to schooling adopted nearly a century ago, which invested in an administrative bureaucracy to design, monitor, and inspect teaching, rather than in the knowledge of the people doing the work. As a consequence, preservice and inservice investments in teacher knowledge have been quite small compared to those in many other countries.

In contrast to the traditions of U.S. education, teachers in these countries make virtually all decisions about curriculum, teaching, and assessment because of the greater preparation and inservice support they receive. They are almost never hired without full preparation, a practice enabled by subsidies that underwrite teacher preparation and by salaries that are comparable to those in other professions.

In former West Germany, for example, prospective teachers earn the equivalent of two academic majors in separate disciplines prior to undertaking two additional years of rigorous teacher preparation at the graduate level. This training combines pedagogical seminars with classroom-based observation and intensively supervised practice teaching (Burns et al., 1991; Kolstad, Coker, & Edelhoff, 1989; OECD, 1990).

Preparation in Luxembourg, a seven-year process, extends beyond the baccalaureate degree to professional training that blends pedagogical learning with extensive supervised practice teaching (OECD, 1990).

In France, new models of teacher education send candidates through two years of graduate teacher education, including an intensively supervised year-long internship in schools.

Most European and Asian countries are extending both their preservice education requirements and inservice learning opportunities for teachers (OECD, 1990). Five-year programs of teacher preparation and intensive internships are becoming the norm around the world (Darling-Hammond & Cobb, 1995).

Beginning teachers in Japan receive at least 20 days of inservice training during their first year on the job, plus 60 days of professional development. Master teachers are released from their own classrooms to advise and counsel them (OECD, 1990; Stigler & Stevenson, 1991).

In Taiwan, candidates pursue a four-year undergraduate degree, which includes extensive courses on child learning, development, and pedagogy, prior to a full-year teaching practicum in a carefully selected and supervised setting.

After their preparation as apprentices, beginning teachers in the People's Republic of China work with a reduced teaching load, observing other teachers and preparing under the supervision of master teachers. They work in teaching teams to plan lessons and conduct peer observations (Paine, 1990). Schools in China provide ongoing support for collegial learning.

In most of these European, and many Asian, countries, teachers spend between 15 and 20 hours per week in their classrooms and the remaining time with colleagues developing lessons, visiting parents, counseling students, pursuing research, attending study groups and seminars, and visiting other schools.

By contrast, most U.S. elementary teachers have three or fewer hours for preparation per week (only eight minutes for every hour in the classroom), whereas secondary teachers generally have five preparation periods per week (13 minutes for every hour of classroom instruction; NEA, 1992). In most U.S. schools, teachers are not expected to meet with other teachers, develop curriculum or assessments, or observe one another's classes—nor is time generally provided for these kinds of activities.

INVESTING IN TIME FOR TEACHER LEARNING

Other countries are able to afford these greater investments in teachers' knowledge and time for collaborative work because they hire fewer nonteaching staff and more teachers who assume a broader range of decision-making responsibilities.

In the United States, the number of teachers has declined to only 53% of public school staff, whereas the number of nonteaching specialists and other staff has increased (NCES, 1993). Furthermore, only about 75% of the teachers take primary responsibility for classrooms of children. The remainder work in pullout settings or perform nonteaching duties. A system in which lots of staff work outside the classroom to direct and augment the work of teachers unintentionally increases the need for greater coordination, raises class sizes, and reduces time for classroom teachers to collaborate.

Although fewer than half of all public education employees in the United States work primarily as classroom teachers, classroom teaching staff comprise more than three fourths of all public education employees in Australia and Japan, and more than 80% in Belgium, Germany, the Netherlands, and Spain (OECD, 1992). These hiring patterns give a greater number of teachers per student more time each week for professional development activities, studies with colleagues, and meetings with parents and individual students. In their study of mathematics teaching and learning in Japan, Taiwan, and the United States, Stigler and Stevenson (1991) noted that one reason

> Asian class lessons are so well crafted is that there is a very systematic effort to pass on the accumulated wisdom of teaching practice to each new generation of teachers and to keep perfecting that practice by providing teachers the opportunities to continually learn from one another. (pp. 12-47)

In addition, teaching in most other countries is not as bureaucratically organized as it is in the United States. It is not uncommon, for example, in Germany, Japan, Switzerland, and Sweden, for teachers to teach multiple subjects, counsel students, and teach the same students for multiple years (OECD, 1990; Shimahara, 1985). When similar arrangements for personalizing teacher–student relationships have been tried in the United States, student achievement is significantly higher because teachers know their students better both academically and personally (Gottfredson & Daiger, 1979; NIE, 1977).

Professionalizing teaching may call for rethinking school structures and roles and reallocating educational dollars. If teachers assume many instructional tasks currently performed by others (e.g., curriculum development and supervision), the layers of bureaucratic hierarchy will be reduced. If teachers have opportunities for collaborative inquiry and learning, the vast wisdom of practice developed by excellent teachers will be shared across the profession. If teachers are more carefully selected and better trained and supported, expenditures for management systems to control incompetence will decrease. Furthermore, if we make investments at the beginning of teachers' careers for induction support and pretenure evaluation, we should see a decline in the money needed to recruit and hire new entrants to replace the 30% who leave in the first few years.

These early investments will also reduce the costs of band-aid approaches to staff development for those who have not learned to teach effectively and the costs of remediating, or trying to dismiss, poor teachers—not to mention the costs of compensating for the effects of their poor teaching on children. In the long run, strategic investment in teacher competence should free up resources for innovation and learning.

RETHINKING SCHOOLING AND TEACHING TOGETHER

Ultimately, the quality of teaching depends not only on the qualities of those who enter and stay, but also on workplace factors. Teachers who feel enabled to succeed with students are more committed and effective than those who feel unsupported in their learning and in their practice (Haggstrom, Darling-Hammond, & Grissmer, 1988; McLaughlin & Talbert, 1993; Rosenholtz, 1989). Those who have access to teacher networks, enriched professional roles, and collegial work feel more efficacious in gaining the knowledge they need to meet the needs of their students and more positive about staying in the profession.

Teachers in schools with shared decision making, according to a recent survey, were most likely to see curriculum reforms accompanying transformations in teaching roles (LH Research, 1993). For example, 72% of the teachers in site-based managed schools believed that cooperative learning had had a major impact on their schools, compared to only 35% of the teachers in schools that had not restructured. Also more prevalent in restructuring schools were more rigorous graduation standards, performance-based assessment practices, emphasis on in-depth understanding rather than superficial content coverage, accelerated learning approaches, connections between classroom practices and home experiences of students, and teacher involvement in decisions about school spending (LH Research, 1993).

Teachers in such schools were more likely to report that their schools were providing structured time for teachers to work together on professional matters—for example, planning instruction, observing one another's classrooms, and providing feedback about their teaching. More opportunities to counsel students in home visits and to adapt instruction to students' needs were also cited. In addition to feeling less constrained by district routines or standardized curriculums, teachers were more optimistic about their relationships with principals, their working conditions, and the educational performance of students. In brief, teachers in restructured schools were more confident about the professional status of teachers and more likely to view themselves as agents, rather than targets, of reform (LH Research, 1993).

The attempts across the country are still embryonic and scattered rather than systemic, but the possibilities for rethinking teacher preparation and revamping how schools structure teacher time and responsibilities are probably greater now than they have ever been. Although current efforts are impressive, it is important to realize that U.S. education has been down this path before. The criticisms of current educational reformers—that our schools provide most children with an education that is too passive and too rote-oriented to produce learners who can think critically, synthesize and transform, or experiment and create—are virtually identical to those of progressive educators at the turn of the century, in the 1930s, and again in the 1960s.

An underinvestment in teacher knowledge and school capacity killed all these efforts to create more universal, high-quality education. Progressive education, Cremin (1965) argued, demanded infinitely skilled teachers, and it failed because such teachers could not be recruited in sufficient numbers. Because of this failure, during each wave of reform, learner-centered education gave way to standardizing influences that "dumbed down" the curriculum: in the efficiency movement of the 1920s, the teacher-proof curriculum reforms of the 1950s, and the back-to-the-basics movement of the 1970s and 1980s. Disappointment with the outcomes of these attempts to simplify and prescribe school procedures, however, led in turn in each instance to renewed criticisms of schools and attempts to restructure them.

Current efforts at school reform are likely to succeed to the extent that they are built on a strong foundation of teaching knowledge and are sustained by a commitment to structural rather than merely symbolic change. Major changes in the productivity of U.S. schools rest on our ability to create and sustain a highly prepared teaching force for all, not just some, of our children.

REFERENCES

Burns, B. P., Hinkle, R., Marshall, C., Mangold S., Chideya, F., Waldrop, T., Foote, D., & Pedersen, D. (1991, December 2). The best schools in the world. *Newsweek*, pp. 50-64.

Cremin, L. A. (1965). *The genius of American education.* New York: Vintage Books.

Darling-Hammond, L. (1994). *Professional development schools: Schools for developing a profession.* New York: Teachers College Press.

Darling-Hammond, L., & Cobb, V. L. (1995). *A comparative study of teacher training and professional development in APEC members.* Washington, DC: U.S. Department of Education.

Ebmeier, H., Twombly, S., & Teeter, D. (1990). The comparability and adequacy of financial support for schools of education. *Journal of Teacher Education, 42,* 226-235.

Gottfredson, G. D., & Daiger, D. C. (1979). *Disruption in six hundred schools.* Baltimore: Johns Hopkins University, Center for Social Organization of Schools.

Haggstrom, G. W., Darling-Hammond, L., & Grissmer, D. W. (1988). *Assessing teacher supply and demand.* Santa Monica, CA: Rand.

Kolstad, R, K., Coker, D. R., & Edelhoff, C. (1989) Teacher education in Germany: An alternative model for the United States. *The Clearing House, 62*(5), 233-234.

LH Research. (1993). *A survey of the perspective of elementary and secondary school teachers on reform* (Prepared for the Ford Foundation). New York: Author.

McLaughlin, M. W., & Talbert, J. E. (1993). New visions of teaching. In D. K. Cohen, M. W. McLaughlin, & J. E. Talbert (Eds.), *Teaching for understanding: Challenges for policy and practice.* San Francisco: Jossey-Bass.

National Center for Education Statistics (NCES). (1993). *The condition of education, 1993*. Washington, DC: Author, U.S. Department of Education.

National Education Association (NEA). (1992). *The status of the American school teacher.* Washington, DC: Author.

National Institute of Education (NIE). (1977). *Violent schools—Safe schools: The Safe School Study Report to Congress.* Washington, DC: Author.

Organization for Economic Cooperation and Development (OECD). (1990). *The training of teachers.* Paris: Author.

Organization for Economic Cooperation and Development (OECD). (1992). *Education at a glance, OECD indicators.* Paris: Author.

Paine, L. W. (1990). The teacher as virtuoso: A Chinese model for teaching. *Teachers College Record, 92,* 49-81.

Rosenholtz, S. (1989). Teacher's workplace: *The social organization of schools.* New York: Longman.

Shimahara, N. K. (1985). Japanese education and its implications for U.S. education. *Phi Delta Kappan, 66,* 418-421.

Stigler, J. W., & Stevenson, H. W. (1991, Spring). How Asian teachers polish each lesson to perfection. *American Educator,* pp. 12-47.

Sykes, G. (1985). Teacher education in the United States. In B. R. Clark (Ed.), *The school and the university* (pp. 264-289). Los Angeles: University of California.

2 Redirecting the Professional Development of School Administrators: Collaborative Approaches

Anne M. Gargan
Rita E. Guare

Fordham University

VIA: PATHS TO VISIONARY LEADERSHIP

> I want to find a way of speaking of community, an expanding commu-
> nity, taking shape when diverse people . . . come together in speech
> and action to constitute something common among themselves.
> (Greene, 1993, p. 13)

As the United States approaches the new millennium, the enormity of the
educational, social, political, economic, and ethical issues the country faces
makes visible the need to search for a new language and practice of leadership (Giroux, 1988; Starratt, 1995). For the last decade or more, the intense
search for excellence in school reform and renewal efforts has been a national priority. The search has been no less intense at the level of administration
preparation reform (Mulkeen & Cambron-McCabe, 1994). In the changing
context of administration preparation, the VIA (Vision, Instruction &
Administration) program at Fordham University represents a model for inte-

21

grated, collaborative leadership and a metaphor in the search for a new way of speaking about leadership.

The impulse to search is deeply rooted in who we are as human beings. We seek to find a way, a path that will help us make sense of our lives. As sojourners, each of us seeks meaning in the realms within which we live, labor, and love. This search for meaning is a primary force, unique and particular for each person. In literature and in art, the search and the seeker are dramatically presented, and through these aesthetic representations we are reminded of our own vocation as meaning seekers and meaning makers. The vocation to seek and to create meaning finds particular expression in schools as administrators, teachers, students, and parents "come together in speech and action to constitute something common among ourselves" (Greene, 1993, p. 13).

However, it may not be enough to work at constructing the world as meaningful. Human excellence points school communities toward deconstruction as a way to complement what has been learned in the past. To deconstruct is to practice the intentional displacement of the dominant system (Derrida, 1982). This practice challenges the binary oppositions imbedded in our thinking and in our language: objectivity/subjectivity, autonomy/community, male/female, cognitive/affective. The VIA program supports the disclosure of such patterns of thought and speech by encouraging administrators to develop the art and action of critique. Through reflective journals, administrators are challenged to examine their underlying beliefs and assumptions and to engage their school communities in similar reflection. In educating for reflective practice, VIA seeks to affirm and challenge what Donald Schon (1987) calls

> knowing-in-action, the sorts of know-how administrators reveal in the intelligent, spontaneous, skillful action of their practice. Whatever language we may employ, however, our descriptions of knowing-in-action are always constructions. They are always attempts to put into explicit, symbolic form a kind of intelligence that begins by being tacit and spontaneous. (p. 25)

The meaning that we seek and the actions that engage us in joint construction, deconstruction, and reconstruction summon forth a profound truth: Our lives are inescapably linked with each other. Charles Taylor (1989) argues that the quest for meaning is dialogical. Moreover, this character is rooted in the crucial role language plays in each person's journey toward meaning:

> We become full human agents, capable of understanding ourselves, and hence of defining our identity, through our acquisition of rich human

languages of expression . . . including the "languages" of art, of ges-
tures, of love, and the like . . . we learn these modes of expression
through exchanges with others. (p. 32)

Rather than the journey of isolated individuals, the search for
meaning is one that communities must make together. Leaders who recognize the quest for meaning in themselves as well as with others, and who
search for languages that do justice to our lives together, sense the "deep-
down" drama inherent in human life. The search for meaning, and the creation of languages for honoring a multiplicity of meanings when diverse
people come together to form some common bond, deeply informs the kind
of visions school communities create. These visions help us find our way
and inspire the very best in leadership.

Creating Visions Collaboratively

Where there is no vision, the people will perish. (Proverbs 29: 18)

Over the past decades, a new literature of leadership has evolved, with theories that are both complex and conflicting. With the development of an integrated bureaucratic system over a century ago, efficiency, rationality, and
precision drove the enterprise as educational administrators built a stable,
predictable, and controlled hierarchy for teachers and students. Bureaucratic
and scientific management principles set the stage for the development of
administrative training programs that advanced a functionalist view of
schooling (Mulkeen, Cambron-McCabe, & Anderson, 1994). Grounded in
empiricism, predictability, and scientific certainty, administrators found a
way to make sense of their world. They viewed organizations as rational,
objective, and mechanistic; they understood decision making as a reasoned
and linear process; and they saw power as privileged and hierarchical
(Mulkeen et al., 1994).

   In an age of shifting paradigms, such views are no longer responsive, and they pose a serious threat to school reform and renewal efforts.
There is a growing belief that traditional hierarchies must be dismantled and
replaced with more democratic structures (Clark & Meloy, 1990; Foster,
1986; Giroux, 1988; Mulkeen et al., 1994):

We are certain of one thing. We will never move within the bureaucratic structure to new schools, to free schools. That structure was invented
to assure domination and control. It will never produce freedom and
self-actualization. We cannot get there from here. This risk of move-

ment from here to there is not great. The bureaucratic structure is failing in a manner so critical that adaptations will not forestall its collapse.
It is impractical. (Clark & Meloy, 1990, p. 21)

The complexities that educational leaders face in social, cultural,
and political contexts, the problem-posing and problem-solving strategies
expected of reflective practitioners (Schon, 1983, 1987), and the organizing
networks of interest groups necessary for decision making (Peters &
Waterman, 1982) demand alternative organizational structure.

Major shifts have taken place in both theory and research on leadership that have informed practices within new structures. In particular,
there has been a move away from functional leadership, with its emphasis
on efficiency and technical problem solving, to substantive leadership, with
its emphasis on meaning and purpose. Although school leaders are always
working within the demands of both these zones, what will be needed in
creating the schools of the future are leaders with vision.

Robert Starratt (1995) offers compelling analysis of what vision
means and suggests that, if vision is to be important for administrators, it
must be connected to other complex and interrelated elements that constitute leadership. Starratt's (1995) theory of leadership illuminates the depth
dimension of vision and positions it within a core of meanings and values.
Briefly, the major elements of this theory are:

- Leadership is rooted in the personal and collective meanings that
  ground our identities and inspire our deepest beliefs.
- Leadership emerges out of a vision, a dream grounded in those
  essential meanings that give our lives purpose. The power in
  leadership flows from a shared vision.
- Leadership is rooted in the drama of life in which action is
  charged with meaning and value and in which the heroic dimensions are summoned.
- Leadership involves paying attention to the communal voice in
  creating the vision and in building a covenant among people who
  are committed to the dream and its celebration.
- Leadership involves institutionalizing the vision in the everyday
  life of the school through procedures, programs, and policies.
- Leadership calls for renewing the vision in the communal cele-
  brations of people and restructuring the vision in response to
  new hopes that surface in and for the school community.

Vision is central to this theory of leadership and thus provides a
solid grounding in visionary leadership for the preparation of administrators

in VIA. In his ground-breaking book, *Leadership,* James MacGregor Burns (1978) offered another clue in designing the VIA program. Burns believes that "the most powerful influences consist of deeply human relationships" (p. 11) that we experience with each other. Intimacy is at the heart of collaborative leadership and is shared through vision and story. Howard Gardner's (1993) latest study of leadership affirms the relational and highly interactive nature of leadership. Echoing the contribution of Bennis and Nanus (1985), Gardner describes the leaders as ones who must have a central story and who must be the embodiment of that story:

> Stories and narrative, whether personal or fictional, provide meaning and belonging in our lives. . . . The story fabric offers us images, myths, and metaphors that are morally resonant and contribute both to our knowing and our being known. (Witherall & Noddings, 1991, p. 1)

The leader dwells inside the beliefs and meaning and calls attention to them through the story vision. The VIA program encourages administrators to work in teams within the cohorts and within their own school communities in creating visions of leadership. In a continuous process of detecting distortions of the vision throughout the layers of the organization's structure, administrators are challenged to examine their beliefs and practices regarding the essence of the human person, the nature of the teaching/learning process, and the complexities of the social, political, and cultural contexts.

Within the program, administrators are called to be risk takers working collaboratively with all members of their school communities in defining, articulating, and sharing the visions they create. Through carefully designed action learning projects, the leaders develop strategies to support multicultural, multilingual, and multiracial models to achieve and to actualize the vision. Through cases and simulations, administrators develop problem-posing and problem-solving skills, strategic planning, prioritizing, and critical reflection. The active learning process within the cohort and in the field enables administrators to recognize, sooner rather than later, the formal and informal structures within organizations that are barriers to change. Visions rooted in community, connectedness, commitment, and celebration are pathways in which the language is one of collaboration and in which they critically challenge the current reality.

Collaboration is an alternative value system that has at its core noncompetitive cooperative behavior, nonhierarchical networks and processes, and a displacement of power from the top to the center. This represents a fundamental reordering of the organization. Thus, what is needed are participating structures in which problems are solved in terms that share experiences and specialized knowledge. Effective teamwork demands specific skills. Examples of these include cooperation, consensus building, and conflict resolution. The skills must be learned and practiced not only by the formal leaders, but by all members in the community before these new values become part of the decision-making culture of the school. Obviously, unless developmental learning of these skills takes place, and unless development for the new roles and responsibilities promised in reordering organization is a priority, efforts to collaborate will be blocked. However, we are encouraged by Paolo Freire's challenge that, "Today, the task of overcoming our lack of democratic experiences through experiences in participation still awaits us" (cited in Kraus, 1984, p. 17).

"A revolution in education requires competent, skilled, and visionary leadership" (Griffiths, Stout, & Forsyth, 1988, p. xiii). Such leadership, we believe, demands that administrators' preparation programs find an integrated and collaborative way of speaking about leadership. VIA represents that hope.

CREATING THE COLLABORATIVE INSTRUCTIONAL LEADER: THE VIA APPROACH

The emerging learning communities of the 1990s that forecast the teaching/learning structures of the 21st century possess certain commonalities. Interactive, interdisciplinary instruction abounds, as does students' work in cooperative, heterogeneous groups to solve real, complex problems and to exhibit their solutions through a series of authentic assessments such as performances, projects, or portfolios (Drake, 1993; Johnson, Johnson, & Holubec, 1994; Kagan, 1990; Wiggins, 1993a; Wolf, 1989). These schools will be, as Peter Senge (cited in O'Neil, 1995) avers, true learning organizations in which all constituents continually and collectively strive to reach their greatest potential. Principals of these schools "tend to see their job as creating an environment where teachers and students can continually learn" (p. 22).

To achieve this optimum learning situation for all school members, and to remove the structural, social, psychological, and developmental barriers to collaboration, the school leaders must possess certain interpersonal abilities. The creation of trust (Starratt, 1993), the implementation of administrator, teacher and student instructional teams, and the creation of flexible schedules that increase the possibility of integrated instruction are all facets of these necessary empowering leadership skills.

However, if the primary purpose of schooling is to increase and augment student learning so that the 21st-century graduates have the knowledge and ability to perform the higher order thinking and complex tasks of the technology age, then the school leader must possess and be able to demonstrate professional competency in the area of instruction. In short, he or she must become a viable instructional leader. To achieve this goal, it seems reasonable to assume that schools of education that seek to develop school supervisors and administrators would incorporate, within their programs, those skills, attitudes, and knowledge bases that produce a person capable of leading the school learning program.

In the past, common practice had been to insure the attainment of managerial skills by administration students; now many schools of education are moving to a holistic, collaborative, integrated approach to instruct future administrators who will model the expected behaviors of those graduates in their workplace—the 21st-century school. Indeed, as the National Council for Accreditation of Teacher Education (NCATE) (1995) *Curriculum Guidelines* indicate:

> As new programs evolve, a new rationale for preparation programs is emerging, one based on the integration of professional practice with subject content and theoretical constructs. This new rationale acknowledges the deficiencies of old intellectual paradigms and seeks a framework that includes reflective practice, problem-based instruction, understanding and creating learning communities, contemporary leadership models and problem-centered field research. In addition, a trend toward organizing by student cohort is visible. (p. iii)

The VIA program follows this model, and through the creation of action learning cohorts, attempts to instill in students a variety of research-tested, reflective curricular strategies and instructional practices. These habits of mind will enable the new administrator to demonstrate knowledge, not only about the organization, scheduling, and professional development necessary to affect thematic, interdisciplinary, active learning units within and among classrooms, but also about the concepts, essential understandings, outcomes, prompts, activities, and authentic assessments of the units themselves. At the present time, many administrators have not been able to assume instructional leadership roles because they have felt inadequate about their expertise in this area. This most important and essential aspect of education has, too frequently, been removed from the purview of the school administrator, who is nevertheless expected to be in the vanguard of curricular decision making for the school.

An examination of the proposed New York State Certification Requirements for School Administrator/Supervisor (1994), the NCATE (1995) *Curriculum Guidelines, A New Compact for Learning* (University of the State of New York, 1991), the National Evaluation System's (1995) *Building-*

level/District-Level Administrator Assessment Frameworks, and the new certification requirements of other states, such as Vermont, Kentucky, Illinois, and Texas, reveal that there is a general consensus about the knowledge, skills, and attributes that school leaders should possess so that they can collaborate with others to design appropriate curriculum and instructional programs. Furthermore, they should also be able to work with other members of the school community to develop active learner-centered environments, to assess student outcomes, and to plan long-term professional development activities aimed at improving collaborative, interdisciplinary instruction (Miron, 1995).

The research and literature from the field seem clear about the outcomes that schools of education must pursue if they are to produce the instructional school leaders needed for today as well as for the next century. However, there is a vast chasm that separates the ideal of collaborative, knowledgeable, instructional leadership from today's reality. Fullan (1991) cites "abstract theorizing, lack of problem and skill focus, distance from actual settings and absence of applications and follow-through" (p. 336) as the chief reasons so many university administration programs are ineffective. For example, they teach about these strategies and performance assessments while the aspiring administrators are passively seated in rows, dutifully taking notes on the "cooperative grouping lecture."

Moreover, although the concept of a cohort is a popular one today, it means more than marching lockstep with a selected group through a series of prescribed, disparate courses. A cohort demands teaming and a belief that the gestalt is more than the sum of all its component parts. High-performance teams are created, not born (Cross & Reitzug, 1996) through a series of unified experiences that are designed to instruct through the active involvement of the learner during the process and reasoned reflection on completion of each phase of the unit.

To work successfully with an adult cohort, particularly in the final two of the four teaming phases (forming, storming, norming, and performing), the professor must be prepared to be a highly collaborative resource person and must truly exemplify the "guide on the side" model. These empowered administrative adult cohorts, having experienced the collaborative model through a process approach, will be better prepared to practice these behaviors and share them with teachers and students so as to improve the quality of the school instructional program. In the VIA program, this collaborative process has become part of the university division itself, in which VIA courses are planned cooperatively and integrated by professors and in which input from all members of the team is the expectation.

The VIA classroom models the student-centered, active learning classroom of the 21st-century school. Outcomes of the units are understood from the beginning by administration students, as are the modes of assessment. These assessment criteria, or rubrics, include rigorous standards and authentic assessments and involve both individual and team projects. Everyone assesses everyone else in the VIA classes. Professors assess individual student drafts and give timely, specific feedback to improve student achievement. Professors and other students collaborate to assess completed group projects and performances through vehicles such as debates and oral presentations. Each team member assesses the other members of the team and gives specific feedback to increase grouping skills. A journal of the VIA—the journey—is kept by each student, and professors are encouraged to provide feedback in writing. A variety of instructional models are employed to deliver instruction (Joyce & Weil, 1986). However, the problem-solving, case-study methodology, in which students are actively engaged and construct their own possible solutions, is prevalent. The professor is the facilitator who assists the groups of adults to link new learning to old knowledge to solve significant school problems.

Other collaborative aspects of VIA include internship at the school site under the joint supervision of the university professor and the school-based mentor, who design the intern's projects together with the intern. This internship, which is woven throughout the program, provides opportunities for the student to apply the knowledge and skills learned and practiced through performances and projects in the more sheltered classroom environment to a real situation, with guidance throughout the process.

In this manner, the VIA program assists aspiring school administrators to overcome the structural, social, psychological, and developmental blocks to collaborative, instructional leadership.

VIA: POINTING THE WAY TO COLLABORATIVE ADMINISTRATIVE LEADERSHIP

Perhaps the functions that enjoy the least collaboration in a school setting are those that are deemed to be purely administrative in nature. The structural, social, psychological, and developmental blocks to collaborative leadership are strongest in this arena.

Traditionally, the planning, management, and monitoring of school facilities and budgets as well as the ensuring of compliance with legal mandates and regulations have rested totally within the purview of the principal and other school administrators (Knoll, 1987). School instruction schedules, plant safety/cleanliness guidelines and routines, lunchroom, busing and fire drill procedures, the ordering and distribution of school supplies—

these mundane but necessary tasks have been left to the supervisor by the rest of the school community with the proviso that he or she understand fully that this is a mere addendum to the real work of schools (Glickman, Gordon, & Ross-Gordon, 1995).

The advent of site-based management (Murphy, 1991) and flexible scheduling have made collaboration among all members of the school community in the area of school administration a necessity, even at the present time (Fullan, 1991). Extended school days and years; block and parallel programming to support thematic, interdisciplinary instruction; distance learning technology; the formation of smaller units such as the "house" concept; differentiated staffing; as well as open campuses—all endorse the urgency of this communal need. However, neither the building principal, the teachers, nor the parents have received the training necessary to meet the challenge of administrative cooperation and collaboration throughout the entire organization that the 21st-century school demands.

The VIA program has addressed this concern. Through an active learning, problem-solving, case study approach involving contract management and conciliation practices in grievance procedures, adult students have a chance to practice the knowledge, skills, and attitudes learned in a risk-free environment (Krupp, 1982; Oja, 1991). Supervisory personnel issues become collegial rather than hierarchial (Rooney, 1993), thus permitting both teacher and supervisor to reach self-actualization (Maslow, 1970) through the design and implementation of mutually agreed-on goals.

Multiculturalism will be one of the hallmarks of the schools of the future. Indeed, in our large cities today, diversity is a clear and present reality. The question of staff recruitment and hiring has, to date, been largely within the scope of the administrator's duties. However, site-based management teams, which include parents and teachers in addition to administrators, now have decision-making capabilities in this area. The building supervisor must be able to work as part of this group to set criteria for hiring, ensure equitable procedures, and advance the cause of staffing diversity, while insuring excellence of instruction within the vision of the school. Professional development in this area has not been characteristic of university programs in general. However, the VIA program provides both in-class and supervised in-school experiences to promote the integration of these necessary skills and attitudes among its students.

A singularly unilateral administrative school function has been the management of the school budget. Although it is true in many instances that, to date, this has involved a rather small sum of money (because salaries and additional federal and state monies have historically been distributed from the district level), there has still been little input from the majority of the school community on the disposition of the actual funds. However, this facet of school governance has already undergone a metamorphosis and is continually devolving to the school level at a rapid rate (Murphy, 1991). Site-based management gives a much greater degree of autonomy over the actual budget to the individual school. This may be highlighted in the present reality of differentiated staffing that permits schools to blend hitherto discrete categorical funds to create their own staffing patterns to meet individual school needs (Fernandez, 1989). This change in school operations makes previous university school finance courses almost obsolete. A more in-depth look at budgeting as a support to thematic, interdisciplinary, technology-assisted cooperative student learning, as well as a support to the teacher and parent as action researchers, must be provided. Coursework should also include techniques for conducting budget meetings so that they can be productive and responsive to the school's vision.

Through a combination of direct instruction and problem solving, the VIA program encourages students to work in teams with "messy" real-life situations, in which a scarcity of resources demands a strict prioritization of goals and needs. In addition, experts in the field such as principals and superintendents, who deal effectively with these issues on a daily basis, are part of the program. In this manner, future administrators will be better prepared to deal with the new, competitive world of public education in which state deregulation, charter schools, and parent vouchers are becoming prevalent and in which fiscal accountability and efficiency, linked to student achievement, will be a hallmark for the school leader of the future.

Scheduling is often seen as a fairly low-level administrative function and, as such, has often been given short shrift in programs that prepare school administrators and supervisors. However, in reality (if not in espoused theory), the schedule both drives and reflects the school instructional program. All too frequently, this priority of the schedule is maintained at the expense of good instructional practices.

The current research on teaching and learning (Bomer, 1995; Crowder, 1992; Darling-Hammond & Quinones, 1992; Gardner, 1993; Glatthorn, 1994; Hargreaves, 1992; Johnson et al., 1994; Merenbloom, 1991; Peterson, 1992; Wheelock, 1992; Wiggins, 1993b) clearly delineates the manner in which children learn optimally and efficiently—in thematic, interdisciplinary, active learning classrooms, in which new learning is linked to old. In this classroom, a variety of learning modalities are accommodated, and students are encouraged to pursue their interests and to produce real work in cooperative groups. There is only one problem vis-à-vis this constructivist learning environment and the school schedule. This instructional model takes "too much time" and does not fit into the traditional 40-minute frame currently in place in so many schools, particularly in middle and high schools. In other words, instruction is subordinated to the schedule, even though such isolated, disparate, episodic learning is diametrically opposed to the current research.

Through direct instruction and problem-solving work groups that use real school schedules as their basis, the VIA program introduces the administration and supervision students to alternatives such as block schedules and four-by-four schedules, as well as trimester and parallel programming (Canaday & Rettig, 1995), that support the current views on teaching and learning. To insure that this reformed schedule will be implemented by the school community, VIA participants also learn methods of collaborating with teachers, parents, and students in alternative schedule design (Hackmann, 1995). Practice in these new learnings is facilitated through projects at the student's own school.

Thus, collaborative leadership is fostered in the administrative arena in which functions that have historically been "I will" now become "We can!"

CONCLUSION

Today's schools are caught in a whirlwind of social and political change, shifting paradigms and promises, and intense public debate about the nature of schooling. As the United States enters the millennium, efforts at school renewal and reform are mounting. Voices are calling for the fundamental transformation of U.S. public schooling and envision a new model of alternative, democratic structures. Advocates of restructuring call for smaller schools, site-based management teams, and a curriculum with accountability for student outcomes. The idea that problem solving and decision making require a radical reordering of the relationships within school communities has propelled a reorganization in favor of participatory cultures. These major educational reforms underway in school systems throughout the nation require a radical recasting of administration preparation programs.

In the current climate of criticism and controversy about schools, preparing administrators for the demands of practice is greater than ever. External criticism and internal doubt mark the terrain of the professional development of administrators. At the same time, professional development schools have sought to attain high levels of academic rigor and status (Mulkeen et al., 1994). Although debates rage and responses are offered, creating a solid link between administrator preparation programs and school renewal efforts must be seen as critical.

Administrators will need to see their leadership as a way of working toward more participatory arrangements. They will need to have a commitment to building visions with others of what schools can be. Above all, administrators will need to reclaim their role in administering the instructional programs within communities of excellence. School communities that are renewing their meaning and purpose will need to work with administrators skilled in the visionary, instruction, and administrative demands of leadership. The most important areas of professional practice lie beyond the conventional boundaries of professional competence (Schon, 1987). VIA sets a new boundary in our search for integrated and collaborative leadership. We believe it represents a WAY.

EPIGRAM

The teachers told us quietly that the way of experts had become a tricky way. They told us it would always be fatal to our arts to misuse the skills we had learned. The skills themselves were mere light shells, needing to be filled out with substance coming from our souls. They warned us never to turn these skills to the service of things separate from the way. This would be the most difficult thing, for we would learn, they told us, that no fundi [religious leader or educator or healer] could work effectively when torn away from power, and yet power in these times lived far, immeasurably far from the way. This distance from the seats of power to the way, this distance now separating our way from power usurped against our people and our way, this distance would be the measure of the fundi's pain. They told us there was no life sweeter than that of the fundi in the bosom of his people, if his people knew their way. But the life of a fundi whose people have lost their way is pain. All the excellence of such a fundi's craft is turned to trash. His skills are useless in the face of his people's destruction, and it is as easy as slipping on a river stone to see his craftsmanship actually turn like a weapon against his people.

. . . Our way, the way, is not a random path. Our way begins from coherent understanding. It is a way that aims at preserving knowledge of who we are, knowledge of the best way we have found to relate to each, each to all, ourselves to other peoples, all to our surroundings. If our individual lives have a worthwhile aim, that aim should be a purpose inseparable from the way.

. . . Our way is reciprocity. The way is wholeness.

—Ayi Kwei Arhah, Two Thousand Seasons. (the introductory frontispiece to Alice Walker's Living by the Word)

REFERENCES

Bennis, W., & Nanus, B. (1985). *Leaders: The strategies for taking charge.* New York: Harper & Row.

Bomer, R. (1995). *Time for meaning: Crafting literate lives in middle and high school.* Portsmouth, NH: Heinemann.

Burns, J. M. (1978). *Leadership.* New York: Harper & Row.

Canaday, R. L., & Rettig, M. D. (1995). The power of innovative scheduling. *Educational Leadership, 53*(3), 4-11.

Clark, D. L., & Meloy, J. M. (1990). Recanting bureaucracy: A democratic structure for leadership in schools. In A. Lieberman (Ed.), *Schools as collaborative cultures: Creating the future now* (pp. 3–23). New York: Falmer Press.

Cross, B. T., & Reitzug, U. C. (1996). How to build ownership in city schools. *Educational Leadership, 53*(4), 16-19.

Crowder, B. (1992). *R-BEM: The results based education model.* Albany, NY: Educational Vistas.

Darling-Hammond, L., & Quinones, N. (1992). Building a learning centered curriculum for learning centered schools. In *Interim report of the New York State Assessment Council to the Commissioner and the Regents.* Albany, NY: New York State Education Department.

Derrida, J. (1982). *Margins of philosophy.* Chicago: University of Chicago Press.

Drake, S. M. (1993). *Integrated curriculum: The call to adventure.* Alexandria, VA: Association for Supervision and Curriculum Development.

Fernandez, J. A. (1989). *Dade county public schools: Blueprint for structured schools.* Paper presented at the Conference on Choice and Control in American Education, University of Wisconsin-Madison, Madison, WI.

Foster, W. (1986). *Paradigms and promises: New approaches to educational administration.* Buffalo, NY: Prometheus Books.

Fullan, M. G. (1991). *The new meaning of educational change.* New York: Teachers College Press.

Gardner, H. (1993). *Multiple intelligences: The theory in practice.* New York: Basic Books.

Giroux, H. (October, 1988). *Rethinking the purpose of educating school administrators: Dreaming about democracy.* Paper presented at the Danforth Foundation Meeting for Professors of Educational Administration, Oxford, Ohio.

Glatthorn, A. (1994). *Curriculum renewal.* Alexandria, VA: Association for Supervision and Curriculum Development.

Glickman, C. D., Gordon, S. P., & Ross-Gordon, J. M. (1995). *Supervision of instruction: A developmental approach* (3rd ed.). Boston: Allyn & Bacon.

Greene, M. (1993). The passions of pluralism: Multiculturism and the expanding community. *Education Researcher,* 22(1), 13.

Griffiths, D.E., Stout, R.T., & Forsyth, P.B. (Eds.). (1988). *Leaders for America's schools: The report and paper of the national commission on excellence in educational administration.* Berkeley, CA: McCutchan.

Hackmann, D. G. (1995). Ten guidelines for implementing block scheduling. *Educational Leadership,* 53(3), 24-28.

Hargreaves, A. (1992). Cultures of teaching: A focus for change. In A. Hargreaves & M. G. Fullan (Eds.), *Understanding teacher development* (pp. 216-241). New York: Teachers College Press.

Johnson, D., Johnson, R. T., & Holubec, E. J. (1994). *Cooperative learning in the classroom.* Alexandria, VA: Association for Supervision and Curriculum Development.

Joyce, B., & Weil, M. (1986). *Models of teaching.* Englewood Cliffs, NJ: Prentice-Hall.

Kagan, S. (1990). The structural approach to cooperative learning. *Educational Leadership,* 47(4), 12-15.

Knoll, M. K. (1987). *Supervision for better instruction.* Englewood Cliffs, NJ: Prentice-Hall.

Kraus, W.A. (1984). *Collaboration in organizations: Alternative to hierarchy.* New York: Human Sciences Press.

Krupp, J. A. (1982). *The adult learner: A unique entity.* Manchester, CT: Adult Development and Learning.

Maslow, A. (1970). *Motivation and personality.* New York: Harper & Row.

Merenbloom, E. Y. (1991). *The team process: A handbook for teachers.* Columbus, OH: National Middle School Association (NMSA).

Miron, L. F. (1995). Pushing the boundaries of urban school reform: Linking student outcomes to community development. *Journal for a Just and Caring Education,* 1(1), 98-114.

Mulkeen, T. A., Cambron-McCabe, N. H. & Anderson, B. J. (1994). Educating leaders to invent "tomorrow's" schools. In T. A. Mulkeen, N. H. Cambron-McCabe, & B. J. Anderson (Eds.), *Democratic leadership: The changing context of administrative preparation* (pp. 15–28). Norwood, NJ: Ablex Publishing.

Murphy, J. (1991). *Restructuring schools: Capturing and assessing the phenomena.* New York: Teachers College Press.

National Council for the Accreditation of Teacher Education (NCATE). (1995). *Curriculum guidelines.* Alexandria, VA: Educational Constituent Leadership Council, c/o Association for Supervision and Curriculum Development (ASCD).

National Evaluation System (NES). (1995). *Building-level/district-level administrator assessment frameworks.* Amherst, MA: Author.

New York State Education Department. (October, 1994). *Proposed certification regulations for administrative and supervisory service: SAS/SDA.* NY: NYSED

Oja, S. N. (1991). Adult development: Insights on staff development. In A. Lieberman & L. Miller (Eds.), *Staff development for education in the nineties* (pp. 37-61). New York: Teachers College Press.

O'Neil, J. (1995). On schools as learning organization: A conversation with Peter Senge. *Educational Leadership, 52*(7), 20-23.

Peters, T., & Waterman, R. (1982). *In search of excellence.* New York: Harper & Row.

Peterson, R. (1992). *Life in a crowded place: Making a learning community.* Portsmouth, NH: Heinemann.

Rooney, J. (1993). Teacher evaluation: No more "super"vision. *Educational Leadership, 51*(2), 43-45.

Schon, D. A. (1983). *The reflective practitioner: How professionals think in action.* New York: Basic Books

Schon, D. A. (1987). *Educating the reflective practitioner.* San Francisco, CA: Jossey-Bass.

Starratt, R. J. (1993). *The drama of leadership.* London: Falmer Press.

Starratt, R. J. (1995). *Leaders with vision: The quest for school renewal.* Thousand Oaks, CA: Corwin Press.

Taylor, C. (1989). *Sources of the self: The making of the modern identity.* Cambridge, MA: Harvard University Press.

The University of the State of New York. (1991). *A new compact for learning: Improving elementary, middle and secondary school results in the 1990s.* New York: New York State Education Department.

Walker, A. (1988). *Living by the word: Selected writings. 1973–1987.* San Diego, CA: Harcourt Brace Jovanovich.

Wheelock, A. (1992). *Crossing the tracks.* New York: New Press.

Wiggins, G. (1993a). *Assessing student performance.* San Francisco: Jossey-Bass.

Wiggins, G. (1993b). Assessment, authenticity, context and validity. *Kappan, 75,* 200-214.

Witherell, C., & Noddings, N. (Eds.) (1991). *Stories lives tell: Narrative and dialogue in education.* New York: Teachers College Press.

Wolf, D. P. (1989). Portfolio assessment: Sampling student work. *Educational Leadership, 47*(7), 35-39.

3 THE TASK CHARACTERISTICS OF TEACHING: IMPLICATIONS FOR THE ORGANIZATIONAL DESIGN OF SCHOOLS

Brian Rowan

University of Michigan

One of the most common assumptions in research on educational organizations is that teaching is a complex and nonroutine task (Bidwell, 1965; Lortie, 1975; Meyer & Rowan, 1978; Weick, 1976). Yet virtually no quantitative, empirical evidence exists on this point. Despite this, a view of teaching as complex and nonroutine is central to the literature on school restructuring. This literature argues that schools are overly bureaucratic and centralized, and that a shift is needed to more "organic" or "professionalized" forms of management that involve supportive forms of administrative leadership, participative forms of school decision making, and staff collaboration. These forms of management are assumed to be better suited to the management of complex and nonroutine forms of teaching because they capitalize on the commitment and expertise of a professionalized teaching force (for a review of these arguments, see Rowan 1990a, 1990b).

Based on these observations, this chapter addresses three research questions:

1. To what extent can teaching be considered a nonroutine task?
2. Is there a relationship between the presence of nonroutine forms of teaching and the emergence of organic forms of management in schools?
3. Is organic management in schools associated with an increase in teacher motivation and on-the-job learning?

These research questions are examined using survey data collected from over 600 teachers in 16 high schools located in California and Michigan. The sample consists mostly of comprehensive high schools located in urban or suburban areas, although there are two small, "alternative" high schools in the sample and several "Magnet" high schools. The data reported here were collected in 1991 as part of a three-year field study conducted by the Center for Research on the Context of Secondary School Teaching, an OERI-funded research and development center housed at Stanford University.

FINDINGS

Readers are cautioned that the analyses reported in this chapter are preliminary and in need of refinement. Moreover, due to restrictions on the length of American Education Research Association papers, discussion of the approach and data analytic methods used in the chapter are minimal.

The data reported here are teachers' perceptions of organizational structure and climate. Articles by Rowan, Raudenbush, and Kang (1991) and Raudenbush, Rowan, and Kang (1991) establish the importance of using hierarchical linear models in the analysis of these kinds of data. In addition, an earlier work used a different procedure for measuring the task characteristics of teaching and analyzed the relationship between this measure and the emergence of organic management in schools (Rowan, Raudenbush, & Cheong, 1992). Finally, a paper by Raudenbush, Rowan, and Cheong (1992) examined the effects of organic management in schools on one type of motivational variable—teacher efficacy. All these papers provide more extensive detail on the approach and methods used in this chapter.

Teaching as a Nonroutine Task

We turn first to the problem of whether teaching is a nonroutine task. To investigate this issue, we administered a series of questions to teachers based on scales developed by Withey, Daft, and Cooper (1983). These scales were intended to measure the two dimensions of "technology" discussed in Perrow (1967): task variety and task uncertainty. Task variety occurs when workers perform many different tasks as part of their job, with routine jobs having low levels of task variety and nonroutine jobs having high levels of task variety. Task uncertainty occurs when there is an absence of clear and reliable knowledge upon which to base task activities. Tasks with an uncertain knowledge base are nonroutine, whereas tasks with a certain knowledge are routine.

The scales used here have certain advantages over the measure we used in our previous study. In Rowan et al. (1992), we measured the task characteristics of teaching using Hage and Aiken's (1969) classic measure of job routinization. However, analyses of a variety of measures of organizational "technology" suggest that this measure is inadequate, in large part because it reflects task variety but does not tap task uncertainty (Withey et al., 1983). In addition, an interesting feature of the scales used in the present analysis is that we can compare the answers of teachers to the answers given by members of other occupations using the research reported by Daft and McIntosh (1978).

Measures of task characteristics. In the analyses presented here, we asked teachers to respond to a series of questions about their jobs and developed scale scores for each teacher. The following measures were used in the analyses:

- *Task variety,* a 4-item scale with an internal consistency of .80 as measured by Chronbach's alpha. Teachers responded on a 6-point scale to the following items: (a) many of my tasks are the same from day to day, (b) my work is basically routine, (c) my work activities vary considerably from day to day, and (d) my job duties are quite repetitious. All responses were coded so that higher scale scores indicate higher levels of job variety, and
- *Task uncertainty,* a 3-item scale with an internal consistency of .66. Teachers responded on a 6-point scale to the following items: (a) there is a clearly defined body of knowledge that guides my work, (b) I rely on established procedures and practices in my work, and (c) there is an understandable sequence of steps that can be followed in my job. All items were coded with high-scale scores indicating higher levels of task uncertainty.

Although the scales we use have fewer items than those described in Withey et al. (1983), they have comparable psychometric properties. The two scales have a correlation of .42. We could have increased the internal consistency of our measures by combining the two scales; however, other researchers have argued against such a combination because the two dimensions of task certainty and task variety have been found to show different relationships to the same criterion variables.

Findings. One way to analyze the response of teachers to these measures is to empirically place teachers into the fourfold classification scheme used by Perrow (1967) to describe types of technologies. Perrow's classic work identified four types of technologies: routine (low in task variety and low in task uncertainty), craft (low in task variety and high in task uncertainty), engineering (high in task variety and low in task uncertainty), and nonroutine (high in task variety and high in task uncertainty).

In order to classify teachers, we calculated an average score for each teacher for each scale and coded those teachers with an average below 3.5 as low on that scale and those with an average of 3.5 or above as high on that scale. The results are presented in Table 3.1.

The data in Table 3.1 are not consistent with the widespread assumption of educational researchers that teaching is a nonroutine task. Instead, using the procedure described earlier, we find that 47% of the teachers see teaching as a routine task, 35% see teaching as an engineering task, 14% see teaching as a nonroutine task, and 3% see teaching as a craft.

One major reason for these results is that teachers do not report working under high levels of task uncertainty. Table 3.1 shows that 82% of the teachers rate teaching low on this dimension. An inspection of item responses shows that 83% of the teachers agree that "there is a clearly defined body of knowledge that guides my work"; 76% agree that "there is an understandable sequence of steps that can be followed in my job", and 74% agree that they "rely on established procedures and practices" in their job.

Table 3.1. Cross-Tabulation of Teachers' Responses to Measures of Task Variety and Task Uncertainty.

Task Uncertainty	Task Variety	
	Low	High
Low	Routine (286) 47%	Engineering (211) 35%
High	Craft (19) 3%	Nonroutine (87) 14%

There is more variation on the task variety scale with about 50% of the teachers seeing teaching as having high task variety and the other 50% seeing the job as having low task variety. An inspection of the item responses shows that 74% of the teachers agreed that "many of my tasks are the same from day to day." However, teachers also reported variety in their work. For example, 67% agreed that "my work activities vary considerably from day to day," only 45% agreed with the statement that "my job duties are quite repetitious," and only 25% agreed that "my work is basically routine."

We can also use the results from Table 3.1 to compare the responses of teachers to the responses of members of other occupations, as reported in Daft and McIntosh (1978). In our data, the average teacher response fell just to the left of the boundary between a routine task and an engineering task. Other occupations found by Daft and McIntosh to have routine work include: bank tellers, clerical personnel, machine shop workers, draftsmen, sales personnel, and auditors. Occupations found to have engineering-like work were lawyers, engineers, and accountants. University teaching, it is worth noting, fell into the craft category in Daft and McIntosh's research.

In order to better understand the educational philosophies and approaches underlying these various perceptions of the task of teaching, we correlated teachers' responses on the measure of task variety and task uncertainty to teachers' responses on various items asking their views about teaching, learning, and curriculum. These data are presented in Table 3.2.

The pattern of correlations in Table 3.2 suggests that a nonroutine view of teaching is associated with:

- A dynamic view of subject-matter knowledge;
- An interactive style of teaching that emphasizes class discussion, writing about ideas, and having students revise assignments; and
- A student-centered pattern of instruction that provides different students in the same class with different assignments and that encourages student choice in assignments.

By contrast, the correlations in Table 3.2 suggest that a routine view of teaching is associated with:

- A static view of subject-matter knowledge as "cut and dried" and "well defined";
- A hierarchical view of learning that emphasizes student grouping based on past achievement and a sequenced program of learning in which students first learn basic skills before proceeding to more complex learnings; and
- A standardized view of the curriculum in which teachers feel it is important to "cover" an agreed-upon curriculum and for all students to learn the same content regardless of achievement level.

Table 3.2. Correlates of Task Uncertainty and Task Variety.

	Task Uncertainty	Task Variety
Views About Subjects		
1. Academic subject well defined	-.35	-.10
2. Subject knowledge always changing	.11	.26
3. Subject "cut and dried"	-.18	-.41
Views About Curriculum		
1. Little disagreement about what to teach	-.18	-.41
2. Teach basic skills before complex skills	-.25	-.14
3. Must cover the curriculum	-.26	-.18
4. Low achievers learn best in small chunks	-.16	—
Views About Teaching		
1. Emphasize class discussion	.09	.25
2. Emphasize revising assignments	—	.21
3. Emphasize writing about ideas	.10	.20
4. Emphasize choice of assignments	.12	.20
5. Emphasize different assignments	.17	.14
6. Emphasize same content for all achievement levels	-.16	-.10
7. Best to group based on prior achievement	-.12	-.16

As a final step in the analysis, we developed a two-level hierarchical linear model in order to examine the sources of variation in teachers' perceptions of task uncertainty and task variety. In this approach, we are able to decompose variation in the outcome variables into within- and between-school components and to examine the effects of independent variables measured at the teacher level on teachers' conceptions of task, controlling for school effects on these conceptions.

The independent variables for the analysis were: (a) a series of dummy-coded variables representing the subjects teachers taught, such as English, math, social studies, science, and others; (b) measures of teachers' background characteristics, including sex and years of experience; (c) a measure of the extent to which teachers perceived students as needing differing forms of instruction based on different needs; and (d) a measure of the extent of ability grouping in the academic department to which teachers were assigned. In a previous study, we found that many of these teacher-level variables affected teachers' perceptions of task routinization (Rowan et al., 1992).

The results of the analysis are presented in Table 3.3. First, the variance decomposition shows that very little of the variance in teachers' ratings of task uncertainty or task variety lies between schools—only about 4% of the variance for task uncertainty and above 15% for task variety. In addition, the table shows that several of the independent variables in our model account for this within-school variance.

With respect to the regression models shown in Table 3.3, it should be noted that these are "trimmed" models. Independent variables that failed to achieve statistical significance in a first-round analysis were trimmed from the model, and then the models were reestimated. The results show that task uncertainty was: (a) higher for teachers who viewed students as needing differentiated instruction, (b) lower for teachers who worked in departments with academic tracking, and (c) lower for more experienced teachers. Task variety was: (a) higher for teachers who viewed students as needing differentiated instruction, (b) lower for male teachers, and (c) lower for math teachers.

Summary. Our results fail to confirm the assumption that teaching is a complex and nonroutine task, at least for the teachers in this study. In fact, in our sample of high school teachers, nearly half the teachers viewed teaching as a routine task with low task variety and low task uncertainty, whereas 35% viewed teaching as an engineering task having high task variety but low task uncertainty.

The correlation analysis suggested that a routine conception of teaching is associated with a highly rationalized view of education that emphasizes ability grouping, a sequenced and hierarchical approach to learning, and a standardized and static view of subject-matter knowledge. The regression analysis suggested that experience in teaching reduces task uncertainty, and that math teaching is characterized by less task variety. With respect to nonroutine teaching, both the correlation and regression analyses suggest that a conception of teaching as a nonroutine task is associated with a dynamic view of knowledge, an emphasis on differentiating instruction for students, and an interactive style of teaching.

The Effects of Task Conceptions on Organic Management

We now turn to the hypothesis that nonroutine tasks give rise to organic forms of management. To examine this hypothesis, we developed a series of measures of organic management in schools based on teachers' responses to a series of questionnaire items. In previous research, we demonstrated that teachers' perceptions of organic management vary predictably within schools as a function

Table 3.3. HLM Analysis of Sources of Variation in Task Uncertainty and Task Variety.

	Task Uncertainty	Task Variety
Variance decomposition:		
% between schools	3.6%	15%
Within-school regression:		
Intercept	.737	.228
	(.118)	(.115)
Differentiated Instruction*	.074	.206
	(.035)	(.036)
Tracking	-.103	
	(.026)	
Sex		-.174
		(.067)
Experience	-.022	
	(.003)	
English		
Math		-.354
		(.121)
Science		
Other		

*Note: First coefficient is unstandardized regression coefficient; standard error in parentheses; all coefficients statistically significant at p > or = .05, two-tailed.

of: (a) teachers' location in the academic division of labor in schools (i.e., the academic track in which teachers work, the subject they teach), and (b) teachers' background characteristics (i.e., sex and years of experience).

In our previous studies, we have suggested that within school differences in organic management occur because school administrators manage different subunits within schools differently and because teachers working under different conditions and with different conceptions of their task actively construct their work environments to fit their needs. This is not to deny that there are differences among schools in organic management. Indeed, our previous studies have uncovered this kind of school-level variation. However, we also have demonstrated substantial within-school variance in teachers' reports about the managerial environments of schools, and we have developed a number of theoretical arguments to account for these differences (Rowan et al., 1991).

In this chapter, we examine the idea that teachers' reports about organic management will vary within schools as a result of their differing conceptions of the task of teaching. In particular, we expect teachers who report higher levels of task variety and task uncertainty to also report higher levels of organic management in the schools in which they work. We assume that this will occur because: (a) teachers who face uncertainty will actively seek out the support of administrators and colleagues and work to gain control over their working environment in order to cope with the uncertainties of teaching, and (b) because school administrators will be oriented to providing more organizational support to subunits and teachers who face more variety and uncertainty in their work.

Measures of organic management. The measures of organic management used in this chapter are the same ones that we have used in previous research (Rowan et al., 1991, 1992). The three measures are:

- *Staff cooperation*, an 8-item scale measuring cooperation and collaboration among school staff. The measure covers a variety of dimensions of this construct, including the extent to which members help each other in diverse duties, share beliefs and values about the central mission of the school, maintain uniformly high standards of performance for themselves, and seek new ideas (internal consistency = .86);
- *Teacher control,* a 9-item scale measuring teacher participation in and control over decisions about student behavior codes, content of inservice programs, student grouping, text selection, teaching content and techniques, and amount of homework assigned (internal consistency = .75); and
- *Principal leadership*, a 13-item scale measuring the supportive aspects of administrative leadership in schools, including such activities as effectively coping with outside pressures, setting priorities, recognizing, encouraging, supporting staff, and involving staff in decision making (internal consistency = .94).

The measures tap dimensions of organic management described in the general literature on organizations and in discussions of effective schools (e.g., Little, 1982; Rosenholtz, 1985). Correlations among the three scales range from .49 to .66, suggesting that the items tap a single and underlying dimension of school organization. At the same time, however, our previous research demonstrates that each scale has different relationships to both independent and dependent variables. As a result, we have not combined these scales into a single index of organic management.

Key findings. Table 3.4 shows the results of our analyses. As in Table 3.3, the table provides an initial variance decomposition in each dependent measure and then presents the results in a two-level hierarchical linear modeling analysis that estimates the effects of independent variables measured at the teacher level on the dependent measures.

In each of the models, the following independent variables were included in the within-school analysis: (a) the measures of task variety and task uncertainty discussed previously, (b) the dummy-coded variables measuring the subjects taught by teachers, (c) the measure of the extent to which teachers perceive students as needing differentiated instruction, (d) the measure of the presence of ability grouping in a teacher's academic department, and (e) teachers' sex (1 = male) and years of teaching experience. The models shown in the tables are "trimmed," that is, variables that failed to achieve statistical significance in a first-round analysis were deleted from the model, and the model was then reestimated.

The variance decompositions show that 27% of the variance in staff cooperation lies between schools, 19% of the variance in teacher control lies between schools, and about 23% of the variance in teachers' perceptions of principal leadership lies between schools. In previous analyses, we have found that the alternative high schools in the sample show the highest levels of organic management. From the standpoint of organization theory this makes sense. These schools are smaller and are characterized by stronger missions than other schools in the sample, factors that previous research has shown facilitate the development of organic management.

The most important finding from Table 3.4 is that the within-school analyses provide only partial confirmation of contingency theory. First, our two measures of task characteristics have statistically significant effects on only two of the three measures of organic management—staff cooperation and teacher control. More importantly, however, these effects are in opposite directions. As predicted, task variety has positive effects on teacher control and staff cooperation. However, contrary to our expectations, task uncertainty has negative effects on these variables.

The effects of two other variables are worth noting. The measure of teachers' perceptions of the need for differentiated instruction, a variable that was positively related to task variety and task uncertainty, has positive effects on teacher control and principal leadership. The measure of ability grouping, which was negatively related to task variety, also tends to have positive effects on teacher control and principal leadership.

Table 3.4. HLM Analysis of Sources of Variation in Organic Design Variables.

	Staff Cooperation	Teacher Control	Principal Leadership
Variance decomposition:			
% between schools	27%	19%	23%
Within-school regression:			
Intercept	-.464	-.294	-.211
	(.147)	(.101)	(.117)
Differentiated Instruction*		.107	.211
		(.026)	(.034)
Tracking	.119	.078	.083
	(.043)	(.019)	(.024)
Sex			
Experience			
Task Uncertainty	-.149	-.098	
	(.043)	(.032)	
Task Variety	.112	.094	
	(.043)	(.034)	
English			
Math			
Science			
Other	.206	.184)	
	(.091)	(.070)	

*Note: First coefficient is unstandardized regression coefficient; standard error in parentheses; all coefficients in table statistically significant $p >$ or $= .05$, two-tailed.

Summary. What do these analyses imply about the validity of contingency theory in studies of school organization? It seems likely that the causal ordering of variables used in the present analyses is wrong. For example, we might argue that task variety and task uncertainty are affected by (rather than affect) organic design in schools. From this perspective, teachers who report more control over decisions and who work in environments characterized by staff cooperation have greater task variety, perhaps due to the collaborative nature of work in the school and because of participation in school decision making. These teachers might also face less technical uncertainty because they control their working environments and receive support and help from colleagues.

This line of reasoning is not entirely inconsistent with the contingency theory. For example, assume that teachers hold a view of teaching that encourages diversity and complexity in instruction (e.g., they perceive students as needing differentiated instruction—a variable found in Table 3.3 to be positively related to measures of task variability and task uncertainty and a variable found in Table 3.4 to be positively related to organic design). In order to cope with demands presented by differentiated instruction, teachers might be expected to seek control over their work environment and seek out collaborative relationships with colleagues. By participating in organic forms of management, these teachers then might be able to resolve the problems faced by implementing differentiated instruction. Such participation should increase the amount of task variety present in a teacher's job by requiring a teacher to participate in more meetings and committees, but it would reduce the amount of technical uncertainty faced by the teacher by providing him or her with a set of routines that could be used in instruction.

This scenario is consistent with Rosenholtz's (1989) discussion of school organization. However, unlike Rosenholtz, we think the scenario makes a troubling statement about the nature of school culture. Recall that task certainty is associated with a standardized and hierarchical view of curriculum and instruction. That is, lower levels of task uncertainty are associated with a view of teaching that favors ability grouping, emphasizes a standardized curriculum for all students, views knowledge as "cut and dried" and well defined, and asserts that students learn best when they first master basic skills in small steps before proceeding to complex subject matter. From this perspective, the organic forms of management observed in the schools in this sample could be reinforcing the kinds of highly rationalized forms of instruction that many advocates of school reform currently criticize.

In short, the data in Table 3.4 clearly do not support the simple chain of reasoning we began with. However, the alternative interpretation just discussed is not entirely inconsistent with the overall logic of contingency theory. Our discussion suggests that teachers who have adopted a complex form of instruction might seek to participate in school decisions and to find supportive relationships with colleagues. As this occurs, teachers will experience increased task variety and decreased task uncertainty. Although a definitive test of this chain of reasoning requires longitudinal data, we think a reanalysis of the current, cross-sectional data might also shed light on the line of reasoning discussed here.

The Effects of Organic Management

Finally, we turn to an examination of the effects of organic management on such teacher outcomes as commitment, expectations for successful task performance, and on-the-job learning. Our interest in these teacher outcomes derives from research on teaching, which suggests that variables such as commitment, expectations for success, and on-the-job learning are associated with effective performance as a teacher (e.g., Ashton & Webb, 1986). Research in organizational psychology similarly suggests that effective task performance is a function of motivation and skill.

A wide variety of research suggests that organic management will foster these teacher outcomes. For example, organizational psychologists have arrayed an impressive amount of data suggesting that job and organization design schemes that make organizations more "organic" in form increase worker motivation (for a review, see Porter, Lawler, & Hackman, 1975). In addition, research in adult learning has recently connected organic management to gains in workers' on-the-job learning (Marsick, 1989). Finally, there is an emerging body of educational research that is consistent with this view (for a review, see Rowan, 1990b).

Measures. In the analyses reported next, we employ measures of commitment, expectancy, and professional growth to assess the outcomes of organic management for teachers. Our measures are:

- *Commitment,* an eight-item scale that assesses teachers' commitment to students, to the school in which they work, and to teaching in general. Items measure teachers' perceptions of the amount of effort, enjoyment, and enthusiasm with which they approach their work and their interest in remaining in their current teaching assignment, school, and the teaching profession.
- *Expectancy,* a three-item scale that is intended to measure teachers' expectation that their teaching will be successful. It asks teachers to rate the extent to which they think they can reach difficult students, insure that students achieve at a high level, and make a difference in students' lives; and
- *Professional growth,* a three-item scale that asks teachers to rate opportunities for learning on the job. Teachers are asked to assess the extent to which they feel supported by colleagues to try out new ideas, are eager to hear about ways to improve as a teacher, and are improving as a teacher.

Items for these scales were drawn from a wide variety of research studies both in education and in research on organizations more generally. They have face validity and display reasonable psychometric properties. The commitment index has an internal consistency of .75, the expectancy scale has an internal consistency of .68, and the professional growth scale has an internal consistency of .62. The measures are modestly intercorrelated. Growth and commitment have a zero-order correlation of .57, growth and expectancy have a correlation of .32, and commitment and expectancy have a correlation of .40.

Findings. Table 3.5 presents the results of the analyses. Once again, we estimated a series of two-level hierarchical linear models, this time with teacher commitment, expectancy, and professional growth as the dependent variables in the within school models. The independent variables in the with-in-school models were: (a) the three measures of organic design, (b) the controls for teacher sex and years of experience, (c) the dummy-coded variables representing subject taught, (d) the measure of teachers' perceptions of the need to differentiate instruction for students, (e) the measure of tracking in a teacher's department, and (f) the measures of task variety and task uncertainty.

The findings show that only a small percentage of the variance in the teacher outcome of interest here lies between the schools in this sample. About 13% of the variance in teacher commitment lies between schools, about 9% of teacher expectations for success is between schools, and about 12% of the variance in teachers' reported professional growth is between schools.

The within-school regression models lend support to the hypothesis that organic management leads to increased motivation and learning. For example, there are statistically significant and positive effects of all three measures of organic management on teacher commitment and teacher professional growth. However, among the measures of organic management, only the principal leadership scale has statistically significant effects on teacher expectations for success.

Other findings are worth noting. For example, teachers' perceptions of the need for differentiated instruction have consistently positive and statistically significant effects on each of the three teacher outcomes. Given the findings from the analyses on task conceptions and organic management, we must conclude that the perception of students as needing differentiated instruction is one of the most influential of all beliefs. It shapes teachers' conceptions of the task, spurs the construction of a supportive working environment, and positively affects valued teacher outcomes.

The consistently positive and statistically significant effects of task variety on teacher outcomes are also worth noting. Job design research has

Table 3.5. HLM Analysis of Sources of Variation in Motivation and Learning.

	Commitment	Expectancy	Professional Growth
Variance decomposition:			
% between schools	13%	9%	12%
Within-school regression:			
Intercept	.014	.159	.212
	(.025)	(.079)	(.070)
Differentiated Instruction*	.061	.321	.123
	(.025)	(.033)	(.030)
Tracking			
Sex			-.135
			(.052)
Experience		-.007	-.007
		(.003)	(.003)
Task Uncertainty		.090	
		(.042)	
Task Variety	.173	.081	.092
	(.029)	(.041)	(.034)
Staff Cooperation	.102		.204
	(.040)		(.047)
Teacher Control	.239		.180
	(.045)		(.053)
Principal Leadership	.151	.197	.202
	(.029)	(.040)	(.049)

*Note: First coefficient is unstandardized regression coefficient; standard error in parentheses; all coefficients statistically significant p > or = .05, two-tailed.

long noted that this aspect of work is motivating and enriching, and the present analysis confirms this point of view. On the contrary, task uncertainty, our other measure of task characteristics, has much less of an effect on teacher outcomes, although, predictably, teacher uncertainty tends to decrease teachers' expectations for success.

Finally, we note that more experienced teachers tend to show lower expectations for success and lower levels of professional growth. These findings suggest an interesting pattern of career related growth in teacher expectations for success. Early in teaching careers, teachers' expectations for success are boosted by a lack of experience, but tempered by task uncertainty. As teachers gain more experience, task uncertainty is reduced, thus enhancing expectations for optimism about task performance and enthusiasm for professional growth.

Summary. In conclusion, teachers' levels of commitment, expectations for success, and amount of professional growth appear to be related in complex ways to factors such as the managerial practices that they experience, their conceptions of the task of teaching, and their beliefs about students. However, it seems safe to conclude that after controlling for teacher experience and beliefs about instruction, organic management increases teacher commitment, expectations for success, and professional growth. The effects of organic management are direct in the case of commitment and professional growth, but are indirect in the case of expectations for success. In the case of expectations, the overall pattern of findings from our analyses suggests that organic management reduces task uncertainty, which in turn acts directly to increase expectations for success.

CONCLUSION

The preliminary results of our work are surprising and call for further analysis. For example, our analysis of conceptions of teaching calls into question one of the most taken-for-granted assumptions in research on schools—that the task of teaching is nonroutine. Teachers in our sample did not view teaching in this way. Instead, the plurality of teachers in our study viewed teaching as a routine task. Thus, our findings suggest that many men and women in the teaching profession view the work of teaching very much like men and women in clerical and sales jobs view their work. At the same time, another third of our sample perceived the characteristics of teaching in much the same way as engineers, lawyers, and accountants view work. What bears notice, however, is that very few teachers reported that teaching was a nonroutine task. Clearly, these findings call for further study, especially among organization theorists who have based their explanations of schools as loosely coupled systems on the assumption that teaching is a nonroutine task.

Our study also suggests that conceptions of teaching as a task have educational importance. Perceptions of task certainty and task variety are not only correlated to important conceptions about the nature of learning and school knowledge, but they are also correlated to the kind of managerial environments in which teachers work. What is especially interesting in our analysis is the tendency for the kinds of "organic" forms of management advocated by proponents of school restructuring and teacher professionalism to be associated with task certainty. To the extent that task certainty is based on a standardized view of the school curriculum, a hierarchical view of learning, and a static view of disciplinary knowledge, one is left wondering whether school restructuring or a movement toward the professionalization of teaching along the lines of engineering or law is, in fact, desirable. Clearly, further work is needed to investigate the correspondence between educational philosophies, managerial practices, and conceptions of teaching as a task.

Finally, we note a positive theme in our results. It is clear that "organic" forms of management motivate individuals and inspire professional growth. The direct effects of teacher collaboration, participative forms of decision making, and supportive forms of school leadership on teacher commitment, expectations for success, and on-the-job learning therefore suggest some potential benefits of school restructuring. However, what remains to be seen is the educational purpose toward which teachers in organically managed and professionalized settings commit themselves. Clearly, further research on this problem is needed, especially in light of our preliminary findings.

REFERENCES

Ashton, P., & Webb, R. (1986). *Making a difference: Teachers' sense of efficacy and student achievement.* New York: Longman.

Bidwell, C. (1965). The school as a formal organization. In J. G. March (Ed.), *Handbook of organizations.* Chicago: Rand McNally.

Daft, R., & McIntosh, N. (1978). A new approach to design and use of management information. *California Management Review, 21,* 82-92.

Hage, J., & Aiken, M. (1969). Routine technology, social structure, and organizational goals. *Administrative Science Quarterly, 14,* 336-386.

Little, J. W. (1982). Norms of collegiality and experimentation: Workplace conditions of school success. *American Educational Research Journal, 19,* 325-340.

Lortie, D. (1975). *Schoolteacher.* Chicago: University of Chicago Press.

Marsick, V. (1989). *Learning in the workplace.* New York: Croom Helm.

Meyer, J., & Rowan, B. (1978). The structure of educational organizations. In M. W. Meyer & Associates (Eds.), *Environments and organizations.* San Francisco: Jossey-Bass.

Perrow, C. (1967). A framework for the comparative analysis of organizations. *American Sociological Review, 79,* 686-704.

Porter, L. W., Lawler, E. E., & Hackman, J. R. (1975). *Behavior in organizations.* New York: McGraw-Hill.

Raudenbush, S. W., Rowan, B., & Cheong, Y. F. (1992). Contextual effects on the self-perceived efficacy of high school teachers. *Sociology of Education, 65,* 150–167.

Raudenbush, S. W., Rowan, B., & Kang, S. J. (1991). A multilevel, multivariate model for studying school climate with estimation via the EM algorithm and application to U.S. high school data. *Journal of Educational Statistics, 16,* 295-330.

Rosenholtz, S. J. (1985). Effective schools: Interpreting the evidence. *American Journal of Education, 93,* 352-388.

Rosenholtz, S. J. (1989). *Teachers' workplace: The social organization of schools.* New York: Longman.

Rowan, B. (1990a). Applying conceptions of teaching to organizational reform. In R. F. Elmore & Associates (Eds.), *Restructuring schools: The next generation of reform.* San Francisco: Jossey-Bass.

Rowan, B. (1990b). Commitment and control: Alternative strategies for the organizational design of schools. In C. Cazden (Ed.), *Review of research in education* (Vol. 16). Washington, DC: American Educational Research Association.

Rowan, B., Raudenbush, S. W., & Cheong, Y. F. (1992). *Teaching as a non-routine task: Implications for the organizational design of schools.* Stanford, CA: Center for Research on the Context of Secondary School Teaching.

Rowan, B., Raudenbush, S. W., & Kang, S. J. (1991). Organizational design in high schools: A multilevel analysis. *American Journal of Education, 98,* 238-265.

Weick, K. (1976). Educational organizations as loosely coupled systems. *Administrative Science Quarterly, 23,* 541-552.

Withey, M., Daft, R. L., & Cooper, W. C. (1983). Measures of work unit technology: An empirical assessment and a new scale. *Academy of Management Journal, 26,* 45–63.

4 THE ROLE OF COLLABORATION IN THE PROCESS OF CHANGE

===

Patricia A. Antonacci
Regis G. Bernhardt
Fordham University

If you are one of the millions of Americans who watch the evening news, almost daily you see the urgency of educational reform highlighted as one of the nation's most pressing needs. For more than 25 years there has been a debate over the effectiveness of the nation's schools, a debate conducted largely by the media, in which the public is reminded that its schools are failing.

In *A Place Called School,* John I. Goodlad (1984) uncovered the nation's eyes to the tragic state of the schools, which sent out a call for immediate school reform. Across the country, educators have begun to respond to the dilemma of their 19th-century factory model schools that are still being used to prepare young citizens for the 21st century. They realize that the traditional model of schooling, once suited for the industrial age, has outlived its usefulness in educating the children of the information age. This status quo of our nation's schools becomes even more dramatic when its context is considered: Schools remain frozen in time within a dynamic society in which change is occurring with undaunted speed.

The questions that continue to arise are: If educators are responding to the need for change within their schools, what prevents successful school reform? What obstructs such admirable attempts by our schools to effect positive change? It is not that schools do not try to improve; it is that the problem of change or restructuring is no small matter. It has now become clear that improving a school is not contingent on the implementation of a new instructional program or the application of more current approaches to teaching. Rather, improving a school is the actual transformation of the school to thoughtful environments in which children learn and teachers teach (Fiske, 1991). Restructuring a traditional school calls for change at the grassroots level: change that goes beyond simple programs that have in the past proved to be a "band-aid cure" for systemic problems. What is more, there is no simple "quick fix" for any school (Allington & Walmsley, 1995). Any grassroots change that brings about a transformation of the school environment is a process that is ongoing and not a one-shot deal (Fullan, 1991).

It is, therefore, no secret that change is difficult at best, no matter how small or worthy its goal. Although educational practice has a history of resistance to any sort of fundamental changes (Fullan, 1991; Sarason, 1990), and although there are indeed many complex factors related to the success or failure of any initiative, to make the change process work demands looking beyond the innovation itself to other factors involved (Fullan, 1991). One major factor involved in change that we address in this chapter is the collaboration among two teachers and an administrator that brought about a significant transformation in the early literacy program and in the learning environment within the school.

HOW COLLABORATION LEADS TO CHANGE

Collaboration among teachers and staff involves talk that has the potential to contribute to the change process. The power of talk in the change process has been well researched and documented (Johnson, 1990; Little, 1981). Such collaboration exists when there is collegiality present within a school or even within part of a school. Little (1981) has defined collegiality through its practice: (a) when staff members talk about instruction, and this type of talk is frequent, continuous, and precise; (b) when teachers and administrators observe each other teach and then talk about what they saw in the lesson; (c) when teachers, administrators, and other staff members come together to plan a lesson, select materials, and design curriculum and instruction; and (d) when there is a sharing of ideas related to what is known about learning.

However, all talk that occurs in a collaborative school environment does not necessarily support effective change. Collaboration is productive when it involves talk that focuses on instruction (Little, 1981). Furthermore, when teachers and administrators collaborate in ways to improve instruction and learning, they have the opportunity to become teacher researchers or reflective practitioners. They are "interested in improving the educational practices within their own settings. They undertake research in order to get a better understanding of events in their particular educational environment" (Strickland, 1988, p. 756). Thus the type of collaboration that contributes to the change process must be deliberate, that is, the dialogues must inquire about a specific area of instruction for the purpose of improving it.

A school that is marked by collegiality and collaboration maintains an environment that can nurture and sustain a community of learners in which members are "committed above all to discovering conditions that elicit and support human learning and to providing these conditions" (Barth, 1990, p. 45). It is within this environment that schools have the efficacy to change, for each member, including the students, is committed to life-long learning and is focused on the conditions that support this goal.

The purpose of this chapter is not to discuss the theory and practice of change; indeed, that is a topic that goes well beyond the scope of a single chapter. Rather, we intend to describe a journey of change that we have taken together. The first steps of this journey began three years ago when two teachers and an administrator were talking about improving the literacy program and the learning context for a first-grade class. Within this small group of three staff members, the seeds of collaboration were planted. In its third year, we see that our community of learners expanded, and that an outgrowth of deliberate focus and study has led to very specific changes in a literacy program for diverse students in one urban school, leaving its effects on the way literacy is taught in other primary classrooms as well.

The chapter is presented in two parts. The first part is a comparison of two contrasting models of teaching: the traditional model of instruction and the transactional model of learning. This discussion of two instructional models represents our journey to meaningful learning within the context of a 21st-century school. The description of the transmission model signifies the point at which the journey begins. The account of the transactional model exemplifies the direction of our journeying toward change. It represents the focus of our talk, which evolved into a deliberate study on changing how literacy was learned in a primary classroom. In the second part of the chapter, the change process is chronicled in a brief narration of how one reading teacher, a classroom teacher, and an administrator collaborated to become reflective practitioners. It traces their movement from the transmission model of teaching literacy in one primary classroom to a transactional model, creating a dialogic approach to the development of literacy for the students in a first-grade class. It is the story of the lessons learned not only by students, but by educators who collaborated for change by entering the community of learners.

PART I: TWO MODELS OF TEACHING

Leaving the Transmission Classroom

Our story unfolds in the context of the classroom in which the first-grade classroom teacher relied on a transmission model of learning. This model was indeed the respected one in this school. Like most classrooms in schools across the United States, this first-grade classroom was traditional with regard to the way instruction and learning occurred. The name of this model is derived from how instruction is delivered and transmitted by the teacher to the students in the form of telling. What follows are the major characteristics that describe teaching and learning in such traditional contexts.

Literacy. In any classroom, literacy is defined by the ways that reading and writing are mostly used. In a transmission classroom, literacy is defined in narrow ways; one may see children spending much of their time practicing decoding words from lists, memorizing the correct spelling of words, filling in the one right answer on worksheets, practicing skills, reading out loud to achieve correct pronunciation of the words, and practicing the mechanics of language and grammar. Rarely do the children read silently the books they have selected for enjoyment or curiosity.

Thus, for teachers and children in a transmission classroom, literacy is the sum total of skill practice, reading aloud correctly, getting the one correct answer, and learning not to think creatively or to respond to stories. These narrow definitions of literacy are confirmed by students who defined reading as decoding and working on skill sheets and with textbooks (Johns & Ellis, 1986).

Learning. The kind of knowledge that students in these century-old transmission classrooms possess has been termed "fragile knowledge" by David Perkins (1990) in *Smart Schools*. Through recitation and by rote learning, children acquire isolated facts of information they later find difficult to use. The knowledge students possess is easily tested by teachers through daily quizzes and weekly tests as well as by standardized achievement tests, usually given at the end of the year. These tests confirm that students possess knowledge. However, although most students may know, they may not understand. According to Perkins (1990), "when we understand something, we not only possess certain information about it but are enabled to do certain things with that knowledge" (p. 77). Students who learn by rote acquire isolated pieces of information that do not go beyond the state of possessing knowledge to the state of enablement. Understanding enables students to use the information they know in novel ways. Within the transmission model of learning, they acquire static knowledge that becomes inert because they cannot use it in the future.

Talk. In the traditional classroom, talk is not used in the process of learning for constructing meaning by the student. Rather, it is used by the teacher for transmitting knowledge to the students. In a lecture format, the teacher tells the students what they need to know, or he or she may clarify the information found in the text. The teacher also uses talk to ask questions, ensuring the students have learned the appropriate facts. The students use talk mainly for expressing what they may know. This kind of discourse used in a traditional classroom has been characterized by Mehan (1979) as an I-R-E pattern of classroom discourse, found in most classrooms in which learning is achieved through rote and recitation. The teacher initiates the talk (I), usually through a question, which is followed by a response (R) or an answer from the student. The teacher then evaluates (E) the student's response, determining whether it is right or wrong. This type of discourse is used for acquiring or possessing knowledge; it does not lead to understanding.

Texts. In a transmission classroom, there is a heavy reliance on a single text for learning to read and for learning in the content areas. When this is the case, the text supplies the content of the curriculum having an authoritative voice, that is, it has the "one right meaning."

In learning how to read or to become literate in a primary classroom, there is a heavy reliance on a single basal reader. One prominent feature that basal readers share is the teacher's guide. The typical teacher's guide provides a script for the teacher's daily lessons, that is, everything that the teacher should say and do in delivering reading instruction is found in the teacher's guide. Weaver (1990) suggests that the basal reading programs may be the prototype of the transmission model of teaching, particularly in the primary grades, because there is little deviation from the teacher's guide.

Assessment. The teacher in the transmission classroom views the end-of-the-year standardized achievement test as the most valid and reliable form of assessment. Therefore, at the beginning of the school year he or she uses the results to shape the literacy program by placing the students into one of three reading groups with respect to their ability. It is this test that defines the development of the students, for they will remain stuck within the ability group all year, performing within the rigid expectations set for it by predictions of last year's achievement test.

The standardized test also plays a significant role in shaping the transmission curriculum. When a teacher and the administrators believe standardized tests are real indicators of literacy performance, the test becomes a major part of the curriculum. Early in the school year, teachers train students for the test by holding regular test preparation sessions.

To summarize briefly, the learning that is promoted in a transmission classroom is passive, and the classroom context is mechanical. The teacher's role is passive, with heavy reliance on single texts and basals that guide him or her through the lesson. The children's role is passive as they practice skills, search for the one right answer, and fill in the spaces on their worksheets. Neither students nor teacher enter the community of learners, nor are they empowered to respond to texts in new ways, to challenge the author's words. Rather, the curriculum is imposed on the students and the teacher, coming not from within but from outside the classroom. In short, the transmission classroom is "structured on the old industrial model that treats students as 'products' coming down the assembly-line and teachers as mass production workers" (Futrell, 1989, p. 16).

Entering the Transactional Classroom

There are classrooms today that are shedding the traditional models of teaching and learning. As we gain entrance to a transactional context, we see the teacher and students as part of the community of learners. They no longer play their passive roles; rather, they are actively engaged in their own learning. Knowledge is not transmitted by the teacher; it is co-constructed with others as students and teachers transact with texts to create new meanings. Learning and literacy have acquired new meanings for the transactional classroom.

Literacy. To reiterate, literacy is defined by the ways children are encouraged to engage in reading and writing. In a transactional classroom, children perceive themselves as readers and writers. Throughout the day, they engage in reading authentic books for a variety of reasons. Reading is meaningful, purposeful, and enjoyable. Children's appreciation of varied types of literature is developed from their many opportunities of reading and from having a freedom of choice.

Students also write for many different reasons: Students write to respond to literature, they communicate with others, they author their own books or co-author books with a group, they write in their journals, they write to remember things, or they make signs for classmates to follow. Students not only see themselves as authors, but they view their classmates as writers as well. Their perceptions are derived from children's published books and writings that are placed on bookshelves next to those of noted authors and are used for reading aloud during the day.

Thus, for students in a transactional classroom, literacy is engaging in reading and writing for authentic purposes; the central reason for reading and writing is to construct meaning. Students do not learn isolated skills; rather, they learn literacy skills as they need them within the context of the task. Both reading and writing are used for thinking, not for filling in spaces on worksheets or for practicing isolated skills.

Talk. In a transactional classroom, talk is viewed as a vehicle for learning. It is quite different from the I-R-E model of discourse described by Mehan (1979), in which talk is used by the students to express what they know. It is the social interaction around a task in which students and a teacher are engaged that empowers the talk. No longer does talk serve as the "expression of thought . . . [but] as the medium in which thought is shaped and developed" (Wells & Chang-Wells, 1992, p. 27). The types of talk used by the diverse members of the community of learners may be, and often is, different. Bakhtin (1986) refers to diverse languages used by people from different social strata or age as social languages. The teacher may represent the official language of the curriculum, whereas the children's talk represents their social worlds. As the teacher and child interact to negotiate meaning and co-construct knowledge, the child appropriates the language of the curriculum. Language is learned through use and not from dictionaries (Bakhtin, 1981). Within the transactional classroom, social languages are not only accepted, but encouraged by the teacher who knows their value for learning.

The tasks in which students engage are often defined through the talk, meaning is negotiated and co-constructed through talk directed at accomplishing the task, and talk is central to assessing performance and learning. Talk holds the primary role in learning, which is what led Wells and Chang-Wells (1992) to declare that "students and teachers engage in the dialogic co-construction of meaning, which is the essence of education" (p. 33).

Learning. In a transactional classroom, students are actively engaged in their own learning. Because learning is social in nature (Vygotsky, 1981), it occurs as a collaborative activity between the teacher and student(s) or between a more capable student and another student who is the learner. Talk or social interaction enables the learner to engage in joint problem solving with the teacher. As the child learns the task, he or she gradually internalizes the talk associated with the activity, which then becomes a tool for thought, for individual thinking, and for further problem solving. This is what Vygotsky (1981) meant about learning when he wrote:

> Any function in the child's cultural development appears twice or on two planes. First it appears on the social plane, and then on the psychological plane. First it appears between people as an interpsychological category, and then within the child as an intrapsychological category. (p. 163)

Thus, central to this co-construction of meaning is the social interaction that takes place around the joint problem solving. In a transactional classroom, talk accompanies learning.

Meaning and the construction of knowledge by the student do not occur just because the child engages in social interaction about a specific concept highlighted by the teacher. Learning occurs within the child's zone of proximal development (ZPD). The teacher who works closely with his or her students, assessing their performance during the task, learns more each day about each child's individual development. With this understanding, the teacher pitches the instruction for the individual needs of those students, or teaches within the student's zone of proximal development.

Vygotsky (1978) claimed the zone of proximal development has implications for teaching, learning, and assessment and defines it as the distance between a child's "actual developmental level as determined by independent problem solving and the higher level of potential development as determined through problem solving under adult guidance or in collaboration with more capable peers" (p. 86). Vygotsky suggested that instruction should be at the student's potential level rather than his or her actual level of development. At this point the learner needs assistance by the teacher or another capable peer to perform a task. The transactional classroom relies on this model of apprenticeship, defined by Rogoff (1990), in teaching. Within this model, the child's zone of proximal development informs the instruction.

It is easy to realize why learning in a transactional classroom leads to understanding performances, things that we can do to show understanding (Perkins, 1990). In other words, students in a transactional classroom are called on to use what they have learned in novel ways; they simply do not learn isolated facts that become inert knowledge.

Texts. The type of texts found in a transactional classroom and the approaches to these texts may be characterized by the word *variety.* The teacher does not use a basal reader with the prescriptive teacher's manual, nor does he or she rely on a single text to provide a framework for the content of the curriculum. Rather, children become literate by reading authentic children's literature, for which there is a wide range that varies both in genre and in content.

In the guided reading part of the literacy program, children learn the concepts about print and the mechanics of language by using developmentally appropriate texts. The teacher is aware of the student's zone of proximal development and selects the text according to the child's development with respect to concepts about print. These texts contain short stories that are written with the child's developing concepts about print. They include repetitive text with explicit pictures that provide a strong support to the meaning of that text. The number of words appearing on each page, the number of pages within the book, and the degree of word difficulty increase as the level of the book increases. Additionally, with the increasing difficulty of the level of the book, there is a decrease in the repetitive text. These leveled readers replace the basal reader with its teacher's guide for direct instruction. There is no script provided in the manual to teach the child how to read. Rather, the teacher and the child generate their own script as they read together. The teacher is the expert in the apprenticeship model who demonstrates, scaffolds, and coaches the children during the lesson with a novel script generated for each new lesson. The lesson evolves as the teacher responds to the children's developing literacy concepts.

Assessment. The teacher in the transactional classroom regards assessment as a critical component of instruction. Because good instruction leads the child's development, the teacher must know the child's zone of proximal development. The teacher turns to assessment that is linked to instruction, assessment that is ongoing, occurring daily. The teacher uses the information that this assessment yields to inform his or her instruction.

Some powerful forms of alternative assessment that the teacher may utilize to shape the literacy lessons are observation of the child's reading and writing, analysis of a child's oral reading and a child's responses to the story, analysis of the child's writing, and interviews with the child about reading and writing. This kind of assessment occurs as part of the instruction process. Its purpose is not to categorize a child's ability, but to provide appropriate instruction to further the child's development.

A mindful comparison of the transmission classroom with the transactional one leads us to the conclusion that such a change could only be brought about by a transformation of the classroom environment, a grassroots change. Such changes do not come quickly; they come after long and collaborative efforts of a focused study. What follows briefly chronicles our attempts at such a change.

PART II: A STORY OF CHANGE

The second part of this chapter is a brief narrative of how the initial stages of change were inaugurated within one school over a period of three years when three members of the staff collaborated. These staff members represented three areas of instruction. The classroom teacher was in charge of the content areas of learning including the developmental reading program. The reading specialist represented a specialized area of literacy instruction; she typically taught those students who were "at risk" for learning, providing them with additional support in reading instruction. She also taught courses at the university in literacy development. The administrator was considered the curriculum leader within the building, who also taught at the university level.

Our journey begins when the reading specialist was transferred into the building where the classroom teacher had been teaching for four years and the administrator had been assigned to the building for five years. All three articulated a concern over literacy instruction for the first-graders.

The First Year

> Voices for change: "There are so many children who are 'at risk'! They leave the first grade not knowing how to read."

It was this problem that initiated the dialogue among the classroom teacher, the reading specialist, and the assistant principal. The data were significant: Each year the number of children who failed mounted with more and more children needing remediation. For years, the students who entered remediation in the first grade stayed in the program, receiving Chapter I services for the tenure of their elementary schooling. Each year the blame was placed on the children, not on the instructional program.

As we talked, we refrained from placing blame, and instead we started to study the context in which literacy was being developed. Our dialogue became animated around singular ideas. Initially, we decided that the missing ingredient was what our students in this urban school needed most—children's literature to provide them with the best models of language and to whet their interest for stories. Gradually, our lunchtimes were filled with talk about the new books we found and how we might relate them to the theme of the month or how we might integrate them with math and literature. Our meetings became more focused on joint planning because we taught together within the same room, collaborating on strategies and observing each other.

By the end of the first year in our journey, it was clear that the context in which literacy was being learned was gradually changing. As we became reflective about our teaching strategies, the students' responses, and our own interactions with our students, we redefined our questions on the appropriate ways to develop literacy concepts for students.

It was at this time that the basal reader was beginning to lose its power for the classroom teacher: It would no longer dictate the scope and sequence of the curriculum, nor would it designate the lessons for this first-grade class. It was finally abandoned as incompetent to develop the children's literacy concepts and skills, much less to bring them to literate thinking. It was at this time that we began to ask our second question.

Second Year

> Voices for change: "What are the most developmentally appropriate materials and strategies that we can use to prevent failure in the first grade?"

We finished the first year of our journey enriched by the literature into which we immersed our children and by the students' responses that these enriched stories have evoked. Yet we agreed something was missing; something was lacking for the most needy students who came from homes with few book experiences. At this time, the reading specialist, who at the same time was teaching courses at Fordham University, was influenced by researchers and educators like Keith Stanovich (1986), who emphasized the importance of fluent reading by children who are leaving the first grade. He cited the Matthew principle to describe the debilitating effects on those students: "The rich get richer, and the poor get poorer" as these children struggle to keep up but each year fall even further behind their peers. In *Whole Language Plus*, Courtney Cazden (1992) claimed that although a whole language (transactional) classroom is essential for promoting learning, some students need more. The "plus" that Cazden refers to is direct teaching strategies that boost their development of literacy skills right from the start. It is what Hiebert and Taylor (1994) refers to in *Getting Reading Right from the Start*. Finally, influenced by the effectiveness of Marie Clay's (1985) Reading Recovery program, we decided that direct teaching was the other piece to our literature program that our students needed.

Our second year of collaboration focused on the guided reading aspect of our literacy program. We designed this specific instruction especially for our students, who come to our classrooms unprepared for school and who come to the first grade with few concepts about print. We knew that there were too many children who would benefit from the very costly, but very effective, Reading Recovery program. We therefore decided to adapt this one-to-one approach to teaching reading for small groups of six students instead of one. Our time and energies in our second year were focused on designing the guided reading program that included some of the strategies of Clay's Reading Recovery program, but were situated within a small group of six students who were targeted to be "at risk" for learning. Because we needed the developmentally appropriate reading books for instruction, the finances to support our change were also needed. Strong administrative support made the acquisition of the leveled stories possible. Many of the other materials that supported instruction were teacher made.

Through collaboration, it was decided that those students who would be part of this guided reading approach would not receive their instruction within the classroom because of the many distractions. They received guided reading instruction in the reading room for 30 minutes a day.

At the end of the year there was excitement. Those children who were targeted at the beginning of the year as unprepared for school and most likely to fail were successful. Out of the 12 children, all but 3 made gains on the standardized reading achievement test. What was more, they were all reading the books and writing responses in their journals daily. They perceived themselves as readers and writers; indeed, they had entered the community of learners. In line with the Matthew principle, these children would be the ones getting richer in the second grade.

Third Year

Voices of change: "How can we extend and refine this developmental guided reading approach for use in the context of the first grade with the rest of the children?"

Our journey of collaborative change is continuing in the third year. The change in our literacy program that started for one classroom with three staff members has expanded to other classes and even to other grades. We now have a new administrator who continued our small literacy initiative in a more formal way. For all teachers in the primary grades, pre-K through second, there has been three full days of staff development and the purchase of the materials that support this approach.

Our original collaborative group has changed. The first grade classroom teacher was transferred to another school. For the two of us who remain, our dialogues are still about the literacy program, but the nature of our questions is changing. We now focus on very specific aspects of a child's literacy development, such as ways in which words are understood and appropriated or how the child shows his or her stage of word development during reading.

VOICES OF CHANGE: WHAT WE HAVE LEARNED

As we reflect on our journey, its initiation, and its direction in which we continue, we only now are beginning to realize its breadth. From within the walls of one school, change was brought about through three voices concerned about an area of instruction.

The power of dialogue was not self-contained. In our third year, other classroom teachers have inquired about initiating changes in their literacy programs. They too are starting to talk about the same areas of study that we began three years ago.

We are no longer the same. Our study of literacy learning has changed not only the context of our classrooms, but the way we understand learning and literacy. It has all commenced with a dialogue on a joint problem by three members of the staff.

REFERENCES

Allington, R., & Walmsley, S. A. (Eds.). (1995). *No quick fix: Rethinking literacy programs in America's elementary schools.* New York: Teachers College Press.

Bakhtin, M. M. (1981). *The dialogic imagination: Four essays by M. M. Bakhtin.* Austin: University of Texas Press.

Bakhtin, M. M. (1986). *Speech genres and other late essays.* Austin: University of Texas Press.

Barth, R. (1990). *Improving schools from within: Teachers, parents, and principals can make the difference.* San Francisco: Jossey-Bass.

Cazden, C. (1992). *Whole language plus: Essays on literacy in the United States and New Zealand.* New York: Teachers College Press.

Clay, M. (1985). *The new meaning of educational change* (3rd ed.). Portsmouth, NH: Heinemann.

Fiske, E. B., with Reed, S. & Sutter, R. C. (1991). *Smart schools, smart kids: Why do some schools work?* New York: Simon and Schuster.

Fullan, M. (1991). *The new meaning of educational change* (2nd ed.). New York: Teachers College Press.

Futrell, M. H. (1989). A most precious resource. *Education Week, 8*(25), 16.

Goodlad, J. (1984). *A place called school.* New York: McGraw-Hill.

Hiebert, E. H., & Taylor, B. M. (1994). *Getting reading right from the start: Effective early literacy interventions.* Boston: Allyn and Bacon.

Johns, J., & Ellis, D. (1986). Reading: Children tell it like it is. *Reading World, 16,* 115-128.

Johnson, S. M. (1990). *Teachers at work: Achieving success in our schools.* New York: Basic Books.

Little, J. (1981). *School success and staff development in urban desegregated schools: A summary of recently completed research.* Boulder, CO: Center for Action Research.

Mehan, H. (1979). *Learning lessons: Social organization in the classroom.* Cambridge, MA: Harvard University Press.

Perkins, D. (1990). *Smart schools: Better thinking and learning for every child.* New York: Free Press.

Rogoff, B. (1990). *Apprenticeship in thinking: Cognitive development in social context.* New York: Oxford University Press.

Sarason, S. (1990). *The predictable failure of educational reform.* San Francisco: Jossey-Bass.

Stanovich, K. E. (1986). Matthew effects in reading: Some consequences of individual differences in the acquisition of literacy. *Reading Research Quarterly, 21,* 360-407.

Strickland, D. (1988). The teacher as researcher: Toward the extended professional. *Language Arts, 65*(8), 754-764.

Vygotsky, L. S. (1978). *Mind in society: The development of higher psychological processes* (M. Cole, V. John-Steiner, S. Scribner, & E. Souberman, Eds.). Cambridge, MA: Harvard University Press.

Vygotsky, L. S. (1981). The development of higher forms of attention in childhood. In J. V. Wertsch (Ed.), *The concept of activity in Soviet psychology* (pp. 79-102). Armonk, NY: M. E. Sharpe.

Weaver, C. (1990). *Understanding whole language: From principles to practice.* Portsmouth, NH: Heinemann.

Wells, G., & Chang-Wells, G. L. (1992). *Constructing knowledge together: Classrooms as centers of inquiry and literacy.* Portsmouth, NH: Heinemann.

5   COLLABORATION AND CONSTRUCTIVISM: A CASE FOR THE NONPUBLIC SCHOOL

Gerald M. Cattaro

Fordham University

> To be truly COLLABORATIVE, an organization must have supportive structures in which the authority to act is shared by the people within the organization. (Johnson, 1995, p. 17)

Facing the new millennium the paradigm of collaborative administrator, the emancipation of the classroom teacher, and the engagement of students, parents, and community in the infrastructure of the organization have given new meaning to the expression of leadership in educational settings. The new standards, which place equalization of these dynamics at the heart of the organization, are paramount to any framework design for leadership in a learning community. The leadership challenge is propelled by the phenomena of the forces that drive multicultural and gender concerns. Bonding in a charismatic complexity, these issues call forth the ethical accountability of leadership. The nonpublic schools are preeminent in the conversation of leadership as they are an undeniable and distinct part of the fabric of the U.S. educational design.

     Organizational culture and the tradition of private and religious schools lend themselves to a palpable force as they encounter the standards set forth in the paradigm that express this concept of leadership. Consequently, identity, governance, transitions, finance and, in the case of the religious school, spirituality are unique characteristics of the nonpublic school conversation. Societal and cultural influences such as globalization, deregulation database, and decision making do not stop at the public school. They also provide an agenda to rethink the role of curriculum leadership as it affects the service and relationship dimensions of respective religious educational institutions.

Recognizing the existing paradigm of the nonpublic school, educators are called on to embrace collaborative efforts, facilitate justice, and reflect on the ethics germane to their own heritage. The strategy that undergirds instruction in the nonpublic school setting is driven by these concerns as nonpublic organizations shift from a linear to a more multidimensional decision-making framework.

CHRONICLE OF CULTURES

Proponents of the nonpublic sector of education are often challenged with an imbroglio demonstrated in the apologetical approach and defense of private and religious education. The win–win dimension is not the usual presentation. Most attempts to compare the nonpublic school with public education and public policy serve to alienate the private and religious schools. A good example of this form of rhetoric is found in the research of James Coleman, Thomas Hoffer, and Sally Kilgore (1982) in their 1980 study, *High School and Beyond*. A population of over 60,000 secondary students was evaluated. The results show that students of Catholic and private schools achieve at higher levels than students in public schools.

These issues of comparison somewhat impede the possibilities of coexistence among private, religious, and public educational organizations. Apparent are the many rebuttals to what was to become the maligned Coleman Report. Professor John F. Whitte (1993-1994) of the University of Wisconsin, as reviewed by Parker (1992), built on the analysis of Chubb and Moe (1990). The rebuttals claim that the organizational culture contributes toward the differentiation of schooling in the United States. If the distinctive organizational behavior is to be fully understood, then the tradition, symbolism, culture, and charisma of the three cultures of public, private, and religious schooling must be understood in the context of the reform movement of education across our nation. The expression of the new paradigm of school leadership that embraces collaboration and constructivism is activated within the instructional process of each organizational configuration.

Randall (1994a) proposes that before undertaking the study of private and public schooling, definitions ought to be clarified. Currently, the use of the term *public* describes an entity that has the support of, or is controlled by, government. This somewhat constricted meaning precludes all those who choose another form of educational sponsorship.

Bailyn (1960) defined *public* as:

> in fact anything that benefitted the community as a whole, and in reference to educational institutions, only to designate the lack of legal barriers to the entrance. . . . Indeed it is anachronistic even to say that private and public functions overlapped and merged before the nineteenth century: the distinctions by which to make such a statement were absent. (p. 133)

With this understanding, it is easy to conjecture that the process relative to the education of our citizenry was not cultivated into the private, private, and religious apportionment that exists today. Ideologies matured adjacent to the historical development of the nation. The mélange of these strong beliefs decree the common good, common discourse, and common understanding in directing the United States' struggle to meet the needs of a pluralistic society.

GOVERNANCE AND DOMINATION

The questions as to who is at the helm and who renders the schematization of the organization are germane to any discussion of collaboration. Currently, the climate regarding government control in the United States is an issue of prominence. The Oklahoma City bombing and the rise of militia groups in 1995 are testimony to the United States' contrariety with the issue of government control.

The nation's public schools as a commodity of the government cannot escape the controls of federal legislation, state mandates, and local governments. Combine the controls with the respective court rulings in each of these jurisdictions and the bureaucratic association with government unfolds. Ziegler, Tucker, and Wilson (1977) characterize four phases of control in the history of the public schools of the United States:

- Lay control   1835–1900
- Local professional control   1900-1968
- The nationalism of education   1954-1975
- Educational and social goals   1975-present

Boards of education were representative of the community at the opening of U.S. lay public educational history. Board members had opportunities to interact with their fellow citizens, and concerns regarding educational policies were rooted in the community. The period known as the lay control of public schools allowed for the direct control and administration of the public schools by boards of education. The term *lay* is a reference to the nonprofessional status of the early board of education members. The communities in which these hands-on folks lived were, for the most part, homogeneous and accommodating. Accordingly, this allowed for a manageable situation regarding the governance and superintendence of the community public school.

Circa 1900, the school systems entered a new era inherent upon the growth of U.S. urban centers. The responsibilities of education became too burdensome for board of education members as they felt overwhelmed, and their sense of rationalism provided the quest for professional educators to administer newly apportioned school districts. On that account, responsibilities of education were shifted to the new professionals known as superintendents. School board members were no longer elected within the regular elections, and authority and governance of the public domain of education were centralized. This marked a significant change in the way the nation viewed the public school, as power was no longer in the hands of local nonprofessional citizens. This metastasis was brought about by progressive theorists, most of whom were White, upper middle class, well educated, and Protestant. According to Graham (1970), one of the main functions of the progressives was to eliminate special-interest groups that were influencing certain boards of education. McConnell (1970) notes, however, that the progressives themselves were a special-interest group who attempted to use power in this new system of public education. Interestingly enough, the progressives more often than not politicized their own philosophy of education. Even though there were important curricular changes, the result was one of control (Link, Link, & Catton, 1986). Tyack (1974) notes that power in educational matters was transferred to an "interlocking directorate of urban elites" and a growing educational bureaucracy with vested interest in the "one best system" of education.

Brown v. Board of Education of Topeka, Kansas (1954) and subsequent court decisions, in addition to federal and state legislation, have contributed to the ascendancy of government education in the public sector of education. The infusion of state aid and the disposition of the pandect regulations as well as the distribution of these funds have contributed to the augmentation of centralized agencies. Federal government and state control have added to the financial standing and popular attitude toward public educational institutions in the United States. During the same time, the rise of the teachers' unions and their impact on the collective bargaining process also contributed to the mechanisms of control. The increase in the degree of federal mandates by way of affirmative action and the acknowledgment of the rights of women and handicapped individuals allowed for even more control over local educational agencies. By the early 1980s, the economic conditions of the nation and its global links increased this control. Thus, as Randall (1994b) stated in the *Journal of Research on Christian Education,* "American society has forged an ideological link between state sanctioned schools and support of school systems with the preservation and progress of the nation" (p. 175).

Private schools in the United States, as previously implied, have their origins preceding public education. Each of these schools is governed by a board of directors or similar governing board that selects its own members, determines the school's philosophy, and accepts responsibility for the school. The board is also responsible for resource and financial obligations. Furthermore, the governing board appoints a chief administrator in charge of the day-to-day operations. Each school is free to determine its own philosophy and practice it. Accordingly, it is possible for each private school to maintain a distinct educational and organizational environment that allows them to be independent schools, a name they prefer to use. These schools do not belong to any large formal system, but many share information among their own organizations (Bobette & Danbridge, n.d.).

Eighty-six percent of the youngsters attending private schools attend schools that have a religious affiliation, according to the *Digest of Educational Statistics* (Synder, 1988). The religious schools operate on an underpinning agendum that is associated somewhat with private schools. Together, they seek markets that are decentralized and allow for competition and choice in schooling. Religious schools, by their nature, are obviously moored into an ecclesiastical and theological framework. Their governance is usually based on the ecclesiology of a particular tenet. Currently, the Catholic school system educates the greatest number of nonpublic school children in our nation. It is the largest of the religious school systems (Doyle, 1995).

Most Christian denominations have canonical jurisdictions regarding their organizational structure or a mandate from a scriptural reference as to the education of their youth. In the Catholic educational system, the bishop of a particular diocese is technically the chief educational officer, and he has an ecclesiastical mandate to teach. In the United States, the administration of Catholic schools is usually delegated to a superintendent of education.

In reality, most decisions are made at the local level, especially as they relate to finance, living out the mission of the school, personnel, and marketing. The aftermath of the blizzard of January 1996 in the Northeast illustrated the autonomous nature of each Catholic school. As announcements were made in regard to school closings in the media, the list grew longer and longer as each school made its own decision to close. Chubb and Moe (1990) observed that the local administrators make the curriculum decisions for the religious schools. Principals are appointed by pastors with direction by diocesan educational authorities or boards of education. In the Catholic school system, schools were first established by religious congregations that were loosely linked to the Diocesan Ordinary. Later, during the Baltimore Councils of the 1800s, bishops challenged their pastors to establish grammar schools in every parish, a dream never fulfilled (Buetow, 1970). In a review of Convey's (1992) research on Catholic schools, we find that the secondary schools remained almost totally autonomous as they were owned primarily by religious congregations. According to the National Catholic Educational Association, increasingly dioceses are allowing their schools to be independent and governed by boards of trustees (*Board of Trustees*, n.d.).

In marked contrast to the historical development of the public schools, private and religious schools have a fierce, almost fanatical, consciousness to foster their independence of any government controls. Randall (1994a) makes this perfectly clear as he examines the development of the nation's private and religious schools. He traces the development of nonpublic schools beginning with colonial schools, including the common and progressive schools era up to contemporary schooling. In the colonial era, most early U.S. citizens set out to replicate the system of life they had had in England. This gave way to different ideologies as, for example, settlements in Massachusetts demonstrated a puritanical outlook, the Middle States a diversity of beliefs and ideologies, and what was then the South an Anglican flavor. Power was not in the hands of any particular group and fragmentation of power was reflected in their structure of educational governance. Each religious or cultural group decided for itself its substance and process of educational endeavors (Cremin, 1970; Curti, 1974; Meyer, 1957).

During the transition toward common schools we find the control factor and homogenization of schools a threat to the philosophies of private and religious schools. Progressives made every effort to forward their pedagogies in reaction to xenophobia and religious and racial bigotry (Randall, 1994b). The educational reformers saw to it that states protected their rights and those of parents *in loco parentis*. States mandated attendance laws and regulated activities of private schools. California tried to mandate that children could attend nonpublic education facilities only with the permission of the local school board (Jorgenson, 1987). The concern of control over education in the private sector reached its culminating point when private and religious schools joined forces against the state of Oregon. In *Pierce et al. v. Hill Military*

Academy (1925) and *Pierce et al. v. Society of Sisters* (1925), the Supreme Court established the right of the nonpublic school to exist. The decisions also permit the state to issue reasonable regulation of private and religious schools. The struggle for independence of nonpublic education from what Randall (1994a) terms the coercive power of the state continues to the present time.

POLITICAL INFLUENCES ON REFORM

Pundits of U.S. education made their own attempt as they perused their goals as to the character of the U.S. polity. For Jefferson, it was to diffuse knowledge, inculcate virtue and patriotism, and thus cultivate the citizen. It is interesting to note that Jefferson made no provisions for the African American in his discourse on education. Mann remained mute on the common understanding of the mixing of the races. Dewey (1897), on the contrary, enlarged the social responsibility of the school and together with many progressives, harnessed schooling to social needs. Education was not politicized; ideologies gave way to interest groups that subsequently developed constituencies. Once the state and federal government permitted funding of various educational reforms, the doors were left wide open for the politicization of education and reform movements. Who determines the values that are germane to the U.S. student gave way to the relevance of political models in educational institutions: "the language of power, coalitions, arenas, bargaining, negotiations, interest ambiguity and so on" (Glatter, 1982, p. 16).

Politics has influenced each phase of school reform in the United States and continues to have its influence on the current debate on school reforms. The McGuffy Readers reflected a puritanical Protestantism. Later, pragmatism was faulted by conservative opponents as a substituted hedonism for idealistic standards. The National Educational Association's (NEA) Committee of Ten who tried to standardize college entrance, was accused of perpetuating high schools for the elite. The NEA's Cardinal Principles, which incorporated Dewey's philosophy of progressive education, were slowed by traditionalist advocation. Social reconstruction has had a short-lived resurgence as it flexes with political sentiment. Open education was panned by opponents as chaos (Parker & Parker, 1995).

EFFECTS OF CONTROL AND POLITICIZATION

Influential forces such as control and politics have paved the way for the development of two distinct partners in the education of U.S. citizenry. These two forces have directed the path of public and nonpublic schools as they have faced the inevitable flow of change in pedagogy and leadership. Control and politicization seem to strengthen the case for the nonpublic school and the implementation of school reform, embedded in the new paradigm of leadership and curriculum. The new framework calls for the collaboration of leadership and the construction of curriculum. Control and politicization are the provisos that distinguish public and nonpublic cultures.

The public culture of schooling in the United States is based on a tax structure that allows for monies to flow to schools. Stakeholders do not have to be satisfied with the educational processes, outcomes, or nonsuccesses of schooling. U.S. adults, 75% of whom do not have children attending public schools, likewise need not be concerned about success (Randall, 1994b). Distant authorities, such as elected board members and superintendents of schools, have the power to appoint, interfere, and stop the flow of funding, even in site-based efforts at school leadership. Systems support structure that may be liberating or a barrier to the implementation of school reform. Organizations and school cultures must have supportive, lean infrastructures in the organization to narrow the gap between policy and practice.

ORGANIZATIONAL CULTURE

Organizational culture and its development seem germane to our discussion at this juncture. It is maintained by theorists that each organization has its own culture. By organizational culture, it is meant that the organization has a set of practices, rituals, shared meanings, language, and tradition. Cultural elements give all human organizations internal meaning, purpose, and cohesion (Deal, 1987).

Erickson (1982) views culture as knowledge, a set of interpretive frames or metaphors for making sense of experience and behavior. Research on the issue of culture illustrates the observability of the culture of organizations. Bates (1987) stated:

> Culture is constituted and expressed through institutions, social relations, customs, materials, objects, and organizations. To this extent, culture is observable; empirical descriptions can be provided of the ways in which the meanings, values, ideas, and beliefs of social groups are articulated through various cultural artifacts. These artifacts constitute the structures through which individuals learn their culture. (p. 188)

Each system of education in our nation has developed its own culture under the umbrella of education and schooling. The way the institutions live out the particular vision of culture differs, based on a continuum provided for by their particular culture. What is known is that the culture of each of the three structures—public, private, and religious—will be lived out in their particular schools. The force for change in governance style and curriculum innovation as per the new paradigm is linked to how the culture allows for change within its structure.

Waller observed as early as 1932 that:

> Schools have a culture that is definitely their own. There are, in the school, complex rituals of personal relationships, a set of mores, folkways and irrational sanctions, a moral code based on theme. There are games which are sublimated wars, teams and an elaborate set of ceremonies concerning them. There are traditionalists waging their world-old battle against innovators. There are laws and there is the problem of enforcing them. (p. 103)

Elmore (1995) interpreted the regularities of schooling as a genetic code and likened school organizations to the DNA molecule that forms a template for the transmission of life. The premise allows for systemic enculturation of policies that dictate control and politics in the culture of public, private, and religious schools. It permits the pattern of behavior to trickle down to the school from the macro system, depending on the genetics of the organization. The culture of the school cannot be ignored; the history of the organization must be understood. Comprehending and responding to school culture is a critical dimension if we are to set about a school restructuring effort (Conley, 1993).

COLLABORATION AS LEADERSHIP

Organizations are open systems that need careful management to balance internal needs. There is no one best to organize. The appropriate form depends on the task involved. Leaders must be concerned with "good fits" that formulate in a simplistic manner the contingency approach to organizations. Bartlett and Sumatra (1994) investigated 20 companies in regard to management based on the familiar aphorism: Structure follows strategy; systems support structure. They concluded that the maxim is no longer applicable in today's business market. Based on the research of these 20 companies, their work proposed an organic model of organization that reflected the collaborative approach to leadership.

The organic model is actualized in a framework of purpose. Consequently, engagement of purpose is important and control of the employee diminished; accordingly, employees identify with the organization aligned with an emotional link and take pride in themselves and the organization. Organizational culture is mapped out in the educational environment. Smith and Scott (1990) extended their research on collaboration in school cultures to include the following:

- The belief based on effective schools research that the quality of education is largely determined by what happens at the school site.
- The conviction, supported by research, that instruction is most effective in a school environment characterized by norms of collegiality.
- The belief that teachers are professionals who should be given responsibility for the instructional process and held accountable for its outcomes.
- The use of a wide range of practices and structures that enables administrators to work together on school improvement.
- The involvement of teachers in the decisions about school goals and the means of achieving them.

Engagement-of-purpose and good-fit seem to designate the characteristics for the collaborative model in the nonpublic school. Added to this fabric are elements of a shared moral order. Cibulka and Boyd (1989) recognized that the policies affecting private schools are inherently moral and value-laden. In retrospect, the culture of the nonpublic school seems to be a better fit for the collaborative process. Organizational design, organization to deliver, and the ability to construct a new future are discussed to show the purpose and "good fit" that the collaboration model maintains for nonpublic schools.

Organizational Design

Mintzberg (1979) identified five sectors that he believed all institutions possess: (a) the operating core, what the organization makes happen; (b) the middle-line persons responsible for supervision; (c) the strategic apex or those responsible for sustaining the mission; (d) the technistructure, finance, and budgeting; and (e) the support staff who guides the infrastructure.
A review of the following organizational charts focuses on Mintzberg's institutional sectors as lived within the structures of the organi-

zation of the public and nonpublic educational genres. The model that represents the nonpublic sector is an example that expresses most organizational charts of key Jesuit high schools (Figure 5.1). Jesuit schools, as private Catholic schools, would be the most representative of nonpublic education, which has been reduced to include only those who have an instructional voice. Representing the public school model of design is a typical structure of a state school system (Figure 5.2). The hierarchical diagrams, although simplistic, clearly indicate the path of resistance toward collaborative models and curriculum innovation in nonpublic and public organizations.

Organization to Deliver Change

Chubb and Moe (1990) have documented how private schools differ from public counterparts. The main focus of the nonpublic schools is on organizational delivery. In private schools, higher distant authorities like boards and supervisors have less power. Even for Catholic schools, higher ecclesiastical authorities meddle less than their public school colleagues. Private schools have more flexibility in personnel policies. The researchers found that although each school's approach may differ within each of the nonpublic schools visited, the schools' goals were focused. Also noted was less disagreement among the staff than prevailed in public schools.

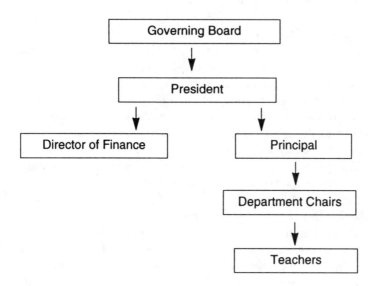

Figure 5.1. Typical nonpublic school

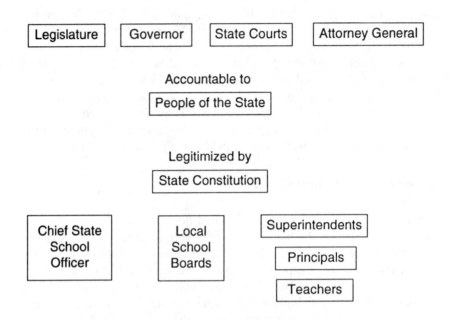

Figure 5.2. Typical state structures

The study further indicated that private school principals were less likely to seek career advancement. Teachers found work more rewarding in nonpublic schools, and there were better principal–teacher and teacher–teacher relationships. Teachers have more influence in every phase of the nonpublic school from choosing text, deciding what to teach, and establishing standards for discipline and homework. More importantly, teachers do not feel that success is beyond their control. The pivotal piece is the concept that control for schooling lies with the teachers. Thus the new paradigm that emphasizes the collaboration of leadership and looks on the teacher as leader would be easy to implement in the nation's nonpublic schools.

The gap between retrace and action seems to widen in public education. Conversation for educators in the public sector must begin with the historical nature of their organization and infiltrate the existing culture. The many stockholders of public education have to be brought into the conversation. Albert Shanker (1993), president of the American Federation of Teachers, refers to the public schools as our "chaotic nonsystem." He suggests that there is no consensus among the 15,000 school districts and 50 states as to deciding what students should know. He agrees with Chubb and Moe (1990) that the current democratic control can be blamed for school failure, but only as it is practiced in the United States.

Shanker (1993) would like to see more control in the hands of the professionals. He goes further to explain that due to "educational bankruptcy" in some local districts, we see them turning toward privatization, as in the case of Dade County, FL, Baltimore, MD, and Duluth, MN. Shanker (1993) calls for a focus on standards. He seems to reflect the thinking of many of his colleagues that change must be focused on the product of the organization, as opposed to focusing on the infrastructure of the organization. The link in public schools between what Mintzberg called the operating core for schools would be teachers and the strategic core, which in the organization of public schools (See Figure 5.3), would be boards of education and superintendents' ideas because of the macromanagement of public schools. The union also under its "protection" rules has created in some districts a misalignment in the organization of the public schooling.

In context, the nonsystem may be currently dysfunctional, and restructuring toward a collaborative model will demand leaders who will be able to balance the symbolic concerns of the organization and deal with the ambiguity of the decision-making process. Collegial models characterize decision making as a participatory process with all members of the institution having an equal opportunity to influence policy and action. As Noble and Pym (1970) stated:

> The most striking feature of the organization to the newcomer or outsider seeking some response from it is the receding locus of power. In complex organizations in the spheres of education, industry, administration or commerce, the Kafkaesque experience is very common; wherever or at whatever level one applies to the organisation, the "real" decisions always seem to be taken somewhere else. (p. 63)

Ability to Build a New Future

Paradoxes in implementing a collaborative organization confuse us because they prove that things do not behave the way we expect them to behave and because we are asked to live with simultaneous apparatuses. We have the ability to plan a move for next year and choose the dinner menu within the same hour. Paradoxes are part of postmodernist society. To help successful organizations deal with paradoxes, Charles Handy (1994) suggested the use of the Sigmoid Curve (See Figure 5.4). He explains how the S-shaped curve, which intrigued people since time began, sums up the story of life itself, starting slowly, experimentally, and flatteringly; we wax and then we wane. The units of time have become shaken in modern society, and the accelerating pace of change shrinks every Sigmoid Curve. The secret to organizational success is in dealing with the paradoxes of postmodernism to begin a new Sigmoid Curve before the first one fizzles out.

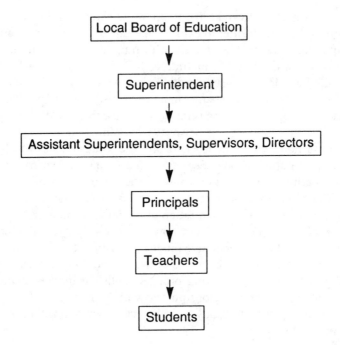

Figure 5.3. Typical line staff organization

Organizations that can predict the point of change at point A, when everything is going well, that is, before point B comes along and they are faced with disaster, are the organizations that will grow in our postmodern times.

The bureaucratic complexities of public schools, their culture, and the numbers of stockholders do not allow for an easy pathway through paradox. Nonpublic schools that depend on the marketplace for their existence must keep their eye on point A at all times. They will not continue to exist if they do not function at point A. Currently, we are in a time of great flux as we meet the new century. Most organizations that adhere to the hierarchical and bureaucratic models of organizations will not be able to create a new Sigmoid Curve. The challenge is how to convince people to abandon the first curve, to take the leap into the future and thus avoid failure. In the public school sector, which is interested in protecting its teachers and administrators, this will be difficult.

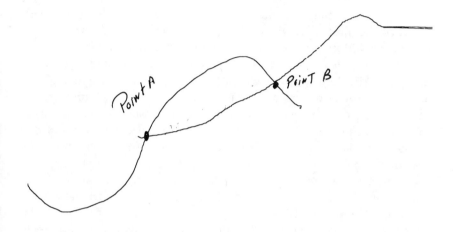

Figure 5.4. The Sigmoid Curve

WORKING WITH PARADOXES

During the first half of the 1990s, the pressure for change in the curriculums that primary and secondary school teachers teach has grown to new levels. Teachers often complain that the work is too difficult for today's students. Businesses often challenge the role of academia in defining what education ought to be by stating that graduates are not prepared to enter the workforce. Educators work with new and rapidly changing technology while parents ask for a return to basics. Infusing values into an instructional program is frequently praised, provided that the values that parents perceive as being reserved for the home are not part of the curriculum.

Moreover, teenage students have grown up in a world in which technology has been blossoming all around them. CNN and its worldwide news coverage, MTV and its global music perspective, the appearance of virtual reality in shopping malls and flea markets, and the Internet with its huge information classes have created new and meaningful learning experiences for children and young adults away from the school setting. For the first time in recent history, the generation gap is not defined by the magnitude of mischief, misbehavior, or risk taking, but rather by the use of and familiarity with technology, particularly computers. Students complain of boredom or of curriculums that do not seem relevant to them in today's world. Moreover, students bring with them a new level of social issues that was never the case in earlier times. Problems of date rape, violence, drugs, early-age sex, teen pregnancy, the threat of AIDS, weapons, and sometimes unsafe school environment affect education and introduce an unwritten curriculum.

Tyler (1989), in *Basic Principles of Curriculum and Instruction*, described curriculum development as a four-step process, beginning with the development of objectives, *meaningful* learning activities, organization and sequencing of learning activities, and finally assessment—measuring the success of meeting the objectives. One of the principles that Tyler stated is that there are many particular experiences that can be used to attain the same educational objectives. Consequently, as long as the educational experiences meet the various criteria for effective learning, they are useful in attaining the desired objectives. This means that the teacher has a wide range of creative possibility in planning particular work. Tyler continued by stating that learning activities should include developing a skill in thinking and problem solving. In the first place, it has been shown that information can be acquired at the same time that students are learning to solve problems. Hence, it is more economical to set up learning situations in which the information is obtained as a part of a total process of problem solving than it is to set up special learning experiences just for memorizing information.

A logical question that grows out of experience in curriculum development using the Tyler model is: Who decides what meaningful learning activities are? Brooks and Brooks (1993), in their work on constructivism, stress that students should be given problems that are relevant and make use of active inquiry activities. They also stress that "Curriculum materials must be responsive to students' problem-solving suppositions" (p. 160). Henderson and Hawthorne stressed that "the constructivist interpretation of curriculum focuses on teachers' and students' actual educational experiences as they construct meanings over past, present, and anticipated future learning activities" (p. 16). The constructivist approach clearly necessitates collaboration between and among teachers *and* between teachers and students in defining what are meaningful learning experiences. In the process of curriculum development, reference is often made to a curriculum continuum.

The case study presented by Peter Senge (1994) of Emily R. Meyrs is an example of someone who was able to face the paradoxical worlds of the public and nonpublic school organization. Ms. Meyrs was given the assignment five years ago to bring computing into the Chadds Ford, PA, public elementary school. She began with high hopes, creating an interactive instructional situation to build "microworlds" to simulate the real world and build their own learning environments. Although the district gave her an award for outstanding service, the concept of computer-based interactive learning did not begin to make a dent in the rest of the school organizations. The limiting factor was an "us-versus-them" management structure that virtually incapacitated teachers by setting them against administrators. Eventually, she resigned. Two years ago she began designing a learning laboratory at the Media-Providence Friends School, where she designed the "Learning Habitat."

Imagine then, a school in which people join together to learn, regardless of their age, occupation, or home address. Relationships between people are encouraged because they facilitate learning. In Quaker schools, this guiding principle is based on the religious belief that every person contains the light of God within him- or herself. Beliefs make a profound difference; they provide a constructive mental model in which students and faculty may flourish. It provides an alternative to the competitive mechanisms of most schools that punish teamwork and collaboration.

The case for the nonpublic school is meaningful only when viewed through the lens of the paradigm that incorporates purpose and complexity of the culture of the organization confronting the world of paradoxes facing us in the new millennium and building the relationships between teaching methods and the structures of schools.

REFERENCES

Bailyn, B. (1960). *Education in the forming of American society.* New York: W. W. Norton.

Bartlett, C. A., & Sumantra, G. (1994, November/December). Changing the role of top management: Beyond strategy to purpose. *Harvard Business Review,* pp. 79-88.

Bates, R. J. (1987). Corporate culture, schooling, and educational administration. *Educational Administration Quarterly, 23*(4), 79-115.

Boards of trustees: Members responsibilities (Thumbnail Series). Washington, DC: National Association of Boards of Catholic Eduction of the National Catholic Education Association.

Bobette, R., & Danbridge, W. (n.d.) *Minority leaders for independent schools.* Boston: National Association for Independent Schools.

Brooks, J. G., & Brooks, M. G. (1993) *In search of understanding: The case for constructionist classrooms.* Alexandria, VA: Association for Supervision and Curriculum Development.

Brown vs. Board of Education, 347 U. S. 483 (1954).

Buetow, H. A. (1970). *Of singular benefit: The story of U.S. Catholic education.* New York: Macmillan.

Chubb, J. E., & Moe, T. M. (1990). *Politics, markets and America's schools.* Washington, DC: Brookings Institution.

Cibulka, J. G., & Boyd, W. L. (1989). Introduction: Private schools and public policy. In J. G. Cibulka & W. L. Boyd (Eds.), *Private schools and public policy: International perspectives.* London: Falmer Press.

Coleman, J. S., Hoffer, T., & Kilgore, S. (1982). *High school achievements: Public, Catholic, and private schools compared.* New York: Basic Books.

Conley, David T. (1993) *Managing change in reconstructing schools. Culture, leadership, and readiness.* Washington D.C: OSCC Bulletin 36.

Convey, J. J. (1992). *Catholic schools make a difference: Twenty-five years of research.* Washington, DC: National Catholic Education Association.

Cremin, L. (1970). *American education: The colonial experience: 1607-1783.* New York: Harper & Row.

Curti, M. (1974). *The social ideas of American educators.* Totowa, NJ: Littlefield & Adams.

Deal, T. E. E. (1987). The culture of schools. In L. T. Sheive & M. B. Schoenheit (Eds.), *Leadership examining the elusive* (p. 315). Alexandria, VA: Association for Supervision and Curriculum Development.

Dewey, J. (1897). *My pedagogic creed.* New York: E. L. Kellogg.

Doyle, D. (1995). *Where connoisseurs send their children to school.* Eugene, OR: ERIC Clearinghouse on Educational Management, ED 384–982.

Elmore, R. (1995). Principles of practice and the regulation of schooling. *Education Administration Quarterly, 31,* 355-373.

Erickson, F. (1982). Conceptions of school culture: An overview. *Educational Administration Quarterly, 23*(4), 11-24.

Glatter, R. (1982). The micropolitics of education: Issues for training. *Educational Management and Administration, 2*(2), 160-165.

Graham, O. I. L., Jr. (1970). *The great campaign: Reform and war in America: 1900-1928.* Englewood Cliffs, NJ: Prentice-Hall.

Handy, C. (1994). *The age of paradox.* Boston: Harvard Business Press.

Hodgkinson, H. (1993). American education: The good, the bad, and the task. In S. Elan (Ed.), *The state of the nation's public schools: A conference report* (pp. 13-23). Bloomington, IN: Phi Delta Kappa

Johnson, S. M. (1995, December). Headers for change. *Education Bulletin of the Harvard Graduate School of Education,* p. 17.

Jorgenson, L. P. (1987). *The state and the non-public school, 1825-1925.* Columbia: University of Missouri Press.

Link, A. S., Link, W. A., & Catton, W. B. (1986). *American epoch: A history of the United States* (Vol. 3). New York: Alfred A. Knopf.

McConnell, G. (1970). *Private power and American democracy*. New York: Random House.

McLaughlin, M. W. (1987). Learning from experience: Lessons from policy implementation. *Educational Evaluation and Policy Analysis, 10*, 171-178.

Meyer, A. E. (1957). *An educational history of the American people*. New York: McGraw-Hill.

Mintzberg, H. (1979). *The structure of organization*. Englewood Cliffs, NJ: Prentice-Hall.

Morgan, G. (1993). *Images of organization*. Newbury Park, CA: Sage.

National Education Association Commission on Reorganization of Secondary Education. (1918). *Cardinal principles on secondary education* (Bulletin 35). Washington, DC: Bureau of Education.

Noble, T., & Pym, B. (1970). Collegial authority and the receding locus of power. *British Journal of Sociology, 21*, 431-445.

Parker, F. (1992). Review: Chubb and Moe. *National Forum, 72*, 47.

Parker, F., & Parker, B. J. (1995, Spring). A historical perspective on school reform. *The Educational Forum, 59*, 278–287.

Pierce et al. vs. Hill Military Academy, 268 U.S. 510 (OR. 1925).

Pierce et al. v. Society of Sisters, 268 US 510 (1925).

Randall, E. V. (1994a). *Private schools, public power: A case for pluralism*. New York: Teachers College Press.

Randall, E. (1994b). The state and religious schools in America: An overview of a rocky relationship. *Journal of Research on Christian Education, 10*, 175-198.

Senge, P. (1994). *The fifth discipline fieldbook*. New York: Doubleday.

Shanker, A. (1993). The task before us. In S. Elam (Ed.), *The state of the nation's public schools: A conference report* (pp. 88-107). Bloomington, IN: Phi Delta Kappa.

Smith, S. C., & Scott, J. J. (1990). *The collaborative school*. Alexandria, VA: National Association of Secondary School Principals.

Synder, T. D. (1988). *Digest of education statistics*. Washington DC: National Center for Educational Statistics.

Tyack, D. B. (1974). *The one best system: A history of American urban education*. Cambridge, MA: Harvard University Press.

Tyler, R. T. (1989). *Basic principles of curriculum and instruction*. Chicago: University of Chicago Press.

Waller, W. (1932). *The sociology of teaching*. New York: John Wiley.

Ziegler, H. L., Tucker, H. J., & Wilson, L. A. (1977). How school control was wrestled from the people. *Phi Delta Kappan, 58*, 534-539.

6   STAFF DEVELOPMENT PLANNING: TEACHER RESPONSES TO THE NEEDS OF AT-RISK STUDENTS

Daniel L. Duke
Bruce Gansneder

University of Virginia

A curriculum, as Mauritz Johnson (1967) reminds us, is a set of intentions. Students sometimes experience difficulties achieving intended learning outcomes. All the good curriculum intentions in the world are worth little if teachers are unable or unwilling to respond to student difficulties with appropriate instructional interventions. Helping teachers to develop and use effective intervention strategies with students experiencing learning problems or related difficulties should be a primary focus of staff development.

To assist educators responsible for planning and implementing staff development, this chapter draws on a large study of teacher responses to at-risk students. The authors worked with colleagues from five other universities with support from the Danforth Foundation.[1] The chapter opens with a rationale for and description of the study, followed by a review of selected findings and a discussion of their implications for staff development.

---

[1]Fellow researchers on the project included Charles Burckett, Dennis Butterfield, Mary Jane Connelly, Michael Gillespie, and Larry Frase.

RATIONALE

In the aftermath of calls for educational reform in the early 1980s, cries of concern were heard for students who might suffer as a result of efforts to raise academic standards and increase school requirements. These students came to be known as *at-risk students*. Although the term has been used by some educators to describe a wide range of youth problems, we decided that it would refer specifically to students who, by virtue of low grades and poor academic performance, were at risk of not advancing to the next grade level or graduating.

Educational researchers and practitioners over the years have developed a variety of techniques and strategies to help at-risk students. These practices are referred to as *instructional interventions*, by which are meant any treatments selected or recommended by teachers for the specific purpose of helping a particular student succeed in his or her school work. Slavin and Madden (1989) reviewed many group-based interventions and found some evidence of effectiveness under certain conditions. A large-scale study by Phi Delta Kappa (Frymier & Gansneder, 1989; Lombardi, Odell, & Novotny, 1990) found that teachers and administrators were aware of and reported using a number of interventions to help at-risk students in general. What researchers outside of special education have not investigated systematically, however, are the instructional interventions that teachers select for particular at-risk students. One purpose of the Danforth Instructional Intervention Study, therefore, was to identify the interventions teachers choose to use with specific nonspecial education students experiencing academic difficulties.

The focus of this study is important because pressure is increasing for regular classroom teachers to handle student problems that typically have been referred to specialists (Evans, 1990). Some pullout programs, for example, have been criticized as disruptive and ineffective (Madden & Slavin, 1989). Are regular classroom teachers, however, prepared to address the needs of individual at-risk students? Our findings provide insights concerning teachers' awareness of different instructional interventions and their preferences for particular interventions. These data may help teacher educators, school administrators, and staff developers determine preservice and inservice training needs.

DESIGN OF THE STUDY

The primary focus of the Danforth Instructional Intervention Study was the regular classroom teacher and his or her efforts to help particular at-risk students. Trained interviewers at sites in five states (California, New York, Tennessee, Utah, and Virginia) were instructed to select teachers of academic subjects who had given two or more students low grades at the end of the first grading period in the fall of 1989. Students identified as disabled who had received special education services prior to the study were excluded because they were likely to have available a variety of individualized services. Interviewers randomly selected one struggling student on whom to concentrate for the remainder of the school year. A control student also was chosen, but teachers were not informed of this selection. Only the grades of control students were monitored. Pseudonyms were created to protect the identities of all students.[2]

A total of 229 teachers were interviewed three times—at the end of the first grading period, the first semester, and the second semester—to determine the instructional interventions they reported using with individual students. Teachers were drawn from urban, suburban, and rural sites. Table 6.1 shows the gender, grade level, and subject matter areas for each of the 229 at-risk students in the study.

Interview questions were designed to determine which interventions teachers already had used and were considering using with the at-risk students in question. Questions included the following:

Interview No. 1 (end of first grading period):

- Why did this student receive a low grade in your course?
- What efforts were made to help prevent the subject from receiving a low grade [prior to the end of the first grading period]?
- What efforts to help the subject now should be made?

Interview No. 2 (end of first semester):

- Since the end of the first grading period, what specific efforts have been made either by you or at your suggestion to help the subject?
- Do you intend to continue any of these efforts during the second semester? If so, which ones?
- Do you intend to try any new approaches with the subject during the second semester? If so, which ones?

---

[2]The complete results of the study were reported by the authors in a paper entitled "The Identification of Effective Strategies for At-Risk Students" (1991). This paper was presented at the 1991 Annual Convention of the American Educational Research Association.

Table 6.1. Gender, Grade Level, and Subject Matter Area of 229 At-Risk Students.

Gender	Male	153
	Female	67
	Unknown	9
Grade Level	K	3
	1st	8
	2nd	11
	3rd	25
	4th	29
	5th	26
	6th	27
	7th	14
	8th	18
	9th	29
	10th-12th	30
	Unknown	
Subject Matter Area	Elementary Reading	77
	Elementary Math	51
	Math (Grades 6-9)	9
	Algebra 1 or 2	8
	Geometry	1
	English (Grades 6-9)	23
	English (Grades 10-12)	14
	General Science	11
	Earth Science	4
	Chemistry	2
	Biology	3
	Social Studies	15
	Foreign Language	4
	Unknown	7

Interview No. 3 (end of second semester):

- Do you feel that any strategies or techniques were particularly successful or unsuccessful with the subject during the year?

To illustrate the kind of information collected in the interviews, a sample transcript follows. The teacher taught a first-grade class in a rural Virginia school district. The student referred to in the transcript received an unsatisfactory grade in October because he was struggling with reading readiness. By the end of the school year in June, he had progressed to a point at which he was reading in a primer and using word attack skills, short vowels, and beginning and ending sounds. The teacher felt it was appropriate to recommend that the student advance to the next grade level.

October Interview (1)

Why did this student receive a low grade in your course?

Basically, he doesn't have the slightest clue as to what is happening. He wants to read desperately, but he can't retain sight words nor letter sound connections to use any decoding skills. His strength is that he has a good immediate auditory visual memory. When we are reading from the board, he can do what I do, but tomorrow he won't be able to remember it. He can do worksheets while I'm saying "Circle the one that begins with F," but tomorrow he can't consistently tell you the sound it makes. So his worksheet grades might be a little higher than his actual grade should be because I don't feel he's mastering what he needs to master. He's trying hard though. I'm not giving him an actual F because I don't want to kill all of his enthusiasm.

I don't think mistakes are well tolerated at home. He's not a risktaker at all. He's beginning to feel free to take risks with me. I think a lot of it is motivational.

What efforts were made to help prevent the student from receiving a low grade?

The efforts were made with a whole group because they were all having some problems. We use groups of two to have them tutor each other. They play computer games, and we have whole language experiences.

I spoke with his Chapter 1 teacher and she is remediating in the same area—total reading skills.

I sent an interim report home asking his parents to come for a conference. They did not respond in any way.

We made individual books using repeated vocabulary from their reader. All these things were being done in Chapter 1 too. He was getting a double dose. He needs more higher thinking practice. We did journal writing using vocabulary words. We have done word searches. We are making alphabet books for each child. We use a lot of *Little People Books* too.

I created a classroom library using vocabulary words. Every time they pick up a book, they have to look at these same words. We constantly go over letters and sounds. We do music experiences to emphasize listening. We try to bring all that stuff that makes it fun and will get them going.

We have a typing center. They type all their new words. We use sentence strips and a word bank to put words in order. All these activities are done as a whole group, but it is a remedial group. They all need it.

What efforts to help the student now can be made?

I will keep on with what we're doing, and I think a referral is in order. He seems to have some organizational processing problems that are not normal for his age. As motivated as he is, it should come easier for him. If he doesn't get some kind of identification and placement, he just won't be able to keep up.

He probably won't go to second grade, and I don't know how strong he would be next year in first grade. That's about it. I want to keep him having a positive image about himself and school work.

January Interview (2)

The above student received a low grade at the end of the first grading period. Since that time what specific efforts have been made either by you or at your suggestion to help the student? What were the reasons for each of these efforts?

Flashcards went home again. I conferenced with his mother again and she asked what she could do. I told her he just knew very little vocabulary. So I asked her to help him to get some sight connections and to discuss beginning sounds with him. I sent sight words home and she has been helping him. It has made a big difference. He's getting a C this time in reading. He's really beginning to make the sound-letter connections. He's still weak though.

He's a straight A student in math. He's still not really motivated to work on anything but math on his own. His reading is always going to be low.

Do you intend to continue any of these efforts during the next grading period? If so, which ones?

Yes. I'm sending home stories and that will continue. I'm sending home word lists too. What I do for him I do for all of them, but I do seem to concentrate on him more. The word lists are for his mother to use to make flash cards. I'm hoping his mother will come to conferences again this time.

Do you intend to try any new approaches with the student during the next grading period? If so, please list each approach and the reason for trying it.

He is in a new reader. We've gone to the Scott Foresman because it is slower paced for vocabulary. They're much less frustrated as a group. I'm doing more in their journals with them. They know more words, so it's easier for them. We're also keeping a vocabulary book. They're really excited about it because they can refer to it when they write in their journals. We're also doing a lot with complete sentences. What I'm finding is they're perfectionists because they're insecure in their knowledge. They aren't willing to take risks.

June Interview (3)

Do you feel that any strategies or techniques were particularly successful with this student during the year?

Whole language strategies worked. He didn't do well with isolated skills lessons. He couldn't use that to attack words. Dictated stories, journal writing, language experience worked. He loved reading; he loved writing. Success in math gave him some confidence. I think it carried over. Word banks and vocabulary books worked for him. The McCracken Spelling Program—I initiated that after the first of the year. It takes one sound a week and the children identify whether the sound is at the beginning or end of a word. He just took off after that. It pulled it all together for him. Nursery rhymes were good for him too.

Do you feel that any strategies or techniques were particularly unsuccessful with this student?

Alphabet books were not helpful. As I said before, isolated skills lessons didn't seem to help him. He couldn't apply the skills to reading. Interviews such as the one above suggest the thinking process in which teachers engage as they try to figure out how to address the needs of students experiencing difficulties.[3]

FINDINGS

A review of all the interview data yielded a variety of specific interventions intended by teachers to help struggling students. When these interventions were condensed and organized into discrete categories, 98 distinct interventions were identified. Table 6.2 includes a comprehensive list of all the interventions.

Some interventions obviously were more popular than others. Table 6.3 presents the most frequently mentioned interventions. Column 1 contains the percentages of teachers who claimed to have used particular interventions between the beginning of school and the end of the first grading period. During this time period, for example, 22.3% of the teachers indicated using a parent–teacher conference, 13.1% tutoring during class, and so forth. Column 2 contains percentages of teachers who claim to have used particular interventions after the end of the first grading period. The most frequently mentioned intervention for this time period was positive verbal reinforcement (14.0%).

What is striking about these data are the relatively small percentages of teachers who indicated using any of the interventions. Why, for example, were parent–teacher conferences not called for in almost all of the cases? A second interesting finding is that the likelihood of a particular student receiving a particular intervention seemed to drop in most cases after he or she had received a low report card grade. Why this should be the case is uncertain. Do teachers give up on students? The only interventions that increase after the end of the first grading period are relatively "low energy" interventions. Do teachers get caught up in the complexities of school life after the first grading period and find themselves unable or unwilling to expend additional energy on struggling students? Perhaps many classes function like battlefield surgery units, with teachers adopting a kind of triage mentality. Students deemed most likely to benefit from interventions receive more attention than those perceived to be least likely to benefit.

---

[3]No effort was made in the study to verify that teachers actually used interventions mentioned in the interviews; so the data from the study must be regarded with caution.

Table 6.2. Inventory of Interventions for At-Risk Students.

1.0 Adjustment of Expectations

    1.1   Reducing requirements or expectations
    1.2   Giving student "second chances" to complete work
    1.3   Returning unacceptable work without a grade and asking student to redo it
    1.4   Allowing student to retake tests and quizzes
    1.5   Assigning student to a different ability group in class
    1.6   Permitting student to be examined in an alternative mode

2.0 Adjustment of Instruction

    2.1   Placing student in a self-pacing or "mastery" format, allowing more time to complete work
    2.2   Utilizing special materials appropriate to student's ability level
    2.3   Utilizing special materials of interest to the student
    2.4   Assigning special homework
    2.5   Providing opportunities for more practice (in terms of assignments and activities)
    2.6   Providing opportunities to take practice quizzes and tests
    2.7   Breaking down complex tasks/assignments into simpler, more easy-to-handle units
    2.8   Modeling desired performance for student
    2.9   Providing additional "structure"—such as sequencing work in a logical, easy-to-follow order
    2.10 Pre-teaching or reviewing vocabulary prior to lesson
    2.11 Providing "hands on" assignments
    2.12 Reading aloud to student
    2.13 Listening to student read
    2.14 Providing opportunities for independent study

3.0 Instruction in Supplementary Content

    3.1   Study skills
    3.2   Problem solving, metacognitive strategies
    3.3   Social skills
    3.4   Self-monitoring skills
    3.5   Content related to self-esteem

4.0 Teacher-Initiated Counseling and Advisement

    4.1   To diagnose problems and concerns
    4.2   To explain expectations
    4.3   To review assignments, tests
    4.4   To brainstorm ideas for resolving problems
    4.5   To apprise student of seriousness of situation
    4.6   To review grades or progress

Table 6.2. Inventory of Interventions for At-Risk Students (cont.).

5.0 Tutoring or Re-Teaching by Teacher

    5.1   During class
    5.2   During regular school hours, but outside of class
    5.3   Before or after school

6.0 Supervision and Monitoring

    6.1   Reminders, friendly nagging
    6.2   Close supervision during class
    6.3   Assignment sheets
    6.4   Student contract
    6.5   Removing distractions, changing student's seat
    6.6   Repeating/clarifying directions and instructions
    6.7   Regular review of assignments, notebooks, etc.
    6.8   Calling on student regularly during class

7.0 Encouragement

    7.1   Positive verbal reinforcement
    7.2   Other forms of recognition (i.e., written, tangible rewards, etc.)
    7.3   Behavior modification protocol
    7.4   Grade "bargaining"
    7.5   Opportunities for extra credit
    7.6   Extra attention and caring
    7.7   Assigning extra responsibilities as a form of recognition (peer tutoring, for example)
    7.8   Focusing on what a student does well
    7.9   Providing numerous opportunities for success

8.0 Discipline

    8.1   Time out or isolation (also can be used as a reward)
    8.2   Lowering student's grade
    8.3   Detention during school (recess, lunch)
    8.4   Detention after school, Saturdays, etc.
    8.5   Loss of privileges
    8.6   Ignoring, withholding attention
    8.7   Testing student on rules/consequences

9.0 Technology

    9.1   Use of computers for remediation
    9.2   Use of computers as incentive
    9.3   Use of computer to develop cognitive ability
    9.4   Tapes of lessons (for follow-up, reinforcement, review of missed lessons)
    9.5   Tapes of lessons (for parent review, self-as-model)
    9.6   Requiring student to make tape as part of assignment

Table 6.2. Inventory of Interventions for At-Risk Students (cont.).

10.0 Instructional Assistance in Class

    10.1   Tutoring by teacher aide
    10.2   Tutoring by adult volunteer
    10.3   Peer tutoring
    10.4   Cooperative learning
    10.5   Consulting teacher

11.0 Parent Communication and Involvement

    11.1   Home instruction or tutoring
    11.2   Parental monitoring at home (homework review, signed assignment sheets, etc.)
    11.3   Parental monitoring at school
    11.4   Progress reports to parents
    11.5   Parent-teacher conferences
    11.6   Parent-teacher phone calls
    11.7   Parent-teacher notes
    11.8   Contact with a nonparent "significant other" (sibling, grandparent, employer, minister, etc.)

12.0 Referral and Fact Finding

    12.1   Roundtable or team meeting
    12.2   Child study
    12.3   Psychological assessment
    12.4   School psychologist
    12.5   School counselor
    12.6   Private psychologist or counselor
    12.7   Pediatrician or other physician
    12.8   Chapter 1
    12.9   Resource room
    12.10 Private tutor or learning center
    12.11 Study hall
    12.12 Reading or math lab
    12.13 Cross-age tutor
    12.14 ESL
    12.15 Special summer school program
    12.16 After-school program
    12.17 Peer group or activity
    12.18 Public agency
    12.19 Reassignment to another teacher
    12.20 School administrator
    12.21 School social worker

Table 6.3. Danforth Instructional Intervention Study: The Percentage of At-Risk Students Receiving Selected Types of Intervention.

Intervention	Percentage Who Received Prior to Getting Low Grade	Percentage Who Received After Getting Low Grade
Parent-Teacher Conference	22.3	12.2
Teacher Tutors During Class	13.1	10.0
Teacher Counsels/Advises Student	11.8	5.2
Unspecified Teacher-Parent Communication	11.8	13.5
Teacher Gives Student "Second Chance" to Complete Work, Make-Up Test, etc.	10.0	5.2
Unspecified Teacher Tutoring	9.6	5.7
Student assigned to Volunteer or Aide for Tutoring	9.6	6.1
Referral to Chapter 1	9.2	3.5
Positive Verbal Reinforcement	8.7	14.0
Referral to Resource Room	7.9	8.3
Teacher Communicates with Parent in Writing	7.9	2.2
Peer Tutoring in Class	7.0	4.8
Referral to Counselor	6.6	2.6
Home Instruction/Tutoring	6.6	2.6
Unspecified Peer Tutoring	6.6	5.7
Friendly "Nagging" and Reminders	6.6	2.6
Assignment of Special Homework	5.7	3.9
More Opportunities for Practice	4.8	3.9
Close Supervision During Class	4.8	3.9
Parent Sign-Off Sheet for Assignments/Homework	4.8	7.0
Removing Distractions/Changing Student's Seat	4.4	5.2
Teacher Tutors Student Before or After School	4.4	5.7
Use of Special Materials Appropriate for Student's Ability Level	4.4	2.2
Teacher Phones Parent(s)	3.9	2.6
Teacher Gathers Background Data on Student	3.9	1.7
Referral for Special Education Testing	3.9	1.3
Teacher Reduces Expectations/Requirements	3.9	5.2

Table 6.3. Danforth Instructional Intervention Study: The Percentage of At-Risk Students Receiving Selected Types of Intervention (cont.).

Intervention	Percentage Who Received Prior to Getting Low Grade	Percentage Who Received After Getting Low Grade
Teacher Regularly Checks Assignments/Notebooks	3.9	5.2
Teacher Tutors Student During School Hours, but Not in Class	3.5	4.4
Extra Caring/Positive Attention/Support	3.5	4.4
Teacher Places Student in Self-Pacing, Continuous Progress Format	3.1	2.2
Study Skills Instruction	3.1	2.6

Had data analysis stopped with Table 6.3, the results would have been pretty depressing. We decided to divide the students into two groups, those whose grade (in the subject under examination) improved by June and those whose grade remained the same or dropped by June. The grades of 54.3% of the students (not counting those who transferred to a new class or dropped out of school) improved, whereas the grades of 45.6% of the students dropped or remained the same. Could it be that the teachers of students whose grade improved relied on certain types of intervention that other teachers did not? To address this question, linear correlations of grade changes and the use of types of interventions (based on generic categories from Table 6.2) were calculated. Linear correlations take into account the size of the grade improvement for each student. As Table 6.4 indicates, one type of intervention—instructional adjustment—was significantly related to grade improvement ($r = .19$, $p < .05$).

A review of Table 6.2 shows why interventions involving instructional adjustment might be more effective than other interventions. They tend to require more teacher time, energy, and competence. Placing an at-risk student in a self-pacing learning format or developing materials especially suited to the student's abilities is more demanding than arranging a parent conference or changing a student's seat. Teachers' comments tended to confirm what the linear correlations indicated. In the final interview, when asked which interventions they believed to be particularly helpful, teachers identified instructional adjustment interventions more frequently than other types.

Table 6.4. Linear Correlations Between Grade Changes and the Use of Interventions (Generic).

	Semester Grade Change	Total Total Year Grade Change (n = 164)
Adjustment of Expectations	.06	.04
Instructional Adjustment	.01	.19***
Nonacademic Content	-.11*	.16**
Counseling and Advisement	-.10*	-.04
Teacher Tutoring	-.08*	.08
Supervision and Monitoring	.10*	.07
Encouragement and Support	.00	.05
Discipline	.07	-.08
Technology	-.11*	-.08
Referral	-.17***	-.08
Peer Intervention	.11*	.09
Parent Intervention	.05	-.08
Parent Communication	.06	.07
Total	.01	.08

*$p < .10$.
*$p < .05$.
**$p < .01$.

IMPLICATIONS

Many studies of the school experiences of at-risk students have focused on special programs and group interventions (Madden and Slavin, 1989; Slavin and Madden, 1989). The present study focused instead on the instructional interventions that teachers reported initiating with individual students who received low grades in academic subjects. A second important feature of this study was its longitudinal nature. Students were tracked to see if their grades improved, and teachers provided periodic commentary concerning their choices of interventions. Let us consider what the findings suggest for those engaged in planning staff development for teachers.

Limited Repertoire

The first implication is that most teachers seem to draw on a limited repertoire of instructional interventions for at-risk students. Although 98 reasonably discrete interventions were mentioned by at least one teacher, only 40 interventions were used by more than 3% of the teachers during the first grading period, and only 24 interventions were used by more than 3% of the teachers during the second grading period. The 98 interventions did not include many of the available interventions associated with specialized instruction for reading problems, behavior disorders, and learning disabilities. It would appear that regular classroom teachers could benefit from staff development dealing with the kinds of instructional interventions used by special education, Chapter 1, and reading teachers.

Commitment or Capability?

A case, of course, can be made that some teachers are aware of and capable of using many more interventions than they actually use. That they refrain from utilizing certain interventions could reflect professional skepticism regarding particular interventions, perceived organizational constraints such as class size, or lack of commitment.

The instructional interventions identified in the study require varying degrees of teacher initiative and energy. For example, tutoring a student before or after school demands far more time and effort on the part of a teacher than referring the student to a counselor or sending a note home to the student's parents. The findings presented in Table 6.3 suggest that the most frequently cited interventions for the first grading period included some high and low-effort interventions. The former included teacher tutoring during class and teacher counseling and advisement. The latter included parent-teacher conferences, referrals to tutors or Chapter 1, and giving students second chances to complete assignments.

An analysis of data from the second grading period reveals that most interventions were used less frequently than during the first grading period. Only 3 of the 11 most frequently cited interventions from the first grading period were used by more teachers during the second grading period than the first. These three—unspecified parent communication, referral to resource room, and use of positive reinforcement—represent relatively low-effort interventions on the part of the regular classroom teacher.

One explanation for the finding that many teachers reduced the number of interventions after giving a student a low grade is that these teachers gave up on the students. The key to helping at-risk students, however, entails just the opposite tack. Once a teacher has given a low grade to a student, he or she should increase the level of commitment to helping that student (Duke, 1986). Lortie (1975) noted in his classic study, though, that some teachers consider working effectively with all their students as something "extra"—"beyond the mere fulfillment of their duties" (p. 115). Convincing teachers that their responsibilities include a commitment to helping every student (Lortie refers to this commitment as "inclusiveness") may constitute one of the greatest challenges facing advocates for at-risk students.

The interventions identified in the study involve different degrees of training as well as effort and commitment. For example, more training probably is needed to provide supplementary instruction in study skills than to change a student's seat in order to eliminate distractions. With the possible exception of teacher tutoring, the most frequently cited interventions in the study necessitated relatively little additional training on the part of teachers. It is unclear, however, whether teachers actually lacked the training to use a greater variety of interventions or simply chose, for whatever reasons, to use relatively few interventions requiring special competence.

Instructional Alteration

There is no reason to believe that every instructional intervention will be equally effective with every student. Therefore, it is vital that teachers are prepared to assess the effectiveness of the interventions they use and alter them when necessary. We refer to a teacher's willingness to abandon ineffective interventions and try new ones as *instructional alteration*. Instructional alteration can be thought of as the first line of defense against the perpetuation of academic difficulties for at-risk students.

The present study provides some clues as to how teachers view instructional alteration. That the number of interventions tended to diminish after the first grading period, despite the fact students received low grades, already has been noted. It is reasonable, of course, for teachers to abandon some interventions after the first grading period, especially when students do not receive good grades. We would expect, however, that new interventions would be tried instead. Such alterations did not occur very often. Struggling students were likely in many cases to be dealt with no differently than other students.

One reason some teachers do not alter instruction so as to meet better the needs of struggling students may be their own uncertainty regarding which interventions are effective. When asked at the end of the school year to identify interventions they regarded as effective, some teachers did not mention anything. Staff development could address this issue by providing opportunities for experienced teachers to share their successful and unsuccessful experiences with various instructional interventions.

A NEED FOR STUDENT-BASED STAFF DEVELOPMENT

There is no reason to believe that the kinds of issues raised by the Danforth Instructional Intervention Study can be resolved quickly or simply. Various reasons can be given to explain why some struggling students receive appropriate help and others do not. The case we wish to make is that one aspect of increasing the chances for success of at-risk students is improving the nature of staff development.

All too frequently, staff development focuses on highly generalized instructional concerns. We believe that a significant portion of staff development should be designed to assist individual teachers in addressing the needs of specific students. In a follow-up to the aforementioned study, the lead author developed a new model of staff development and field-tested it in a Virginia school district where he was serving as acting director of staff development. Referred to as Student-Based Staff Development, the model has been described in detail elsewhere (Duke, 1992-1993).

Student-Based Staff Development calls for staff development specialists to monitor the grades received by students at the end of the first grading period each year. This process allows students experiencing difficulties to be identified early enough that targeted assistance can be provided for their teachers and, ultimately, for them. Armed with a list of students receiving low grades, staff development specialists arrange meetings with classroom teachers and instructional resource teachers to discuss the students, any efforts that already have been made to help them, and possible interventions that could be used in the future. When interventions are identified that require additional training, staff development specialists make arrangements to provide the training, typically in the classroom of each teacher needing help. Those tapped to provide this training often are local special education teachers or other district employees who have received advanced training in particular intervention strategies. Most districts sponsor a variety of training opportunities for teachers and supervisory personnel, thereby creating a rich repository of talent that can be used for teacher-to-teacher staff development. Unfortunately, however, most districts do not maintain a regularly updated directory of these teacher resources. Student-Based Staff Development requires that specialists develop such a directory so they can quickly locate individuals with expertise in particular instructional interventions. When district personnel lack the needed expertise, outside consultants can be retained on a per diem basis.

It is our position that the staff development with the greatest potential for helping teachers deal with at-risk students is staff development that focuses on helping individual teachers alter some aspect of their instruction to better meet the needs of particular students experiencing problems. By relying mainly on local educators with specialized training to provide this help, the costs of Student-Based Staff Development can be kept relatively low. Encouraging teachers to share knowledge on how to assist at-risk students has the added benefit of promoting school- and district-wide cultures of collaboration and caring.

REFERENCES

Duke, D. L. (1986). Understanding what it means to be a teacher. *Educational Leadership, 44*(2), 26-32.

Duke, D. L. (1992-1993). How a staff development plan can rescue at-risk students. *Educational Leadership, 50*(4), 28-33.

Duke, D. L., Gansneder, B., Burckett, C., Butterfield, D., Connelly, M. J., Gillespie, M., & Frase, L. (1991). *The identification of effective strategies for at-risk students.* (Paper presented at the annual convention of the American Educational Research Association).

Evans, R. (1990). Making mainstreaming work through prereferral consultation. *Educational Leadership, 48*(1), 73-77.

Frymier, J., & Gansneder, B. (1989). The Phi Delta Kappa study of students at risk. *Phi Delta Kappan, 71*(2), 142,146.

Johnson, M. (1967). Definitions and models in curriculum theory. *Educational Theory, 17*(2), 127–139.

Lombardi, T. P., Odell, K. S., & Novotny, D. E. (1990). Special education and students at risk: Findings from a national study. *Remedial and Special Education, 12*(1), 56-62.

Lortie, D. C. (1975). *Schoolteacher.* Chicago: University of Chicago Press.

Madden, N. A., & Slavin, R. E. (1989). Effective pullout programs for students at risk. In R. E. Slavin, N. L. Karweit, & N. A. Madden (Eds.), *Effective programs for students at risk* (pp. 52–74). Boston: Allyn & Bacon.

Slavin, R. E., & Madden, N. A. (1989). Effective classroom programs for students at risk. In R. E. Slavin, N. L. Karweit, & N. A. Madden (Eds.), *Effective programs for students at risk* (pp. 21-51). Boston: Allyn & Bacon.

7 THE NATIONAL STANDARDS MOVEMENT: TRANSFORMING MATHEMATICS EDUCATION

===============

Martha Stone Wiske

Harvard University

The mathematics education community has taken bold steps in developing a consensus around new standards for curriculum and teaching. In 1989, the National Council of Teachers of Mathematics (NCTM, 1989) issued *Curriculum and Evaluation Standards for School Mathematics,* followed two years later by *Professional Standards for Teaching Mathematics* (NCTM, 1991). Together, these reports outline a comprehensive transformation of both the substance and process of mathematics education. They advocate curriculum focused on key ideas, higher order thinking, and analysis of practical problems; learning focused on active inquiry, dialogue, and sense making; teaching by facilitating students' development of understanding through modeling and coaching; and performance-based assessment embedded in and supportive of instruction.

Other groups, across multiple disciplines and levels of the educational system, have subsequently endorsed comparable standards as a lever for raising the performance of teachers and students (California State Department of Education, 1991; National Eduction Goals Panel, 1991; Rutherford & Ahlgren, 1990). Yet none has progressed as far as the mathematics education community in developing consensus around specific standards and strategies for addressing them (Anderson et al., 1994). The roots, scope, and implications of the NCTM Standards illuminate the contours and dynamics of the broader movement toward national educational standards.

The standards movement is commonly discussed with phrases like "implementation of educational reform" and "teacher training." These words connote a reengineering of outmoded methods that may sound pleasingly crisp and efficient at first. On second thought, they imply a rather technical, narrow, and authoritarian endeavor. *Implementation* suggests the application of a concrete, inert implement. Both *reform* and *standards* have punitive connotations reminiscent of juvenile delinquents and lapsed ideals. Teacher training sounds like a way of fixing what is wrong by modifying misbehaviors. All these terms make the process of transforming practice appear to be mechanical and remote, as if viewed through the wrong end of a telescope. From such a perspective, implementing new standards resembles a fairly technical matter of issuing mandates and distributing new materials.

Looking more closely at the NCTM Standards and the innovations they imply makes the enterprise appear more life-sized, humane, complex, and collaborative. It reminds us that curriculum standards are not so much implemented as interpreted by people, primarily teachers, operating in complex, dynamic, cultural systems. We must sustain support for this interactive, dialogic, and systemic process of individual and institutional learning if we are to accomplish the fundamental transformations that the new curriculum standards endorse.

ORIGINS OF THE NEW STANDARDS MOVEMENT

Pressure for significant changes in education developed from several sources during the 1980s. One was a growing dismay about the quality and focus of education in U.S. schools. Two of the most influential reports in galvanizing action were *A Nation at Risk* (National Commission on Excellence in Education, 1983) and *Educating Americans for the Twenty-first Century* (National Science Board, 1983). Both lamented declining test scores and criticized the content and methods of mathematics and science education in the United States. They linked the output of the education system with economic prosperity. In contrast to some earlier waves of educational reform, these reports endorsed a common, more intellectually adventurous curriculum for *all* students.

Meanwhile, cognitive scientists were concluding that students did not learn much or well from traditional information transmission lessons. Pupils did not retain or understand much from the sort of frontal teaching that was typical in many schools and especially prevalent in math classes (Goodlad, 1984; Sizer, 1984). Learning theorists demonstrated that students arrive at school, even from their first day, with many well developed and resilient ideas. Their minds are not empty shelves to be filled sequentially with whatever their teachers and textbooks dispense, but are already well stocked with ideas developed from everyday experience, common sense, and conventional wisdom. Students' prior concepts, regularly reinforced in daily life, are not easily replaced by the kinds of concepts, theories, and modes of inquiry that school teachers might wish students to understand (Resnick, 1987).

Conceptual change, as cognitive psychologists describe it, is a complex process of engaging students in active inquiry, preferably around problems or questions that students themselves have experienced directly, care about, and help to formulate. The elements of inquiry include making observations or otherwise gathering information, analyzing the information for patterns, debating alternative explanations or conjectures, and refining arguments supported by evidence. Learning requires active participation including thinking as well as doing, that is, minds-on as well as hands-on engagement (Nickerson, Perkins, & Smith, 1985; Schoenfeld, 1987).

These conceptions about the learning process suggested very different teaching approaches from the behaviorist learning theories and rather industrialized teaching models that tended to dominate school practice (Romberg, 1990). Good teaching is not simply effective packaging and transmission of information. Instead of delivering the curriculum, teachers must guide students' inquiry and sense making. They must become facilitators and coaches focused not on teaching but on students' learning.

Changing the emphasis from information transmission to knowledge construction implied changes in curriculum as well as pedagogy. Students' work must shift from memorizing isolated facts and formulas to understanding key concepts and ways of thinking. Curriculum content must focus not on superficial coverage of vast amounts of disconnected information but more in-depth analysis of topics central both to the relevant subject matter and to the interests of students and society. Theodore Sizer (1984) summarized much of this thinking in his principles for "essential schools." He argued that "less is more" in choosing curriculum content and recommended that schools focus on essential questions. Assessments should focus on exhibitions of mastery rather than regurgitation of memorized information.

The rapid evolution of new technologies also drove the movement toward new curriculum standards in the 1980s. Sharply increasing access to calculators and computers would make some prominent aspects of the traditional mathematics curriculum less important, if not completely irrelevant.

Furthermore, these new tools promised new ways for teachers and students to represent, manipulate, and analyze data in more fluent, direct, and active ways. The implications of new technologies for revising the emphasis in curricular topics and their potential for enriching teaching and learning were seen as especially important in science and mathematics education.

In tracing the roots of the NCTM Standards, it is also important to note that many leaders in the mathematics education community had learned from the disappointing results of the "New Math" reform effort in the 1960s. Like several other curriculum initiatives of the 1960s, "New Math" was developed by university-based disciplinarians. It was based on conceptions of the discipline that were not well understood by many school teachers or by most parents. These constituencies rejected the new materials and approaches, and the reform effort foundered (Kline, 1973). In its wake, the mathematics education community recognized that changing schools depends on engagement and endorsement of multiple constituencies.

The National Council of Teachers of Mathematics is a professional organization whose membership is unusually broad, including mathematicians, teacher educators, mathematics education researchers, and people involved in mathematics education in schools: teachers, mathematics department supervisors, and curriculum developers. Members of these constituencies worked collaboratively in developing the NCTM (1991) Standards. The NCTM also consulted with other key agents of school change (e.g., policy makers at all levels of government, and teacher and parent organizations, business leaders, and media producers) as they circulated a draft of the Standards and developed support for their dissemination.

CONTENTS OF THE NCTM STANDARDS

The authors of the *Curriculum and Evaluation Standards* (NCTM, 1989) relate the need for new curriculum goals to changes in the needs of society:

> All industrialized countries have experienced a shift from an industrial to an information society, a shift that has transformed both the aspects of mathematics that need to be transmitted to students and the concepts and procedures that they must master if they are to be self-fulfilled productive citizens in the next century. (p. 4)

To be mathematically literate, all students must meet five basic goals: learn to value mathematics, become confident in their ability to do mathematics, become mathematical problem solvers, learn to communicate mathematically, and learn to reason mathematically. Students whose mathematics education is permeated with opportunities to address these goals should gain *mathematical power*, defined as the ability to "explore, conjecture, and reason logically, as well as the ability to use a variety of mathematical methods effectively to solve nonroutine problems" (p. 5).

The authors are explicit about the values underlying their recommendations for curriculum content and pedagogical activities. Content choices reflect three beliefs:

1. Knowing mathematics is doing mathematics.
2. Mathematics provides models, structures, and simulations that are applicable to many disciplines.
3. The nature and methods of mathematics are changed by developments in technologies, including calculators and computers.

Two principles underlie the pedagogical recommendations. First, activities should grow out of problem situations in contrast with traditional practice in which students rehearse algorithms before using them to solve problems. Second, learning entails active involvement with mathematics. The Standards explicitly endorse a "constructivist" philosophy: "In many situations individuals approach a new task with prior knowledge, assimilate new information, and construct their own meanings. . . . This constructive, active view of the learning process must be reflected in the way much of mathematics is taught" (p. 10).

A list of curriculum standards is outlined for three levels: grades kindergarten–4, grades 5–8, and grades 9–12. Four common standards appear at all three levels:

1. mathematics as problem solving
2. mathematics as communication
3. mathematics as reasoning
4. mathematical connections.

Several more specific content standards at each of the three grade levels define and justify the topics to be taught. For example, whole number arithmetic is taught in grades K–4, algebra in grades 5–8, and discrete mathematics in grades 9–12. Each content standard includes examples of appropriate instructional activities, such as work on projects, group and individual assignments, discussion between teacher and students and among students, and practice on mathematical methods as well as the more usual forms of exposition by the teacher. The Standards urge that students regularly be engaged in active mathematical inquiry: "For example, one could expect to see students recording measurements of real objects, collecting information and describing their properties using statistics, and exploring the properties of a function by examining its graph" (p. 5).

The Standards do not recommend a particular sequence or organization of curriculum within a level, but summarize changes from traditional content, including topics that should receive either increased or decreased attention. At the secondary level, the Standards recommend greater integration of algebra, geometry, and trigonometry rather than treating these subjects in separate courses. Throughout the mathematics curriculum, they stress an increased emphasis on connections among mathematical ideas and between mathematics and other subject matters. They "challenge educators to integrate mathematics topics across courses so that students can view major mathematical ideas from more than one perspective and bring interrelated ideas to bear on new topics or problems" (p. 252).

A final set of standards addresses the process of evaluating mathematics education to guide instruction, learning, and the development of educational programs. These standards propose changes not only in the content of tests to address the changed curriculum, but also in the forms of assessment. Student assessment should encompass multiple methods and should be integrated with instruction.

The Standards are explicitly intended to apply to curriculum and evaluation for all students, not just those preparing for postsecondary education. They challenge educators to alter the tracking structures and other programmatic features that discourage girls and minority students from studying mathematics. They seek to improve equity as well as excellence of mathematics education.

The final section of the Standards, called "Next Steps," contrasts two approaches to change (Cuban, 1988). Quality control changes seek to improve the effectiveness and efficiency of operations without altering their basic features. Design changes "fundamentally alter the organization of the systems themselves" (p. 251). The authors see the NCTM Standards as an initial step in the latter kind of process: "However, the redesign we envision cannot be done in a mechanical fashion. Instead, teachers and other educators must come to a consensus and work collaboratively to bring about the changes needed" (p. 251). Thus, the Standards were issued without prescriptions for achieving them in hopes that professional organizations of teachers and other educators would take responsibility for devising ways of implementing them. The authors of the Standards envision the "redesign of school mathematics" as proceeding through a multifaceted process in which steps are taken on "many paths headed in the same direction."

PICTURES OF PRACTICE

To comprehend the nature of the changes sought by the NCTM Standards, it is useful to look closely at life in schools. Let us consider two images of classroom practice. One is traditional, the other more consistent with the Standards. Both focus on high school geometry classes, partly because geometry is one domain in which the Standards call for significant changes. Although geometry classes may have some distinctive qualities, these images share much in common with classes for other mathematical content areas and grade levels.

Transmission of Information

To conjure the complexities of classroom practice in vivid detail, think about your experience in geometry class. Presumably, this takes you back some years or decades (as in my case) before the Standards were issued. My geometry class is taught by Mr. F, balding and rosy-cheeked, congenial, but firm and awesome. He is armed with the tools of his trade: a worn wooden compass fitted with a stub of chalk, a yardstick, and a black felt eraser. He stands at the front of the room, drawing figures on the chalkboard and talking a foreign language, using words like *congruent* and *perpendicular.* Even the familiar words like *line* and *angle* have such special definitions that they sound alien, too. As he talks, he swings the compass around, making crossed hatch marks and writing letters next to their intersections. Gradually, he fills the chalkboard with designs that apparently carry special significance for him.

     He spells out this significance and records it in short lines of letters linked by peculiar symbols. He talks faster and faster, saying, "therefore," and "because we know," pointing back and forth between the diagram and the growing poem of cryptic symbols he is writing at the edge of the board. And then, shortly before the class ends, a look of satisfaction and calm spreads across his face and he puts down his chalk. He seems to think that the poem has come to represent the design in some complete and finished way. From my seat near the back of a row of connected desks screwed to the floor, it appears that this performance has pleased him enormously, although it has not made any sense to me. I know that my older sister thought geometry was hard, so I am not too surprised to discover that the course seems remote and opaque.

     One day early in the year, Mr. F asks whether any of us students would come to the board and show how to construct a perpendicular. I think this is simple enough "because we know" that perpendiculars make

90 degree angles. I raise my hand with a rare burst of confidence and suggest that we use the protractor and yardstick to draw the perpendicular. But no, that is not only too easy, it is flat out wrong. I am so mortified to have given the wrong answer that I can barely follow the logic of Mr. F's complicated sequence of hatch marks with his compass.

I am starting to get the drift of geometry, though. It is a lot like algebra, which I took last year. Both are complicated, interlocking, self-contained rule systems, like hopscotch. You have to move in a certain sequence, everything has its own special name, and the game has nothing to do with anything except itself. Like hopscotch, there is no apparent reason or purpose for most of the rules, but you are automatically out if you do not follow them. Unlike hopscotch, however, in which you can argue with your friends about the rules and sometimes make up new ones, there is no possibility of negotiating or elaborating any of the rules in math class. They are laid out in the text and by the teacher.

At the end of class Mr. F assigns a set of problems from the end of the chapter in the textbook. Most of them are variations on problems we have watched him solve in class. There is one "story problem" in which the geometry exercise is lightly veiled by an improbable situation. Mr. F lists the answers for the homework problems when we arrive in class the next day. Our first task is to exchange homework with a classmate and mark the answers right or wrong.

Construction of Understanding

Ms. S is about to start a unit on parallelism in her integrated math class for sophomores (Wiske & Levinson, 1993). She begins the class by recalling a recent article in the school newspaper about the parking problem for students' cars. The student parking lot does not have enough room for all the cars that students drive to school. Parking on the street next to the school is restricted to two hours so students with cars often sneak out of school between classes (or with a bathroom pass) to move cars or erase chalk marks placed on their tires by the parking enforcement officer. Mrs. S, whose fifth-floor classroom looks out on the student parking lot, opens this unit by asking her geometry class if the lot could be restriped to accommodate more cars.

When they look out the window, students notice there is some wasted space in the lot and question whether parking at right angles is most efficient. They wonder about variations and averages in the width, length, and turning radius for their cars. As students brainstorm about the relevant variables, Ms. S rephrases some of their ideas with terms and topics that are central to her curriculum unit (e.g., parallel line segments, interior and exterior angles). She announces a contest to figure out how to fit the most cars into the student lot. On this day she allows students to pick their own three-person groups, although she sometimes assigns students to groups. As a homework assignment, students must gather relevant data about the parking lot and their cars and develop some ideas about how parking could be maximized.

During the next class, students work with their partners in the computer laboratory. Members of each trio discuss the proposals they designed on paper and collaborate in developing a joint plan. They draw their plan with a software program that allows them to construct a diagram easily, to measure line segments and angles, and to try out adjustments. For homework, Ms. S asks students to read a section in their textbook and to label their parking lot diagram using the list of special terms introduced in the text. She explains that each group will be expected to use these terms in describing and explaining their plans to the whole class. In addition to the group presentation, each student will prepare a written explanation of his or her group's plan. The written report must incorporate the concepts and terms from the textbook in labeling diagrams, discussing some alternative proposals the group considered and justifying their final design.

As the trios develop and discuss their plans during class, Ms. S circulates among them, listening to their proposals and debates. Occasionally, she paraphrases their comments using the discipline-based vocabulary for concepts and modes of discourse that she wants them to develop: "So your conjecture, Jean, is that if the transversal intersects these parallel lines at 45 degrees you will maximize the number of cars you can fit, right? But Jamal is asking if your data really support that. So how could you make a really convincing argument?"

As each group presents its plan, other members of the class are encouraged to ask questions, to clarify the proposal and its rationale, and to decide whether any feasible improvements are possible. Through these interactions, students practice communicating mathematically as they use mathematics to solve a practical problem in their own lives. Ms. S assesses these conversations and other student performances to evaluate both her students' progress and her own teaching plans. She observes as trios discuss their plans during class and critiques the draft plans that students prepare of their parking proposals. She conducts more formal assessments of the trios' oral presentations and their responses to comments from classmates, as well as the final written product prepared by each student. The class debates the merits of the final proposals and participates in choosing the contest winner. A delegation of students from the class decides to write an article for the school paper describing several of the best proposals and explaining the methods by which they were developed.

WHAT IS THE DIFFERENCE? WHAT MUST CHANGE?

Most U.S. teachers learned to teach from models who resembled Mr. F. They have been reinforced by colleagues who teach this way, by the design of mathematics textbooks, by curriculum mandates that require superficial coverage of a wide range of ideas rather than in-depth understanding of concepts, and by multiple-choice standardized tests that reward quick recall of isolated definitions and procedures. At a more subtle level, many teachers are influenced by the common beliefs that teaching is telling, learning is listening, and mathematics is about right answers (Cohen, 1987; Lampert, 1990).

The NCTM Standards sketch a vision of practice more akin to the second example. The dimensions of difference between these two examples are exactly those to be negotiated in transforming practice toward the vision outlined in the NCTM Standards.

Research with teachers who are in the midst of making such transformations has illuminated the nature of the interwoven changes that are sought and the forces that may support or impede the process (Anderson et al., 1994; Ferrini-Mundy, Graham, & Johnson, 1993; Wiske & Levinson, 1993). It reveals that implementing the NCTM Standards entails shifting a whole system of entrenched and mutually reinforcing ideas, skills, behaviors, technologies, policies, organizational structures, and school cultures. Let us consider these various dimensions of change while keeping the two teachers in mind. Imagine yourself as Mr. F trying to become more like Ms. S. Think about the nature of the transformation you would have to undertake and the range of factors that might affect your progress and your feelings about the effort. Anchoring our analysis of these abstract factors in two particular classrooms reminds us of the intensely personal, particular realities of school practice.

Teachers' Knowledge, Skills, and Dispositions

Many mathematics teachers in U.S. schools learned mathematics from teachers like Mr. F and pattern their practice on these models. Transmission-mode teaching focuses on covering a curriculum, usually in the sequence laid out in the textbook, with an emphasis on demonstrating and rehearsing "correct" facts, formulas, and procedures. Teachers may carry out this kind of teacher-led, text-based "frontal teaching" (Goodlad, 1984) without a deep understanding of either their subject matter or their students' understanding.

To shift toward an approach like that of Ms. S, more in accord with the sort of pedagogy recommended by the NCTM Standards, Mr. F could not simply cover a prescribed curriculum. In order to connect the study of mathematics with everyday life, to guide students' inquiry around key ideas, and to help students construct understanding by making sense of their investigations, teachers like Mr. F need to transform their classroom practice. Such a transformation requires not merely using new methods and materials, but also significant changes in knowledge and beliefs (Cohen, 1990).

A growing body of research is clarifying the dimensions of teachers' thinking that are relevant to successful constructivist pedagogy. Building on a framework developed by Shulman and colleagues (Grossman, Wilson, & Shulman, 1989; Shulman, 1986), Hilda Borko and Ralph Putnam (1995) analyzed the research evidence on novice and experienced teachers' knowledge and beliefs in three overlapping domains: general pedagogical knowledge, subject-matter knowledge, and pedagogical content knowledge.

General pedagogical knowledge encompasses "knowledge of strategies for creating environments and conducting lessons; strategies and arrangements for effective classroom management; and more fundamental knowledge and beliefs about learners, how they learn and how that learning can be fostered by teaching" (Borko & Putnam, 1995, p. 39). Although teachers may provide some direct instruction, cultivating students' capacity to conduct inquiry and make sense of their investigations entails more than just presenting the curriculum. Teachers need to devise academic tasks that promote active inquiry, engage and support students in posing and solving problems, create a classroom culture that encourages risk taking and critical respect for fellow students' ideas, and develop assessments that reveal students' thinking (Brophy, 1989).

In order to help students construct their own understanding, teachers need to know how their students think and learn. Many mathematics teachers believe that students understand if concepts have been clearly presented. They often think students must master basic skills and facts before they can be engaged in understanding (Putnam, Heaton, Prawat, & Remillard, 1992). When teachers are given opportunities to study how youngsters think and learn and are supported in researching their own students' thinking, they are often more willing to forego traditional transmission-style teaching (Fennema, Carpenter, & Loef, 1993; Nelson, 1995).

In order to teach for understanding, teachers must develop a rich and flexible knowledge of their subject matter. Borko and Putnam (1995) analyze this domain as encompassing "knowledge of the facts, concepts, and procedures within a discipline and the relationships among them" (p. 43). Researchers at the National Center for Research on Teacher Education (1991) studied preservice and experienced teachers and concluded that many of them do not understand the meanings that underlie mathematical procedures. Teachers whose understanding of their subject matter is based primarily on the linear sequence of topics in their textbook tend to think students must either learn ideas in this sequence or run the risk of becoming confused. This conception provides an impoverished foundation for recognizing and developing connections between students' ideas and the curricular agenda (Wiske & Houde, 1993).

Along with the substance of their subject matter knowledge, teachers must understand the syntactic structures of the discipline and the ways of establishing knowledge and verifying claims (Borko & Putnam, 1995). This aspect is particularly important in mathematics education because the position endorsed in the NCTM Standards (that mathematics is a way of reasoning and communicating about problems encountered in the world) is at odds with the view commonly held in schools, namely, that mathematics is a fixed collection of right answers. The NCTM (1991) *Professional Standards for Teaching Mathematics* explicitly endorse the need for teachers to develop their subject matter knowledge: "Given the nature of mathematics and the changes being recommended in the teaching of mathematics, teachers at all levels need substantive and comprehensive knowledge of the content and discourse of mathematics" (pp. 139–140).

The final domain of teacher knowledge that Borko and Putnam (1995) describe is pedagogical content knowledge, which "consists of an understanding of how a subject area, and the topics and issues within it, can be organized and represented for teaching" (p. 46). Building on Shulman's (1986) conception, Grossman (1990) identified four aspects of this domain: an overarching conception of teaching a subject, knowledge of instructional strategies and representations, knowledge of students' understanding and potential misunderstandings, and knowledge of curriculum and curricular materials. In mathematics education, the last component often includes knowing how to integrate new technologies, such as calculators and computers, into curriculum and pedagogy.

In sum, constructivist teaching requires that teachers develop more flexible conceptions of their subject matter and more detailed understandings of their students' interests and thinking. They need a richer repertoire of strategies for representing mathematics to students and for managing to elicit, document, and organize discourse about students' ideas.

A more subtle, but equally important, aspect of teachers' beliefs concerns their assumptions about the appropriate distribution and negotiation of intellectual authority in school. In traditional mathematics classrooms, authority is invested in the textbook and in the teacher. These are sources and ultimate arbiters of right answers, which is the basic currency of the mathematics classroom. Without explicitly labeling this dimension of change, the NCTM Standards call for a radical reallocation of intellectual authority. When the agenda is understanding rather than memorization of other people's ideas, the rules of traditional classrooms must change (Wiske, 1994). Teachers in the midst of shifting toward more constructivist approaches have acknowledged that changing their assumptions about intellectual authority is one of the most difficult challenges. It requires a reexamination of often tacit values and a redefinition of the ethical and moral dimensions of good teaching (Wiske, Levinson, Schlichtman, & Stroup, 1992). The fact that teachers' values are enmeshed with a corresponding set of beliefs and assumptions held by students, parents, and administrators only adds to the difficulty of change.

Students' Knowledge, Skills, and Dispositions

The changes for teachers implied by the NCTM Standards suggest corresponding transformations for students in mathematics classes. Most students in U.S. schools expect mathematics classes to be similar to Mr. F's lesson. The teacher talks; the students remember the facts, formulas, and procedures the teacher demonstrates, supply right answers quickly when called upon, and reproduce this learning on homework assignments and tests. Students who learn to play their part in this game tend to resist changing the rules. Learning to invent, critique, challenge, and wonder can be threatening to students schooled in traditional classrooms (Schoenfeld, 1992).

Students must develop new vocabulary, forms of interaction, and modes of discourse as part of the transformation of classrooms in accordance with NCTM Standards. Besides developing new kinds of knowledge and skills, students must develop new attitudes and expectations as they shift from information recipients to knowledge makers. David Perkins and colleagues (Tishman, Perkins, & Jay, 1995) have formulated these attitudes as "thinking dispositions," including the tendency to be curious, to think adventurously, and to give thinking time.

For both teachers and students, enacting the new curriculum Standards amounts to creating a different culture in the classroom, one in which the purpose and the rules of the game are fundamentally different from those of traditional math classes (Wood, Cobb, & Yackel, 1991). Learning to negotiate intellectual responsibility and authority for making sense is a complex process of unlearning old habits and gradually developing new knowledge, skills, and dispositions within a learning community.

Curriculum Materials and Policies

Certainly the NCTM Standards recommend alteration of traditional curriculum materials and policies. They imply changes at all levels of curriculum architecture, from the broad outlines of the scope and sequence of kindergarten-12th-grade curriculum topics, down to the detail of how student assignments can be worded and coordinated most effectively. Teachers who were pioneers in trying to implement the NCTM Standards often cited incompatible curriculum policies established by states, districts, and department heads as one of the significant barriers to their efforts (Wiske et al., 1992). Although these individual pioneers might initiate new approaches in their classrooms, they and their students were sometimes penalized by outdated curriculum requirements. Teachers who were expected to cover a broad curriculum scope found it difficult to foster the culture of in-depth inquiry recommended by the Standards.

The lack of compatible textbooks was another of the barriers frequently mentioned by the early implementors of the Standards. Gradually, textbook authors and publishers have developed materials that are more in line with the Standards. Several recent mathematics textbooks are organized according to the topics and goals outlined in the Standards (Anderson et al., 1994). They suggest activities that include the kinds of inquiry and the use of technologies recommended in the Standards.

Yet even teachers who are fortunate enough to work with textbooks and curriculum policies that are aligned with the Standards face a significant challenge in preparing their own curriculum materials. In order to teach the parking lot unit, Ms. S had to develop assignment sheets, assessment activities and criteria, and some new kinds of lesson formats. After teaching the unit once, she knew how to improve the structure of the instructional activities and to revise the materials. Making a significant transformation in the curriculum requires progressive shifts in an interwoven fabric of materials and methods.

Technology

The two classroom examples differ significantly in the nature and uses of technology. The new curriculum standards are driven, in part, by the rapid development of calculators and computer-related educational technologies. In geometry, for example, computer software enables students to construct and analyze geometric figures in ways that were either much too cumbersome or completely impossible with the old technologies of compass, protractor, and straight edge. With these technologies students can use geometry to analyze practical challenges like the parking lot problem Ms. F posed. They can become geometers who conduct their own investigations and may even invent new mathematics (Schwartz, Yerushalmy, & Wilson, 1993).

Graphing calculators and other computer software offer similar advantages in other branches of mathematics. The computer's capacity to link graphic, iconic, and symbolic representations of mathematical ideas can enable students to manipulate mathematics and see connections that were difficult or impossible with old technologies (Kaput, 1992).

Yet the integration of these technologies with the life of school classrooms is far from simple. The hurdles to be surmounted begin with mere access. Purchases of costly new technologies compete with other priorities in the allocation of scarce educational resources. Even when the technologies may exist in a school, teachers often have difficulty gaining access to them at the time they are needed for their students. The schedule for using the computer laboratory or for bringing computers or calculators into the classroom does not always match what is most appropriate for the needs of every class.

Orchestrating the effective use of complex technologies is no simple matter, even if access can be successfully arranged. Integrating new technologies into the curriculum requires teachers to redesign multiple levels of lesson architecture, from the overall conception of curriculum units and the design of specific exercises and homework assignments, to the integration of computer-based work with offline activities (Wiske & Houde, 1993).

Developing technical fluency takes time, practice, and a willingness to risk looking less than smooth at first. Complex technologies are more likely to malfunction than simple chalk and pencil. Both students and teachers must develop something of the engineer's comfort with tinkering through trial and error if they are going to benefit from the advantages of complex technologies.

Assessment Instruments and Policies

The criteria by which student achievement is measured constitute an important aspect of the reward structure influencing students and ultimately their teachers. These criteria may be set by various decision makers in the educational system: standardized achievement and aptitude test publishers, authors of state tests, writers of departmental exams, and classroom teachers who prepare their own quizzes and tests. In many school systems, some or all of these forms of assessment are significantly out of kilter with the curriculum goals endorsed by the NCTM Standards.

Teachers in the vanguard of implementing the NCTM Standards often complained (Wiske et al., 1992) that the kinds of competencies the Standards urged them to develop in their students were not measured by the tests their pupils were required to take. Students who had learned how to develop and defend original arguments might not score well on standardized multiple-choice tests, although their performances amply exemplified the goals of Standards. Teachers whose own professional evaluations are based partly on their students' standardized test scores may be penalized for enacting the new Standards.

There are now multiple initiatives underway to develop assessment instruments and policies that are more compatible with the new curriculum standards and constructivist pedagogy. Performance-based examinations as developed in California and portfolio assessment programs like those in Vermont and Connecticut attempt to base student evaluations on measures that are more consistent with the focus of the NCTM Standards. As the educational system develops such assessments and their credibility spreads, they will constitute a powerful incentive for teachers and students to address the new curriculum standards.

There are other aspects of the assessment process, however, that teachers notice as subtle yet powerful barriers to the implementation of the NCTM Standards. For example, the Standards emphasize the value of dialogue and collaboration as important mediators of learning among members of a community. Teachers are encouraged to organize collaborative groups and to engage students in peer assessment activities. How do teachers assign individual grades to students who collaborate on a team product? Assessment policies that focus solely on individual accomplishments may not adequately address a teacher's goals nor assess all the important aspects of students' achievement.

Community Expectations

Differing expectations about what constitutes evidence of effective teaching and learning is only one of the areas in which parents' assumptions may conflict with the priorities of the NCTM Standards. Parents who attended traditional mathematics classes carry tacit expectations about how effective classrooms look, what homework and tests should be, and how math courses ought to be structured. Parents of students who are preparing for college are often among the most vocal opponents of classroom practices that depart from the traditional patterns.

Helping parents understand the nature of the shifts in curriculum and evaluation and the rationale behind them is an essential part of implementing new standards. The NCTM worked with the National Congress of Parents and Teachers, along with many other stakeholders, in developing and publicizing the new Standards. The same process of education and collaboration with key members of the school community is necessary at all other levels of the educational system by state and local school officials and by classroom teachers.

School Structures and Culture

All these changes within classrooms imply significant alterations of the school organizations surrounding classrooms. One major structural shift is a rearrangement of students and teachers into courses. The Standards recommend some fundamental changes in the way mathematics courses are defined. Algebra is to be taught in middle school grades so that students will already be familiar with much of the traditional freshman algebra material by the time they reach secondary school. The Standards call for secondary school mathematics courses to integrate material that was traditionally separated in the old algebra I, geometry, and algebra II sequence. These shifts in the placement of curriculum topics often necessitate redefinition of courses and reassignment of teachers.

Allocation of time within the school day is another aspect of school structures that the Standards call into question. Teachers who attempt to implement the Standards often feel constrained by the typical class period of 40–50 minutes. Such a block of time is often too brief to allow the kind of inquiry, often with complex equipment, that the Standards recommend. Particularly, teachers who integrate computer-based investigations request longer class periods or more flexible schedules. A further drawback of the typical school schedule is the lack of much time, if any, for teachers to prepare before classes or to analyze and synthesize after class. The absence of planning time is difficult for all teachers, but especially so for those who attempt more student-centered pedagogy. The kind of teaching recommended by the Standards requires teachers not simply to deliver their planned program, but to guide students in active learning. In order to orchestrate classes around students' work, teachers need time to analyze and adjust to students' responses (Wiske et al., 1992).

Besides such visible structures as the assignment of teachers, students, and time, the NCTM Standards also challenge more subtle aspects of the way schools are organized and managed. The process of decision making has proved to be one of the most significant barriers to implementation of the Standards, especially in the highly bureaucratic systems typical of large urban school districts. In such systems, decisions about curriculum materials, class assignments and schedules, assessment instruments, and the focus and allocation of inservice teacher development are often made by district- or building-level administrators. Teachers attempting to implement the NCTM Standards often found that the outcome of centrally made decisions undermined their efforts (Wiske et al., 1992).

Top-down autocratic administrative methods also contradict the kind of collaboration and negotiation that the Standards urge teachers to foster in their classrooms. Teachers who attempt to foster a culture of inquiry must work to create an atmosphere very different from the traditional classroom. Developing students' taste, tact, and tenacity for the pursuit of mathematical truths is a complex process. It is not consistent with passive obedience to authority. Unilateral decision-making procedures and an emphasis on compliance with mandates do not foster the values, beliefs, and behaviors that are consistent with constructivist pedagogy. Although restructuring efforts alone may not cause significant changes in curriculum and practice, a willingness to reorganize school structures and decision making can complement efforts to change educational values and processes (Elmore, 1995). Teachers should be treated in ways that model and reinforce the processes they are expected to endorse with their students. A school system that encourages a culture of inquiry in all its various activities is more consistent with the atmosphere recommended by the Standards.

IMPLICATIONS

The transformations implied by the NCTM Standards amount to a fundamental shift in educational paradigm. The transmission-of-information paradigm is supported and expressed through a complex, interwoven set of goals, beliefs, behaviors, materials, policies, and organizational structures. The construction-of-understanding paradigm implies changes in every one of these aspects of the educational system. Phrases like "implementation of curriculum reform" do not begin to portray the depth or complexity of the process. Indeed, such language is likely to encourage inappropriately technical and autocratic thinking and strategies. There are at least two basic reasons why such approaches are inadequate to accomplish this change in educational paradigm. One derives from the nature of teaching, the other from the complexity of the educational system.

Teachers as Learners

The educational philosophy behind the NCTM Standards underscores the need for learners to be intellectually active in constructing their own understandings. It endorses connecting academic learning with experiences in the world, both as a source of interesting problems and as a venue for using and communicating what is learned. Finally, the Standards encourage teachers to create opportunities for students to learn from and with one another through collaboration and dialogue.

All these premises apply equally well to teachers as learners. Teachers who wish to move their practice in the directions outlined by the Standards must become active learners: about their subject matter, their students, the processes of teaching and learning, and the uses of new educational technologies. They must learn new ways of supporting and assessing students' progress and of cultivating a new classroom culture. Making all these changes inevitably draws teachers into confrontations with multiple stakeholders, so teachers must also learn to explain and negotiate with students, parents, colleagues, and administrators.

Learning new ideas, skills, and beliefs; developing fluency with new educational technologies and approaches; forming new kinds of relationships with students and other members of the school community—all of these kinds of learning go far beyond the narrow confines that are connoted by "teacher training." Inevitably, transforming one's practice in such profound ways entails not merely a retooling of particular aspects of professional expertise. As one of my favorite teachers, Lois Hetland, says, "You teach who you are." Enacting practice consistent with the NCTM Standards involves a transformation of self for most teachers.

How can teachers be provided with the kinds of learning opportunities that they are expected to offer their students? How can they experience worthy pedagogical models, develop the necessary range of understandings, and nurture the kinds of collegial relationships that will sustain their continuing professional development? Single workshops, conferences, or inservice meetings may set the stage by making teachers aware of possibilities. Brief and limited occasions are not enough, however, to support and sustain the ongoing inquiry that teaching to the Standards implies. Recent research on the process of teacher development emphasizes the help teachers need to construct complex new understandings of their educational goals and practice. Teachers need time to learn, to talk with innovative colleagues, to practice and receive coaching on new approaches, and to reflect on the process and implications of changing their practice (Guskey & Huberman, 1995; Nelson, 1995).

Promising approaches to teacher development foster professional networks that involve teachers sustained in study groups or other forms of learning communities (Lord, 1994; McLaughlin, 1994). Within these structures, teachers can learn a common language and develop collegial relationships that support ongoing dialogue. Sustained dialogue about subject matter and teaching and learning permits teachers to develop ideas, exchange resources, reflect on problems, celebrate accomplishments, and restore the faith that fuels all good teaching.

Several promising models of such professional networks or study groups have been developed. The Urban Math Collaboratives (Webb &

Romberg, 1994) provide one set of models for linking teachers with colleagues both within and across schools and with other professionals concerned about mathematics education. Electronic networks hold the promise of linking teachers who share common interests, but who have difficulty meeting face to face. The mathematics community in Montana (Wiske & Levinson, 1992) has created an impressive set of programs, organizations, policies, and alliances that link teachers with mathematicians and mathematics educators in supporting the implementation of the Standards. These examples illustrate ways of supporting teachers as learners that model and promote the educational approaches endorsed by the Standards.

Schools as Learning Organizations

Although teachers as learners are the heart of educational change, teachers alone cannot produce the changes implied by the NCTM Standards. These changes involve a range of interwoven factors working across all parts of the educational system. Piecemeal tinkering with textbooks, technologies, staff development offerings, or assessment policies is not only insufficient, but potentially counterproductive. Partial interventions of these sorts drain precious resources, including the most valuable one of all, the willingness of dedicated professionals to try "one more new thing."

The organizational context that supports constructivist curriculum is well defined by Senge's (1990) vision of the learning organization. His analysis of such organizations focuses on principles or "disciplines," including continual clarification of personal focus and mastery, shared mental models and visions that encompass assumptions about what is valued and how it is to be approached, and team learning. The fifth and most comprehensive discipline is systems thinking that focuses on dynamic complexity rather than discrete components. "The essence of the discipline of systems thinking lies in a shift of mind:

- seeking interrelationships rather than linear cause-effect chains, and
- seeing the process of change rather than snapshots" (Senge, 1990, p. 73).

Principles of systemic change have been the focus of considerable attention in the business world and are gradually being applied to analysis of educational change. From this perspective, lasting change in education depends not on successful "implementation of reform," but on a continuing process of "reforming" schools as centers of ongoing inquiry (Anderson et al., 1994).

CONCLUSION

The NCTM Standards have made a powerful contribution to systemic change. They articulate a hard-won professional consensus concerning a vision of mathematics education, including curricular goals and approaches and strategies for transforming professional practice. The authors of the Standards acknowledged that their document could be effective only if it stimulated a broad range of interested parties to collaborate in working toward this vision.

This chapter emphasizes the dynamic complexity of this process. Words like *interpretation* rather than *implementation*, *vision* rather than *standards*, *development* rather than *training*, *learning organizations* rather than *school reform* connote the essence of this endeavor. Improving curriculum and pedagogy in schools is a process of ongoing inquiry.

REFERENCES

Anderson, R. D., Anderson, B. L., Varanka-Martin, M. A., Romagnano, L., Bielenberg, J., Flory, M., Mieras, B., & Whitworth, J. (1994). *Issues of curriculum reform in science, mathematics, and higher order thinking across the disciplines*. Boulder: University of Colorado, Curriculum Reform Project.

Borko, H., & Putnam, R. T. (1995). Expanding a teacher's knowledge base: A cognitive psychological perspective on professional development. In T. R. Guskey & M. Huberman (Eds.), *Professional development in education: New paradigms and practices* (pp. 35-65). New York: Teachers College Press.

Brophy, J. (1989). Conclusion: Toward a theory of teaching. In J. Brophy (Ed.), *Advances in research on teaching: Vol. 1. Teaching for meaningful understanding and self-regulated learning* (pp. 345-355). Greenwich, CT: JAI Press.

California State Department of Education. (1991). *Mathematics framework for California public schools*. Sacramento, CA: Author.

Cohen, D. K. (1987). Educational technology, policy, and practice. *Educational Evaluation and Policy Analysis, 9*(2), 153-170.

Cohen, D. K. (1990). A revolution in one classroom: The case of Ms. Oublier. *Educational Evaluation and Policy Analysis, 12*(3), 311-329.

Cuban, L. (1988). A fundamental puzzle of school reform. *Phi Delta Kappan, 69*(5), 341-344.

Elmore, R. F. (1995). Structural reform and educational practice. *Educational Researcher, 24*(9), 23-26.

Fennema, E., Carpenter, T. P., & Loef, M. (1993). Learning to use children's mathematical thinking: A case study. In C. Maher & R. Davis (Eds.), *School, mathematics, and the world of reality* (pp. 93–118). Boston: Allyn & Bacon.

Ferrini-Mundy, J., Graham, K., & Johnson, L. (1993, April). *Recognizing and recording reform in mathematics education: Focus on the NCTM curriculum and evaluation Standards for school mathematics and the professional Standards for teaching mathematics.* Presented at the annual meeting of the American Educational Research Association, Atlanta, GA.

Goodlad, J. (1984). *A place called school: Prospects for the future.* New York: McGraw-Hill.

Grossman, P. L. (1990). *The making of a teacher: Teacher knowledge and teacher education.* New York: Teachers College Press.

Grossman, P. L., Wilson, S. M., & Shulman, L. S. (1989). Teachers of substance: Subject matter knowledge for teaching. In M. C. Reynolds (Ed.), *Knowledge base for the beginning teacher* (pp. 23-36). New York: Pergamon.

Guskey, T. R., & Huberman, M. (Eds.). (1995). *Professional development in education: New paradigms and practices.* New York: Teachers College Press.

Kaput, J. J. (1992). Technology and mathematics education. In D. A. Grouws (Ed.), *Handbook of research on mathematics teaching and learning* (pp. 127-146). New York: Macmillan.

Kline, M. (1973). *Why Johnny can't add.* New York: St. Martin's.

Lampert, M. (1990). When the problem is not the question and the solution is not the answer. *American Educational Research Journal, 27*(1), 29-63.

Lord, B. (1994). Teachers' professional development: Critical colleagueship and the role of professional communities. In N. Cobb (Ed.), *The future of education: Perspectives on national Standards in America* (pp. 175–204). New York: College Entrance Examination Board.

McLaughlin, M. (1994). Strategic sites for teachers' professional development. In P. Grimmett & J. Neufeld (Eds.), *Teacher development and the struggle for authenticity: Professional growth and restructuring in the context of change* (pp. 31-51). New York: Teachers College Press.

National Center for Research on Teacher Education. (1991). *Final report: The Teacher Education and Learning to Teach Study.* East Lansing, MI: College of Education, Michigan State University.

National Commission on Excellence in Education. (1983). *A nation at risk: The imperative for education reform.* Washington, DC: U.S. Department of Education.

National Council of Teachers of Mathematics (NCTM). (1989). *Curriculum and evaluation Standards for school mathematics.* Reston, VA: Author.

National Council of Teachers of Mathematics (NCTM). (1991). *Professional Standards for teaching mathematics.* Reston, VA: Author.

National Education Goals Panel. (1991). *The national education goals report: Building a nation of learners.* Washington, DC: Author.

National Science Board Commission on Precollege Education in Mathematics, Science, and Technology. (1983). *Educating Americans for the twenty-first century: A plan of action for improving mathematics, science, and technology education for all American elementary and secondary students so that their achievement is the best in the world by 1995.* Washington, DC: U.S. Government Printing Office.

Nelson, B. S. (Ed.). (1995, December). *Inquiry and the development of teaching.* Newton, MA: Center for the Development of Teaching, Education Development Center.

Nickerson, R. S., Perkins, D., & Smith, E. (1985). *The teaching of thinking.* Hillsdale, NJ: Erlbaum.

Putnam, R. T., Heaton, R., Prawat, R. S., & Remillard, J. (1992). Teaching mathematics for understanding: Discussion case studies of four fifth-grade teachers. *Elementary School Journal, 93*(2), 213-228.

Resnick, L. (1987). *Education and learning to think.* Washington, DC: National Academy Press.

Romberg, T. A. (1990). Evidence which supports NCTM's Curriculum and Evaluation Standards for School Mathematics. *School Science and Mathematics, 90*(6), 466-479.

Rutherford, F. J., & Ahlgren, A. (1990). *Science for all Americans.* New York: Oxford University Press.

Schoenfeld, A. H. (Ed.). (1987). *Cognitive science and mathematics education.* Hillsdale, NJ: Erlbaum.

Schoenfeld, A. H. (1992). Learning to think mathematically: Problem solving, metacognition, and sense making in mathematics. In D. A. Grouws (Ed.), *Handbook of research on mathematics teaching and learning* (pp. 334-370). New York: Macmillan.

Schwartz, J. L., Yerushalmy, M., & Wilson, B. (Eds.). (1993). *The geometric supposer: What is it a case of?* Hillsdale, NJ: Erlbaum.

Senge, P. (1990). *The fifth discipline: The art and practice of the learning organization.* New York: Doubleday.

Shulman, L. S. (1986). Those who understand: Knowledge growth in teaching. *Educational Researcher, 15*(2), 4-14.

Sizer, T. (1984). *Horace's compromise: The dilemma of the American high school.* Boston: Houghton Mifflin.

Tishman, S., Perkins, D. N., & Jay, E. (1995). *The thinking classroom: Learning and teaching in a culture of thinking.* Boston: Allyn & Bacon.

Webb, N. L., & Romberg, T. A. (Eds.). (1994). *Reforming mathematics education in America's cities: The Urban Mathematics Collaborative Project.* New York: Teachers College Press.

Wiske, M. S. (1994). How teaching for understanding changes the rules in the classroom. *Educational Leadership, 51*(5), 19-21.

Wiske, M. S., & Houde, R. (1993). From recitation to construction: Teachers change with new technologies. In J. L. Schwartz, M. Yeurshalmy, & B. Wilson (Eds.), *The Geometric Supposer: What is it a case of?* (pp. 193-216). Hillsdale, NJ: Erlbaum.

Wiske, M. S., & Levinson, C. Y. (1992, November). *Coordinated support for improving mathematics education* (TR92-2). Cambridge, MA: Educational Technology Center, Harvard Graduate School of Education.

Wiske, M. S., & Levinson, C. Y. (1993). How teachers are implementing the NCTM Standards. *Educational Leadership, 50*(8), 8-12.

Wiske, M. S., Levinson, C. Y., Schlichtman, P., & Stroup, W. (1992, February). *Implementing the Standards of the NCTM in geometry* (TR92-1). Cambridge, MA: Educational Technology Center, Harvard Graduate School of Education.

Wood, T., Cobb, P., & Yackel, E. (1991). Change in teaching mathematics: A case study. *American Education Research Journal, 28*(3), 587-616.

THEORETICAL PERSPECTIVES FOR COLLABORATIVE, CONSTRUCTIVIST CURRICULA

8 ACQUISITION OF SELF-REGULATORY SKILL: FROM THEORY AND RESEARCH TO ACADEMIC PRACTICE

Barry J. Zimmerman

City University of New York

Historically, public schools have emphasized the products or outcomes of learning, such as recall and comprehension of academic content matter, but have given relatively little attention to the *processes* or methods by which students learn. Typically, teachers focus on conveying theories, facts, and principles rather than on ways that students acquire them. For example, essential learning skills such as selective reading, systematic note taking, study time planning and management, and test anticipation and preparation are seldom taught formally. Generally, students are expected to develop their own study methods, and available research indicates that many never develop effective ways to direct their academic studying and performance (Zimmerman, 1994).

Recently, there have been several notable efforts to teach key processes using cognitive strategies, which are powerful cyclic approaches to academic tasks that experts use to learn and retain subject matter (Pressley, Woloshyn, & Associates, 1995; Wood, Woloshyn, & Willoughby, 1995). Although cognitive strategy instruction is not recommended as a replacement for regular teaching of subject matter, Rosenshine (1995) described this complementary approach as "the most important instructional advance in the past 15 years" (p. iii).

Along with these instructional training studies, researchers have investigated students' natural use of cognitive strategies and related processes to cope with and succeed in a wide variety of academic subjects (Pintrich & DeGroot, 1990; Zimmerman & Martinez-Pons, 1986, 1988, 1990). These investigators found that successful students not only used these subject matter strategies to self-regulate their learning and achievement with greater frequency than classmates, but they also used a number of closely associated processes such as goal setting, self-monitoring, environmental structuring, and self-evaluation.

Self-regulation refers to students' self-generated strategies, beliefs, and actions that are directed toward attainment of their goals (Schunk & Zimmerman, 1994). Descriptive research on self-regulatory processes has revealed an interesting picture of how students cope with daily problems of achieving under circumstances with inherent limitations and obstacles. Inspiring examples of self-regulation have emerged from the biographies of intellectual success stories such as Ben Franklin, Thomas Edison, and Ernest Hemingway, but troubling examples of poor self-regulation such as academic helplessness and underachievement have been discovered in recent assessments of our nation's youth. The goal of investigating self-regulation is to understand the source of students' metacognitive, motivational, and behavioral capabilities to surmount academic adversities and succeed in school (Zimmerman, 1989). Society's need for research on self-regulatory processes has become especially acute in recent years.

PROVOCATIVE FINDINGS ON THE ROLE OF STUDENTS' SELF-REGULATION

National concern over the cause of the low achievement of many U.S. students has prompted officials at the United States Department of Education to look beyond the regular curriculum for answers, especially to sources of personal responsibility for learning (Willis, 1992). This new emphasis has been the result of increasing evidence that many U.S. students do not spend sufficient time on their schoolwork. According to the 1990 National Assessment of Educational Progress Report, 71% of the 12th-graders studied no more than one hour a day, and 25% did not study at all.

Fortunately, there are unexpected examples of academic success in the United States, such as inner-city minority students who manage to succeed despite the odds (Wibrowski, 1992) and recent immigrant refugee children from Southeast Asia (Caplan, Choy, & Whitmore, 1992). These remarkable youngsters had to overcome economic hardship, discrimination, emotional scars, language barriers, and even gaps in their schooling in order to excel. They were not sons and daughters of highly educated parents, and they did not attend schools having many academic assets. Their success was due, rather, to their persistence, resourcefulness, and self-reliance—such as their willingness to work late into the night and to get up early the next morning to finish assignments that were due. In contrast, their less successful classmates preferred to go to bed early and to copy a classmate's work before class or to ask for help from the teacher in class (Wibrowski, 1992). Despite their lack of educational training, immigrant Asian students studied at the kitchen table each evening, mastering the essential learning methods through repeated practice and assistance from older siblings. They spent more than three hours on their homework nightly, a 300% greater effort than the average U.S. high school senior. These Asian refugees displayed a significantly greater commitment to succeed in school and a stronger sense of personal efficacy to achieve this goal than their resident U.S. classmates. The personal attributes of these achieving students, namely, their academic time management, studying habits, mastery of learning methods, goal directedness, and a sense of self-efficacy, are the hallmarks of academic self-regulation.

Conversely, the inability of students to self-control themselves effectively has been shown to be a major cause of underachievement (Krouse & Krouse, 1981). A recent review (Borkowski & Thorpe, 1994) indicates that underachievers have lower academic goals, are more impulsive, and are less accurate in assessing their abilities. In addition, they are less self-efficacious, more self-critical about their performance, and tend to give up more easily than achievers. These self-regulatory deficiencies appear to have a substantial effect on the personality and emotional development of underachievers: They have a lower self-esteem, have a higher need for approval, are more anxious, and are more influenced by extrinsic factors than achievers. Self-regulation research can explain both students' accomplishments in the face of steep odds as well as their underachievement and low self-esteem; and thus, self-regulatory skills appear to be not only advantageous but necessary.

SELF-REGULATORY ATTRIBUTES AND PROCESSES OF STUDENTS

Academic self-regulation is relatively easy to recognize as a student attribute. Consider the following examples: a Black girl who is pleading to stay after school to finish her term paper on the computer, a Hispanic boy who is holed up in a corner of the library memorizing algebra solution strategies for an important test, an Asian girl who is unhappy with her inability to remember the major characters in a Dickens novel on an English test.

Teachers do not have difficulty in classifying their students by self-regulatory attributes such as self-starters who (a) display extraordinary persistence on learning tasks; (b) are confident, strategic, and resourceful in overcoming problems; and (c) are personally sensitive to task performance outcomes.

There is reason to believe these teacher judgments are accurate because students' reports of personal self-regulatory activities have been shown to be highly congruent with their instructors' ratings (Zimmerman & Martinez-Pons, 1988). During interviews about study practices, we discovered students who were identified as self-starters by their teachers reported more frequent self-initiation of homework, class assignments, and test preparation than their classmates who required much prompting until these tasks were completed. Clearly, self-regulatory attributes of students are salient to their teachers.

However, educational researchers have encountered greater difficulty in identifying and teaching key processes that underlie students' self-regulatory attributes. Many self-regulatory processes that have been discussed are difficult to measure because of their subtlety and covertness. Furthermore, some findings are difficult to interpret because self-regulatory processes have been given more than one label, such as intentions, goals, and planning (Zimmerman & Schunk, 1989). Despite these barriers, considerable progress has been made in uncovering processes that underlie essential self-regulatory attributes. Research has established that self-regulatory processes (a) are measurable, (b) can be taught to students, (c) are distinct from mental ability, and (d) are highly correlated with academic achievement, whether measured using grade point average, achievement track in school, standardized tests, or task-specific measures (Zimmerman, 1994).

Self-regulation has been found to depend on sources of motivation as well as metacognitive strategies. Using causal modeling techniques, Zimmerman, Bandura, and Martinez-Pons (1992; Zimmerman & Bandura, 1994) demonstrated that two key motivational dimensions of self-regulation—self-efficacy and goal setting—can dramatically improve predictions of student achievement outcomes over traditional assessment measures, such as prior grades or general ability tests. *Self-efficacy* refers to personal beliefs about one's capabilities to learn or perform skills at designated levels, for example, the confidence to achieve at least a B in a course. These researchers found that self-efficacy and goal-setting measures increased prediction of final course grades by more than 30% over prior course grades or a well-known ability test. *Goal setting* refers to designating specific outcomes of learning or performance efforts, such as aspiring to earn an A in a course. There is evidence that self-regulated learners set specific, proximal in time, and challenging goals to guide their learning, and they feel self-efficacious about achieving those goals.

Research by Schunk (1990) and others has demonstrated that it is possible to teach goal setting and other self-regulated learning processes in classroom-like settings, and these processes will enhance both students' achievement and their perceptions of self-efficacy. Rather than reviewing these studies, this chapter focuses on an issue of emerging importance: students' development of self-regulatory competence. First, I describe some of the key self-regulatory techniques that have been reported anecdotally. Then I present a model of how human self-regulatory skill emerges developmentally from social learning experiences. Finally, I describe how students can self-regulate their learning using a cyclic intervention model.

KEY SELF-REGULATORY TECHNIQUES

Several self-regulatory techniques have been widely reported in anecdotal literature, such as autobiographies or biographies of prominent individuals, as well as in qualitative and quantitative research on studying. Each technique has been investigated and considerable evidence amassed concerning its effectiveness.

Self-selected Models, Tutors, or Books

This technique refers to social sources of knowledge and skill, such as learning to use a computer word-processing program from live or visually depicted models (via films, video sources, and how-to books). In his *Autobiography,* Ben Franklin describes his selection of literary models for improving his style of writing. He would make notes on a well-written passage by an exemplary model and then attempt to rewrite the passage from his notes. Then he would compare the two versions to see where he could still improve his writing technique. Although his formal training as a writer was minimal, he became one of the most widely read writers of his time. Research (Schunk & Zimmerman, 1996) shows self-regulated learners select models carefully on the basis of their appropriateness, similarity to themselves, and competence for the task in question.

Task Strategies

Task strategies refer to using effective methods of skill execution, such as a memory scheme for retrieving information for a test. For students of music, the letters in the word *face* define spaces in the treble clef, and the saying

"*Every Good Boy Does Fine*" labels the lines in the clef. Research shows that students usually require numerous examples and accompanying explanation for the model's actions to induce a strategy fully (Zimmerman & Rosenthal, 1974).

Self-set Goals

These goals describe intended outcomes of performance, such as reading a book each week to educate oneself. As a school dropout seeking to complete his education, Thomas Edison decided to read every book in his local library and developed weekly reading goals for himself to accomplish this end. Research shows that self-regulated learners set more effective goals than nonregulated students—goals that are more specific, proximal, and challenging in difficulty level (Schunk, 1990).

Planning and Time Management

This key technique involves estimating and budgeting time for studying. Many writers carefully organize their day by writing early in the morning and relegating the afternoon for other activities. Balzac was able to work 12 or more hours a day by carefully planning and managing his time. Researchers have found that unself-regulated students are not aware of wasted study time and typically underestimate the time requirements of tasks (Zimmerman, Greenberg, & Weinstein, 1994).

Environment (Task) Structuring

This technique involves selecting, organizing, and creating effective work settings, such as finding a quiet spot in the library to study or choosing the right problems to practice and master a new statistical technique. Professional writers (Wallace & Pear, 1977) often devote considerable attention to developing an adventitious writing environment, but settings that are conducive for one writer may inhibit another writer's effectiveness. For example, Norman Mailer likes a room with a view, whereas Emile Zola would write only with the window shades down. Marcus (1988) studied the impact of a radio in the writing environment of high school students and found students' adjustment of the sound level was associated with better writing scores. Research (Zimmerman & Martinez-Pons, 1986) shows that students who are low in self-regulation are less aware of the effects of the environment on their studying effectiveness.

Self-monitoring

Self-monitoring requires students to selectively track their own performance, such as keeping a record of foreign words learned. Highly productive writers such as Ernest Hemingway, Anthony Trollope, and Irving Wallace kept a daily diary of their word or page output. Self-monitoring increases self-awareness of progress, but students need to focus on positive outcomes or improvements in performance to enhance motivation and learning.

Self-evaluative Judgments or Reactions

This technique involves using realistic standards to assess one's progress. The psychologist B. F. Skinner used a pressure-sensitive writing pad that registered only the amount of time he spent writing (rather than thinking), which he used to set standards for future writing. Research (Bandura, 1986) shows that performance-based criteria (e.g., prior performances) for self-evaluation have many advantages over normative (e.g., other class members) or inflexible (e.g., a perfect score) criteria.

Self-consequences

Self-consequences refer to making a reward or punishment contingent on personal accomplishment. Hemingway often made his fishing trips in the Gulf Stream contingent on extraordinary levels of writing. If he could get more than a day ahead of his planned writing goals, he felt justified in taking a day off for pleasurable activities. Research (Watson & Tharp, 1993) indicates that positive outcomes usually work better than negative ones, and that they must be contingent to work, that is, they must follow task completion.

Self-verbalization

This technique involves self-instructions to enhance performance, such as self-relaxation statements to reduce anxiety before a student takes a test. Researchers have found that self-instructions work best when they precede actions rather than when they accompany them (Zimmerman & Bell, 1972), and students' self-verbalizations often become more overt with increases in task difficulty (Vygotsky, 1934/1962).

Self-Imagery

Self-imagery refers to visualizing a behavioral sequence or setting to enhance performance, such as creating a vivid image of a solution to a science problem before attempting to solve it. Many inventors can transform vexing problems into simple visual demonstrations before they can work out formal solutions in detail. For example, Einstein imagined bullets passing through moving elevators and riding on a light wave to develop his Theory of Relativity. Desensitization research (Watson & Tharp, 1993) shows that remaining relaxed during imaginal performing can further acquisition and performance.

THE DEVELOPMENT OF SELF-REGULATORY SKILL

Social cognitive researchers suggest academic self-regulation is an acquired skill. Typically, students develop this skill from social sources such as parents, teachers, and peers, and as students acquire imitative competence, they increasingly shift to self-directed sources. Most academic learning strategies are subtle, covert, and difficult to self-assess. As a result, novice learners seek social sources of this strategic knowledge and skill because they lack the background to develop and integrate them into performance on their own.

Modeling can have a powerful impact on students' learning of a wide range of complex skills, whether the model is a teacher, a parent, or a peer (Bandura, 1986; Schunk & Zimmerman, 1996). Even young children can form a stable representation of a model's cognitive performance when it is carefully organized and repeated (Rosenthal & Zimmerman, 1978; Zimmerman & Rosenthal, 1974). To behaviorally perform an academic skill, students usually require imitative practice and often social support from a teaching model, such as verbal feedback, corrective modeling, physical guidance, and encouragement. Advanced strategic learning, because of its subtlety and difficulty, usually requires repeated imitative practice before the skill is incorporated into one's behavioral repertoire. As students acquire imitative accuracy, teaching models can withdraw their support.

Through this social modeling and imitation process, students become able to practice the learning skill in a self-controlled fashion. Social support is no longer necessary during this phase of development because the learner's control of a learning strategy now depends on covert images and verbal representations of the original modeling sequence (Bandura & Jeffery, 1973). Self-controlled learners self-monitor and self-evaluate the effectiveness of their use of the strategy by matching their observations of their practice efforts against their images and self-descriptions of the model's performance. Although the initial source of one's use of a learning strategy is social and external during modeling and imitation, its internalization depends ultimately on self-influences, such as self-generated imagery and self-verbalization, self-monitoring, and self-evaluation.

Eventually, schools expect an even higher level of self-functioning from students. A self-regulatory level enables them to systematically adapt their academic learning strategies to changing personal and academic conditions. When students' learning becomes self-regulated, they can choose when to use an academic learning strategy and how to vary its features with little or no residual dependence on the model. They are motivated to use a strategy on the basis of its perceived effectiveness in achieving outcomes rather than their beliefs about the competence of previously seen models. A self-regulated learner is very sensitive to changing features of the learning situation and to performance outcomes. In order to self-regulate flexibly to changing conditions, strategy execution must become routine (LaBerge, 1981; Neves & Anderson, 1981). Thus, students' attainment of a self-regulatory level of strategic skill is evident by their flexible adaptiveness in making strategic adjustments to changing contextual conditions.

This social cognitive model of self-regulatory development can be segmented into four distinct phases that begin with modeling influences and end with self-influences (Zimmerman & Bonner, in press). These phases, as described in Table 8.1, are assumed to be sequential, but instructional experiences can influence the subskills of more than one phase simultaneously. Although these phases were derived from descriptive research on skill development, there is evidence that they can be used to teach self-regulation as well (Zimmerman & Kitsantas, 1996). Beginning with social processes, such as modeling and imitation, and later shifting to self-processes, such as self-monitoring and self-evaluation, students can become self-reliant learners.

HOW CAN SELF-REGULATION BE ENHANCED?

This social cognitive view of self-regulatory development is seldom used in group instructional situations, such as classrooms, but it is used widely by coaches or tutors seeking to develop high levels of expertise with individual students. In a recent review of the literature on the development of expert performance across diverse areas, such as athletics, performance arts, and chess, Ericsson and Charness (1994) found that personal talent is far less important than one's methods of learning and practice.

Table 8.1. Self-regulatory Phase in Acquisition of Learning Strategy.

Phase	Name	Definition
1	Strategy observation	Seeing strategy used by a model across variations in tasks
2	Strategy imitation	Emulation of strategy often with social guidance and support
3	Self-control of strategy	Independent use of strategy in structured contexts
4	Self-regulation of strategy	Adaptive use of strategy across changing personal and environmental conditions

Several features were noted in the case histories of elite performers. First, as youth, these experts were tutored by expert teachers (often a parent) who could model essential skills and guide high-quality performance. Second, the students' expertise depended more on regular deliberate practice than anything else—a form of practice that is carefully structured to achieve specific goals. Third, the parents of these promising youth were encouraged to monitor and reinforce them by calling attention to small improvements in skill. Fourth, parents were asked to arrange their child's life to optimize learning by eliminating competing demands for their time and by spacing practices to reduce fatigue and boredom. Making practice a habitual part of the child's daily activities was designed to foster a routinized level of skilled functioning. Interestingly, research on the development of high levels of performance indicates that prodigies show the identical sequence of stages seen in normals; they differ only in the speed of acquisition. These same instructional features were discussed as part of a social cognitive view of self-regulatory development. But can such a model be used in classroom situations?

I suggest that self-regulatory skills in goal setting, strategy use, self-monitoring, and systematic practice can be introduced by teachers during class for student use during studying and homework activities. Greater emphasis has been placed on the development of self-regulatory processes underlying expert mastery in schools organized as an academy. Unlike traditional high schools, academies are designed to advance a discipline (e.g., music, dance, art, military regimen, science, etc.), as well as provide instruction to the next generation, and, as a result, the curriculum focuses on developing improved methods of performance as well as imparting established knowledge (Steinberg, 1995). This behavioral focus of academies affects students' methods of learning, with greater emphasis placed on expert and peer modeling, direct social feedback for performance efforts, and practice routines involving specific goals and methods of self-monitoring. For example, drama academies use audio- and videotape recorders to make it easier for students to hear their diction and voice projection as they rehearse parts for plays. There is less distinction between pupil and teacher in academies, and teachers rely more on tutoring and coaching during actual performance episodes rather than on lecturing in passive classroom settings.

Homework exercises can be used as performance experiences in typical high school classes to develop study skills, and modeling and coaching can be used as the primary vehicles of self-regulatory instruction during special class sessions. Unless acquisition of study skills, such as selective reading, note taking, test preparation, and formal writing, lead to more effective goal setting, to greater use of strategies, and to better self-monitoring, the potential of this knowledge will not be realized. However, when self-regulatory processes play an integral role in the development and use of academic study skills, students will experience a heightened sense of personal efficacy and will reap the benefits of superior academic achievement.

A CYCLIC MODEL OF SELF-REGULATORY TRAINING

Self-regulation is a cyclic approach to learning in the sense that it assumes that mastery requires multiple efforts, and the results of each effort provide the basis for further development. Performance outcomes reveal personal sources of needed changes as well as successes. Deliberate practice (i.e., structured and goal directed) is indispensable to higher levels of development among expert performers because it optimizes the effects of self-monitoring. Historically, teachers have used homework as a major source of academic skill practice, but unfortunately the assignment and completion of homework has declined dramatically in many schools in recent years. This self-regulatory cycle is depicted in Figure 8.1.

The first step in the cyclic model, *self-evaluation and monitoring*, occurs when students determine their personal effectiveness, often from observations and records of prior performances. Students' awareness of their study skills varies tremendously, and unself-regulated students have only a vague sense of what and how to learn from a homework assignment (Zimmerman & Martinez-Pons, 1986). These students can benefit from self-observing their functioning and using self-recorded data to ascertain specific areas of strength and weakness. For example, often students are unaware of the inadequacy of their test preparation until after the test is over because they do not test themselves. Teachers can help students interpret their records of passed and failed test items.

Figure 8.1. A cyclic model of self-regulated learning. From Zimmerman, Bonner, & Kovach (Eds.), *Developing self-regulated learners: Beyond achievement to self-efficacy*, p. 11. © 1996 American Psychological Association. Reprinted with permission.

Once the areas of deficiency are identified, the second step in the cycle of self-regulation can be taken—goal setting and strategic planning. This involves setting a specific learning goal for oneself and selecting an appropriate strategy to attain it, such as a memory scheme. Self-regulatory processes, such as task analysis and self-efficacy perceptions, influence the specificity and the difficulty level of the goals that are set. Students who have well-developed self-regulatory skills can break new tasks into components and set goals more effectively than novices. The selection of an appropriate strategy to attain the goal depends on students' repertoire of existing strategies and on access to teachers or peers who can describe a strategy, demonstrate it, and explain its effectiveness. For example, students who determine that their lecture notes are disorganized may set the goal of rewriting them after class using an outline strategy.

The third step in the cycle of self-regulated learning—strategy implementation and monitoring—occurs when students try to execute a strategy in structured contexts and monitor their accuracy in implementing it. Students need to focus on performing all aspects of the strategy the way a skilled model would. Novice learners often require social feedback and guidance as they attempt to carry out the strategy imitatively. For example, a boy trying to remember a French vocabulary list using the keyword method might have trouble coming up with key words (e.g., a word to connect the French word *froid* to its English translation *cold,* such as the keyword *frigid*). The boy might keep a record of the words he developed to analyze and discuss with his teacher later.

The fourth step in self-regulation—strategic outcome monitoring—occurs when students focus their attention on their learning outcomes in order to adapt their strategy to achieve optimal effectiveness. For example, the boy in our example might test himself on each French vocabulary word and analyze differences between keywords that were successful and unsuccessful in producing accurate recall. The quality of strategic outcome monitoring depends on one's routinization of the strategy, the specificity of one's outcome goals, and one's strategy attributions. Students who have not routinized the strategy will have trouble sustaining it while simultaneously focusing on strategy outcomes or making accurate process-product attributions (Zimmerman & Kitsantas, 1996). At the end of test preparation, students should rate their perceptions of self-efficacy for passing a short quiz on the assigned text material. These ratings can be compared to the actual quiz results to assist the students to develop accurate self-evaluative standards. Through repeated practice, the students' sense of self-efficacy for test preparation will increase in accuracy and level.

The model is cyclic because self-monitoring on each learning trial provides information that can change subsequent goals, strategies, or performance efforts. For example, self-monitoring current strategic outcomes may indicate the initial goals are too ambitious or that a particular strategy is not paying off. These results can also lead to setting more appropriate task goals or choosing a new strategy. I turn next to the issue of applying these four steps with a high school girl in a world history course.

TEACHING STUDENTS TO BECOME SELF-REGULATED LEARNERS

According to the first step of Figure 8.2, the girl should self-evaluate her use of various study skills first. By analyzing the tasks into components and determining her current skill level for each component, she develops both personal insight and motivation to change. This can be done through teacher conferences to pinpoint problems underlying her academic work or by asking her to monitor various aspects of her studying. She traces her poor test performance in history to poor recall of assigned readings. Once this general area of deficiency is identified, she focuses on the specific task

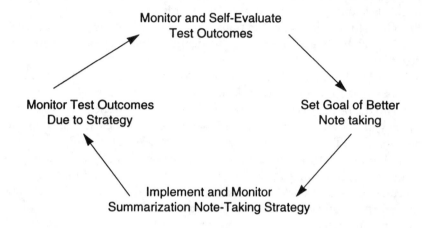

Figure 8.2. Improving note taking during assigned reading through cyclic self-regulation.

skills in question, such as her lack of notes that concisely summarize the assigned readings.

The second step in the self-regulation cycle involves setting specific goals, such as the girl's decision to take notes while she reads all her text assignments. She encounters trouble deciding what to include in her notes and needs to develop an effective strategy, so she asks a classmate who takes outstanding notes. The classmate recommends that the girl write one sentence for each paragraph of text material. She should identify main ideas first and then put these ideas together in a sentence using single words to describe lists of things. For example, regarding a paragraph on the Revolutionary War describing cannons, rifles, sabers, and bombs, the girl could substitute the inclusive word *weapon* in her summary statement. The main ideas could be emphasized using a highlighting pen or written down before drafting the summary sentence. The girl still experiences difficulty in using this summarization strategy and decides to watch her classmate demonstrate this idea selection strategy first on several pages of text.

During the third step, the girl implements and monitors the summarization note-taking strategy; however, she is unable to judge accurately whether any main ideas were omitted. Her classmate goes over her notes with her and gives her feedback regarding successes and omissions. It is suggested that she should monitor her strategy implementation until mastery is achieved and then shift to monitoring strategy outcomes.

During step 4, outcome monitoring will help the girl find out how well the various components of her note-taking strategy are working. The classmate suggests the girl should use the results of her weekly quizzes to go over her notes. If incorrectly answered items were not included in her notes, she should locate them in the book and examine her summary sentence for that paragraph. Inadequate summary sentences should be corrected to include the omitted material, and a more inclusive rule should be used with future summary sentences. If the girl can accomplish this, her sense of self-efficacy for succeeding on future quizzes will undoubtedly increase. Subsequently, she learns that although the summary notes improved her test performance to some degree, she missed many test items that were included in her notes. She decides that she needs to develop better test preparation strategies as well.

Notice how this self-regulatory cycle incorporates key processes from the four phases of the model of self-regulatory development. The girl's initial self-awareness of her poor note-taking skills was due to self-monitoring and recording encouraged by her teacher (step 1). A classmate's modeled strategies vicariously conveyed a better method of note taking—namely, creating summaries (step 2). The classmate's feedback and imitative guidance helped the girl implement her note-taking strategy (step 3). Self-control and self-regulation phases are enhanced by the girl's monitoring of strategic outcomes (step 4). In this way, the girl's development of an effective note-taking strategy grew initially from social sources of knowledge and skill and were displaced eventually by self-regulatory processes.

Although this example involved a single student, self-regulatory training can be implemented for groups of students during regular homework assignments if a skill is more widely lacking. For example, a teacher may assign note taking from selected reading passages in the history textbook as part of a homework exercise. These summary notes can be brought to class and exchanged with peers for grading. The teacher could create a master list of exemplary summary sentences for each paragraph, either personally or from discussions with the class. This procedure would enable teachers to implement self-regulatory learning cycles with the class as a whole.

RESULTS OF SELF-REGULATORY TRAINING STUDIES

Does cyclic self-regulatory strategy training really make a difference? Although the research base has become quite large, I describe here just two studies to illustrate the variety of approaches that have been used. One recent study shows how students' self-monitoring and achievement can be improved by instructor-designed homework exercises in a statistics course. Lan, Bradley, and Parr (1994) developed a monitoring protocol containing a list of the main statistical concepts covered in the text and lectures and a list of studying activities (lecture, text assignments, discussion, tutoring) for mastering the material. For each method of studying, the students recorded the number of times they engaged in it, the amount of time they spent on it, and any increases in perceived efficacy regarding each statistical concept. These researchers found that students in the self-monitoring group performed significantly better on the course exams than those in a control group or a third group that monitored the instructor's presentation of the material.

The salient feature of the self-monitoring condition was the presence of specific definitions of the concepts to be learned. By recording their method of studying each concept, students received continuing feedback regarding utilization of study activities, time devoted to each, and perceived efficacy to solve problems related to the concept. From this feedback, students could decide whether to review a concept, seek additional help, or classify the concept as having been mastered. The students' comments revealed the value of the self-monitoring protocol to them: A "good tool to evaluate myself in understanding materials also helps identify areas that I need to clarify," and "the protocols helped me realize what I didn't understand and how I could study to learn it more effectively" (Lan et al., 1994, p. 37). Clearly, these students perceived the importance of structured self-monitoring in helping them learn more effectively on their own.

Another example of self-regulatory training was reported by Nicaise and Gettinger (1994, August). These researchers worked with four students experiencing reading comprehension problems. The students met with a tutor who taught them four comprehension strategies sequentially: (a) predicting what was likely to come next in text, (b) clarifying difficulties encountered during reading (e.g., stopping when things do not make sense to seek an answer), (c) summarizing, and (d) setting reading goals prior to reading (e.g., to find specific causes of a war). The tutor taught each strategy according to six steps: (a) the strategy was described, (b) the rationale for its effectiveness was given, (c) the tutor demonstrated the strategy and the student imitated it, (d) the student practiced applying the strategy independently using controlled material, (e) the student was tested on three reading passages to determine mastery, and (f) when 90% mastery was demonstrated, the student applied the strategy to self-selected reading material in a test of skill transfer. Although this approach emphasizes certain aspects of self-regulatory development differently than the cyclic model presented earlier, the same process is involved in modeling and explanation, imitative practice with expert feedback, self-directed practice first under controlled conditions (self-control phase) and after mastery is achieved, and under naturally varying conditions (self-regulation phase).

All four students showed gains in each of the four reading comprehension strategies. The results from a multiple baseline design revealed sizable increases in strategy use after modeled training in comparison to baseline levels of performance. The students demonstrated 90% mastery with both controlled and transfer reading tasks. In addition, their average percentile increase in comprehension on the Nelson–Denny Test was 28 points and their posttest scores equaled or exceeded those of local normative groups. The students' self-efficacy perceptions for reading comprehension skills increased from pretest to posttest and subsequently were commensurate with those of classmates. Finally, all students found the program to be highly satisfactory in acceptability.

CONCLUSION

Students' failure to develop effective ways to self-regulate their learning can have devastating long-term effects on their lives. Their inability to be self-directive and self-reliant as learners not only deprives them of needed sources of strategic and corrective information, it also robs them of a continuing sense of personal efficacy and academic accomplishment. The ensuing sense of helplessness or powerlessness undermines their motivation, and it leads these students to devalue and avoid schooling. Disturbing evidence of insufficient studying and underachievement in our nation's schools are two important symptoms of the need to focus greater attention on academic self-regulatory training. Fortunately, we now have scientific evidence regarding the key components of self-regulation, how they interact cyclically, and how self-regulatory processes can be developed as part of regular homework and studying exercises.

REFERENCES

Bandura, A. (1986). *Social foundations of thought and action: A social cognitive theory*. Englewood Cliffs, NJ: Prentice-Hall.

Bandura, A., & Jeffery, R. W. (1973). Role of symbolic coding and rehearsal processes in observational learning. *Journal of Personality and Social Psychology, 26*, 122-130.

Borkowski, J. G., & Thorpe, P. K. (1994). Self-regulation and motivation: A life-span perspective on underachievement. In D. H. Schunk & B. J. Zimmerman (Eds.), *Self-regulation of learning performance: Issues and educational applications* (pp. 45-74). Hillsdale, NJ: Erlbaum.

Caplan, N., Choy, M. H., & Whitmore, J. K. (1992, February). Indochinese refugee families and academic achievement. *Scientific American*, pp. 37-42.

Ericsson, K. A., & Charness, N. (1994). Expert performance: Its structure and acquisition. *American Psychologist, 49*, 725-747.

Krouse, J. H., & Krouse, H. J. (1981). Toward a multimodal theory of academic achievement. *Educational Psychologist, 16*, 151-164.

LaBerge, D. (1981). Unitization and automaticity in perception. In J. H. Flowers (Ed.), *Nebraska symposium on motivation* (Vol. 28, pp. 53-71). Lincoln: University of Nebraska Press.

Lan, W. Y., Bradley, L., & Parr, G. (1994). The effects of a self-monitoring process on college students' learning in an introductory statistics course. *Journal of Experimental Education, 62*, 26-40.

Marcus, M. (1988). *Self-regulation in expository writing.* Unpublished doctoral dissertation, Graduate School of the City University of New York, New York.

Neves, D. M., & Anderson, J. R. (1981). Knowledge compilation: Mechanisms for the automatization of cognitive skills. In J. R. Anderson (Ed.), *Cognitive skills and their acquisitions* (pp. 463-562). Hillsdale, NJ: Erlbaum.

Nicaise, M. A., & Gettinger, M. B. (1994, August). *Fostering the self-regulation of reading comprehension in college students.* Paper presented at the annual meeting of the American Psychological Association, Los Angeles, CA.

Pintrich, P. R., & DeGroot, E. V. (1990). Motivational and self-regulated learning components of classroom academic performance. *Journal of Educational Psychology, 82*, 33-40.

Pressley, M., Woloshyn, V., & Associates. (1995). *Cognitive strategy instruction that really improves children's academic performance* (2nd ed.). Cambridge, MA: Brookline Books.

Rosenshine, B. (1995). Foreword to the second edition. In M. Pressley, V. Woloshyn, & Associates (Eds.), *Cognitive strategy instruction that really improves children's academic performance* (2nd ed., pp. iii-v). Cambridge, MA: Brookline Books.

Rosenthal, T. L., & Zimmerman, B. J. (1978). *Social learning and cognition.* New York: Academic Press.

Schunk, D. H. (1990). Goal setting and self-efficacy during self-regulated learning. *Educational Psychologist, 25*, 71-86.

Schunk, D. H., & Zimmerman, B. J. (Eds.). (1994). *Self-regulation of learning and performance: Issues and educational applications.* Hillsdale, NJ: Erlbaum.

Schunk, D. H., & Zimmerman, B. J. (1996). Modeling and self-efficacy influences on children's development of self-regulation. In K. Wentzel & J. Juvonen (Eds.), *Social motivation: Understanding children's school adjustment* (pp. 154-180). New York: Cambridge University Press.

Steinberg, J. (1995, December 18). Experimental school ideas are afloat, by land and by sea. *New York Times,* pp. B1, B4.

Vygotsky, L. S. (1962). *Thought and language* (E. Hanfmann & G. Vakar, Eds. & Trans.). Cambridge, MA: MIT Press. (Original work published 1934).

Wallace, I., & Pear, J. (1977). Self-control techniques of famous novelists. *Journal of Applied Behavioral Analysis, 10,* 515-525.

Watson, D. L., & Tharp, R. G. (1993). *Self-directed behavior: Self-modification for personal adjustment* (6th ed.). Pacific Grove, CA: Brooks/Cole.

Wibrowski, C. R. (1992). *Self-regulated learning processes among inner city students.* Unpublished doctoral dissertation, Graduate School of the City University of New York, New York.

Willis, S. (1992). Why don't students work harder? *ASCD Update, 34*(4), 1-8.

Wood, E., Woloshyn, V. E., & Willoughby, T. (1995). *Cognitive strategy instruction for the middle and high schools.* Cambridge, MA: Brookline Press.

Zimmerman, B. (1986). Development of self-regulated learning: Which are the key subprocesses? *Contemporary Educational Psychology, 16,* 307-313.

Zimmerman, B. J. (1989). A social cognitive view of self-regulated academic learning. *Journal of Educational Psychology, 81,* 329-339.

Zimmerman, B. J. (1994). Dimensions of academic self-regulation: A conceptual framework for education. In D. H. Schunk & B. J. Zimmerman (Eds.), *Self-regulation of learning and performance: Issues and educational applications* (pp. 3-21). Hillsdale, NJ: Erlbaum.

Zimmerman, B. J., & Bandura, A. (1994). Impact of self-regulatory influences on writing course attainment. *American Educational Research Journal, 31,* 445-462.

Zimmerman, B. J., Bandura, A., & Martinez-Pons, M. (1992). Self-motivation for academic attainment: The role of self-efficacy beliefs and personal goal setting. *American Educational Research Journal, 29,* 663-676.

Zimmerman, B. J., & Bell, J. A. (1972). Observer verbalization and abstraction in vicarious rule learning, generalization, and retention. *Developmental Psychology, 7,* 227-231.

Zimmerman, B. J., & Bonner, S. (in press). A social cognitive view of strategic learning. In C. E. Weinstein & B. L. McCombs (Eds.), *Strategic learning: Skill, will and self-regulation*. Hillsdale, NJ: Erlbaum.

Zimmerman, B. J., Greenberg, D., & Weinstein, C. E. (1994). Self-regulating academic study time: A strategy approach. In D. H. Schunk & B. J. Zimmerman (Eds.), *Self-regulation of learning and performance: Issues and educational application* (pp. 181-199). Hillsdale, NJ: Erlbaum.

Zimmerman, B. J., & Kitsantas, A. (1996). Self-regulated learning of a performance skill: The role of goal setting and self-monitoring. *Journal of Applied Sport Psychology, 8*, 69–84.

Zimmerman, B. J., & Martinez-Pons, M. (1986). Development of a structured interview for assessing student use of self-regulated learning strategies. *American Educational Research Journal, 23*, 614-628.

Zimmerman, B. J., & Martinez-Pons, M. (1988). Construct validation of a strategy model of student self-regulated learning. *Journal of Educational Psychology, 80*, 284-290.

Zimmerman, B. J., & Martinez-Pons, M. (1990). Student differences in self-regulated learning: Relating grade, sex, and giftedness to self-efficacy and strategy use. *Journal of Educational Psychology, 82*, 51-59.

Zimmerman, B. J., & Rosenthal, T. L. (1974). Observational learning of rule-governed behavior by children. *Psychological Bulletin, 81*, 29-42.

Zimmerman, B. J., & Schunk, D. H. (Eds.). (1989). *Self-regulated learning and academic achievement: Theory, research, and practice*. New York: Springer.

9   VYGOTSKY, BAKHTIN, AND IDENTITY FORMATION: APPLICATIONS FOR YOUTH EMPOWERMENT

William R. Penuel

Metropolitan Nashville Public Schools

This chapter examines developmental processes that empower young people to make key program decisions for programs that are designed to serve youth in urban areas in the contemporary United States. Apprenticeship processes, learning to speak using empowering language, and recognizing diverse youth identities are named as key developmental components of these programs. To illustrate these components, specific activities of a youth empowerment program are examined using concepts drawn from sociocultural (Vygotsky and Bakhtin) and psychosocial (Erikson) theories of human development.

THE PARADOXES AND PRINCIPLES OF YOUTH EMPOWERMENT

The fields of public health, health promotion, and disease prevention research and practice have all moved in recent years toward adopting community-focused strategies for prevention (Florin & Chavis, 1990). The research in these fields has increasingly pointed to the need for multistrategic efforts that involve all sectors of the community to solve such problems as HIV/AIDS, violence, and substance abuse (Johnson et al., 1990).

In the process, researchers and practitioners alike have begun to use the word *empowerment* instead of *service delivery* to describe what they do in prevention programs. In the older service delivery model, professionals deliver a preset curriculum designed by a team of experts. Prevention specialists now think of what they do as constructing a partnership with people in communities in which staff assist community members to plan, implement, and evaluate their own programs. Today, in some states, youth themselves—often the target group of prevention programs—are considered to be an important group of partners in efforts to promote community health and to work for social change.

In so-called youth empowerment programs, youth are given the power to choose the direction and strategies of programs that were traditionally designed to serve them. Rather than participating in adult-run activities, youth themselves plan activities that are designed to reduce the risk of their peers getting involved in violence, risky sexual behavior, or substance abuse. Under the banner of youth empowerment, youth take responsibility for carrying out key program tasks, including facilitating meetings, organizing conferences and community coalitions, or supervising and teaching younger children in their neighborhoods.

Many adults who work in youth programs have pointed out that youth empowerment itself is a paradoxical term. It is unclear what it means to *empower* someone, and who is doing the empowering. It is equally unclear what adults can do to support the goal of helping youth to make their own program decisions because youth empowerment could be interpreted to mean that adults must remain silent or absent from the lives of youth. In fact, however, there is an important role for adults, whether as school teachers serving as advisors to peer leadership programs or as community activists working as advocates in youth-serving agencies. In this chapter, I consider three ways in which adults can assist youth in developing, implementing, and evaluating their own programs, acting as partners to and collaborators with youth in efforts to create community change. They are:

- Assisting youth in learning how to change their communities
- Including all youth in constructing a healthy community
- Offering a space for recognizing the diverse identities of youth.

Throughout the chapter I consider how the figures of Vygotsky, Bakhtin, and Erikson provide insight into the sociocultural and developmental processes involved in youth empowerment programs using specific program examples to illustrate these points.

Adult Guidance in Youth Empowerment:
The Case of the Peer Institute

In order to make this chapter valuable to adults who work with youth, I take examples from an annual conference in Massachusetts called the Peer Institute sponsored by the Bureau of Substance Abuse Services of the Department of Public Health. The Peer Institute is an annual four-day residential conference for 250 youth from around the commonwealth, which includes youth from different genders, cultural backgrounds, sexual orientations, and class backgrounds. It is structured to serve as an "advanced training" for youth who have been serving as peer leaders in their local communities, teaching other youth about substance abuse, violence, AIDS/HIV, or the concerns and rights of gay, lesbian, and bisexual youth. The theme of the conference is "Celebrating Differences," and it includes two curricula that are used by staff during the Institute, one focused on creating appreciation for "differences" and another designed to help teams of youth who attend to plan an activity for their group to be carried out after the Institute.

What makes the Peer Institute such a good illustration of youth empowerment in action is that youth and adults work side by side throughout the conference by planning, staffing, and evaluating the conference together. For seven months, a planning team of 350 youth and adults from around the state work in subcommittees to put together the different aspects of the conference that include everything from instructional design to the dance and talent show. Once at the conference, these youth and adults are joined by "alumni" of the Peer Institute, youth who return to the Peer Institute as part of the 50-person staff. They are expected to lead and facilitate different activities, assist with registration and preparation of spaces for different activities, and make the participants feel welcome at the Institute. Finally, one youth assists me each year in conducting the evaluation by collecting data from participants, helping design evaluation instruments, and preparing the final evaluation report.

Adults who serve on the planning team and staff of the Peer Institute themselves often develop their own ability to support youth empowerment goals through the program. By inviting youth to participate and lead alongside them, adults at the Peer Institute give participants a chance to learn valuable tools of organizing for community change, including facilitation skills, problem solving, and cooperation. In addition, by listening to youth's voices, the adults themselves learn how they can be effective in responding to young people's perspectives on the problems of their community and on possible strategies for change. The inclusion of a youth voice in the planning process inevitably means that different activities will be chosen for the conference, different guidelines established, and different goals pursued than would be selected if adults alone planned the conference. Finally, the way in which adults help to create a safe environment for learning and exploration through the planning process and at the Institute and the specific activities that are designed to foster the exploration of diversity afford opportunities for adults to become more effective allies to youth in their struggles.

To provide a closer look at the social and developmental processes involved in planning, implementing, and evaluating the Peer Institute, I now turn to consider in greater detail how each of the three principles of youth empowerment is supported by the instructional and curricular design of both the planning process and the actual Institute. My point here is not to reconstruct the Peer Institute in its entirety but to show how concepts developed by Vygotsky, Bakhtin, and Erikson can direct our attention to how we might better understand and evaluate some of the developmental processes that take place within youth empowerment programs.

ASSISTING YOUTH IN LEARNING HOW TO CHANGE THEIR COMMUNITIES

One of the primary tasks for adult advisors to peer leaders in Massachusetts is to train youth to become peer leaders in their communities. The idea behind this model is that youth can be effective communicators about key social and health issues with their peers and can themselves serve as a source of positive peer pressure for other youth. At the same time, it is recognized that youth need the requisite knowledge and tools for reaching other youth, only some of which they may be able to use when they begin peer leadership. It is the task of trainers of peer leaders to provide youth with such tools.

The Peer Institute's planning team is structured in such a way that it apprentices youth and new adult members into the process (see Lave & Wenger, 1991; Rogoff, 1990). By observing and participating in the planning process with more experienced adults and youth planning team members, new members come to acquire the tools they need to plan and staff the Institute for four days. At the Institute itself, the staff help to facilitate groups in a process of action planning, whereby they design a project to be implemented in their communities. Behind this apprenticeship approach is an application of sociocultural research grounded in the writings of the Russian psychologist Lev Vygotsky. It is important to understand some of the basic themes of Vygotsky's cultural-historical psychology as a context for a discussion of how the Peer Institute apprentices its members into the processes of community change.

Themes of Vygotsky's Cultural-Historical Psychology

One researcher who has written widely on how human mental functioning is socioculturally, historically, and institutionally situated is the Russian psychologist L. S. Vygotsky (1978, 1981a, 1981b, 1987). Whereas many psychologists have examined development as a process taking place within individuals, Vygotsky examined development as a process of transformation of individual functioning as social practices become internalized by individuals (Wertsch, 1985, 1991). Three basic themes characterize this work, each of which overlaps and intertwines with the others: the use of genetic analysis to study individual functioning, the claim that individual mental functioning has sociocultural origins, and the claim that human action is mediated by cultural tools and signs.

The use of a genetic method by Vygotsky is grounded in his view that it is impossible to examine individual functioning without understanding its place in development. For him, any event or phenomenon must be studied from the perspective of its place in development. It is the transformations in individual functioning that are of interest to Vygotsky, that is, how it is that individuals transform their mental functioning through participating in various social activities. At the same time, Vygotsky recognized that simultaneous with individual development, historical and cultural development takes place, changing the context and available resources for developing individuals to use in activity as social practices themselves evolve. For Vygotsky, examining these domains in relation to one another was as important as examining individual development, for to understand individual development, it is necessary to understand how it is culturally, historically, and institutionally situated.

Vygotsky's claim that individual mental processes have their origin in social interaction is a second guiding assumption of his work. His account of the social origins of mental functioning appears in his work in one form as the "general genetic law of cultural development":

> Any function in the child's cultural development appears twice, or on two planes. First it appears on the social plane, and then on the psychological plane. First it appears between people as an interpsychological category, and then within the child as an intrapsychological category. . . . [I]t goes without saying that internalization transforms the process itself and changes its structure and functions. Social relations or relations among people genetically underlie all higher functions and their relationships. (Vygotsky, 1981b, p. 163)

The notion of intermental functioning has a second assumption about the social origins of mental functioning embedded within it. Specifically, Vygotsky applied the term *higher mental functions* (e.g., thinking, memory, and voluntary memory) to processes that exist between people. In other words, intelligence is seen as distributed across persons engaged in joint activity rather than being attributed to individual minds. Vygotsky himself was concerned with the kind of problem-solving dyads studied by Wertsch (1979) and others (see Rogoff, 1990) as young children working in collaboration with adults attempted to solve simple puzzles and perform tasks.

In this connection, Vygotsky (1978) formulated his notion of the *zone of proximal development,* which he defined as the distance between a child's "actual developmental level as determined by independent problem solving" and the higher level of "*potential development as determined through problem solving under adult guidance or in collaboration with more capable peers* (p. 96; emphasis in original). The zone of proximal development is one of the important mechanisms that account for the development of individual functioning, and it has been a particularly useful tool in designing effective instructional interventions (e.g., Palincsar & Brown, 1988; Tharp & Gallimore, 1988). It underlies the approach to teaching strategies that call for adults and more capable peers to provide "strategic assistance" or "scaffolding" to novices as they learn to participate in valued social activities.

A third general theme that organizes Vygotsky's cultural-historical psychology involves the claim that human action is mediated by cultural tools and signs. Language, for Vygotsky, is one of the most important tools for living in contemporary cultures. He viewed language as important, not simply as a representational system, but as a set of structured resources for action. The mediational capacities of language, moreover, are not ancillary for Vygotsky, but integrally related to thinking and other higher mental processes (Vygotsky, 1987). Guiding his work is an assumption that signs and tools are not just servants of individuals' purposes but, in important ways, transform those purposes. As Vygotsky (1981b) noted:

> By being included in the process of behavior, the psychological tool alters the entire flow and structure of mental functions. It does this by determining the structure of a new instrument act, just as a technical tool alters the process of a natural adaptation by determining the form of labor operations. (p. 137)

These tools, moreover, like the problem-solving capacities of individuals, are acquired through participation in social activities, even as they are mastered and transformed by individuals in their own activities. This point is reflected in Vygotsky's (1981a) claim that "a sign is always originally a means used for social purposes, a means of inducing others, and only later becomes a means of influencing oneself" (p. 157).

Learning the Tools of Peer Leadership: Action Planning

One of the greatest challenges for youth empowerment programs is ensuring that youth have the needed tools for accomplishing their goals and helping to create social change and healthy communities. Adults and more capable peers can play a key role here in providing strategic assistance to youth who are participating in youth empowerment programs. One curricular structure that helps facilitate this process at the Peer Institute is that of Action Planning. Action Planning is the process whereby teams of four youth and an advisor determine a goal, strategy, and set of activities for their peer leadership group focused loosely on the topic of celebrating diversity.

Action Planning at the Peer Institute is designed as a six-step process facilitated by one youth and one adult in a room with five to six different teams:

Step 1: Assess Strengths and Needs
Step 2: Assess Strengths and Challenges
Step 3: Brainstorm and Select a Goal
Step 4: Brainstorm Possible Strategies
Step 5: Choose a Strategy
Step 6: Reality Check

Each step of Action Planning is designed to assist peers working in teams along a process of identifying a project that they themselves decide is important to making their community a better place to live. Moreover, these steps closely resemble steps that are used in contemporary approaches to community health planning. The parallels make it easier for young people who participate in action planning to be better prepared to participate in larger community health planning efforts that use a similar approach and similar tools for planning, implementing, and evaluating programs.

The way that many of the activities are structured, moreover, allows for a lot of peer interaction and peer support to shape the process. In Step 4, for example, each team has the opportunity to examine the goals of each of the other teams in the room and suggest possible strategies to assist them in reaching their goal. One team I observed used two of the strategies generated by the other teams rather than those generated by their own team for their action plan. With this structure, the other teams are able to assist teams by suggesting tools and alternatives they might otherwise have left out in choosing a strategy for their Action Plan.

Action Step 5, Choosing a Strategy, invites teams to further develop their thinking about what it will take to carry out their Action Plan. First, they engage in an icebreaker designed to help individuals on each team identify what strengths and gifts they bring to their group. The teams then use a worksheet to assist them in thinking about how much time a particular strategy will take, how much it will cost, and what other resources they will need if they choose this particular strategy. Sometimes, teams come to the Peer Institute having adopted strategies in the past that have been less successful, whether because the time taken was not considered or the scheduling and transportation needs required to carry out a project were not considered. This worksheet acts as a tool for thinking about these issues before a strategy is adopted. This step also provides teams with a tool for decision making, using stickers to represent votes to adopt particular strategies. Although such tools may seem straightforward, many groups find it quite difficult to come to a decision about activities. Without concrete tools for making decisions or a simple agreement to adopt majority rule in the group, teams often get stuck at this step of planning.

What makes this Action Planning curriculum Vygotskian is not just that specific tools are provided through the curriculum for accomplishing the task of designing an action plan, but that the curriculum teaches these tools by engaging teams in participating in the planning process itself. Each team is not simply learning these tools so that a decontextualized set of skills can be mastered; they acquire these tools in the process of designing a project that they themselves are interested in accomplishing. The curriculum itself and the facilitators act as strategic guides, structuring the participation of teams in such a way that the tools incorporated into the curriculum facilitate the process of each team deciding on a goal, a strategy, and a course of action for themselves.

INCLUDING ALL YOUTH IN CONSTRUCTING A HEALTHY COMMUNITY

Participation is just one dimension of the process of fostering a greater inclusion of youth within youth empowerment programs. Inviting youth and adults to work together to plan and implement a project is an important part of youth empowerment, but adults also need to have the capacity to listen to and hear youths' voices about what they hope to accomplish, what they have to offer to action planning, and what obstacles might get in their way. Often this is not so easy for adults because many youth workers have been trained to view youth as needing to be under adult control at all times. They have a difficult time viewing youth as partners and collaborators in their own programs and listening to what youth have to say from that perspective. Often the very language youth workers use to describe situations that come up in programs and to describe what it is they do positions youth more as problems to be solved than as potential contributors to programs. In this connection, youth workers need to have some way to recognize when their own speech and talk with youth and with other adults excludes youth from participating and having a voice. It is in this context, I argue, that Bakhtin's dialogic examination of communicative processes and language is of particular value.

Bakhtin's Dialogic Approach to Communication and Existence

For the Russian literary analyst M. M. Bakhtin, dialogue and human existence are inextricable. It is Bakhtin's (1984) view that dialogic relationships permeate "all human speech and all relationships and all manifestations of human life" (p. 40). From this perspective, one "cannot properly separate existence from the ongoing process of communication" (Morson & Emerson, 1990, p. 50). Bakhtin took this fact to extend to the notion of the self, arguing that the self and other are interdependent, insofar as both self and other are engaged in ongoing dialogue for the length of their existence. For him, there is a "nonself-sufficiency" of the self (Bakhtin, 1979, p. 287). In other words:

> The Bakhtinian self is never whole, since it can exist only dialogically. It is not a substance or essence in its own right but exists only in a tensile relationship with all that is other and most important, with other selves. (Clark & Holquist, 1984, p. 65)

Bakhtin's dialogism is not centered on language as an abstract system of signs alone, but on actual utterances produced by speakers in concrete speech situations. An utterance is itself viewed as part of the ongoing dialogue of existence and is understood as a "link in the chain of speech communication" (Bakhtin, 1986, p. 84). Particular utterances make language real for speakers and listeners by invoking relatively stable or repeatable elements, including the speakers' intentions and tone, the uniqueness of the speech situation, and the particular audience that is present to the speaker.

The repeatable element of utterances refers to the fact that language acts like a resource or cultural tool that mediates a human action. It is an element of an utterance that is repeatable or reusable because stable meanings of words make speech understandable to others:

> Every text presupposes a system of signs understandable to everybody (that is, conventional, valid within the limits of a given collectivity), a "language." . . . To this system belong all the elements of a text that are repeated and reproduced, reiterative and reproducible. (Bakhtin, 1979, p. 283)

The repeatable element of an utterance uses language, then, as if it were "raw materials and means" (Bakhtin, 1979, p. 283) for communication.

Each utterance also reflects another element, something that is nonrepeatable, which contributes to how each utterance is a unique use of some repeatable element of language. Just as every text presupposes something repeatable, a text also represents "something individual, unique, nonreiterative" (Bakhtin, 1984, p. 284). The nonreiterative or nonrepeatable element derives from the fact that any appropriation of a language tool involves, for Bakhtin, an element of novelty or uniqueness, because it is populated with the intentions of speakers and is being used in a new situation. The nonrepeatable points to the way that human speakers make words their own through use, populated with their own intentions, accents, and tones (Bakhtin, 1981).

One of the most interesting of Bakhtin's (1986) claims involves his view that words belong to various social practices and activities. In producing an utterance, a speaker always speaks using a particular speech genre or "relatively stable type" of utterance that belongs to a particular social sphere (Bakhtin, 1986, p. 60). According to Bakhtin, we learn those speech genres just as we learn to speak a national language: We experience recurring situations for a particular style of talk appropriate to the activities of eating a family meal, meeting a new business acquaintance, responding to teachers' questions, and so forth. In addition, Bakhtin also noted that there is another level at which is organized what he called "social languages." Social languages include professional languages, languages of different classes, and the languages of particular ideologies (Bakhtin, 1981). Both social languages and speech genres not only constitute formal organizations of language, but each constructs a "specific way of conceptualizing, understanding, and evaluating the world" (Morson & Emerson, 1990, p. 141).

A fourth important point that organizes Bakhtin's dialogism is that it views each utterance as having the quality of turning to someone else; this Bakhtin (1986) calls "addressivity." The fact that each utterance is characterized by "addressivity" means that it may be read or understood as "oriented toward the response of the other, toward his active responsive understanding" (Bakhtin, 1986, p. 75). This is perhaps one of Bakhtin's most interesting claims because he is articulating a view of speech in which all our meanings are not so much "owned" by individual speakers as they are "rented" (Holquist, 1981). Each utterance for Bakhtin will always be in some sense a response to previous articulations of other utterances because from Bakhtin's perspective:

> Ultimately, an utterance reflects not only the voice producing it but also the voices to which it is addressed. In the formulation of an utterance, a voice responds in some way to previous utterances and anticipates the responses of the other, succeeding ones; when it is understood, an utterance comes into contact with the "counter word" of those who hear it. (Wertsch, 1991, p. 53)

I return to Bakhtin's notion of addressivity in the last part of the discussion, but, for now, I turn to consider how his notion of social language might be used to examine how adult youth workers discuss their program experiences and talk about youth in their programs.

Two Social Languages Among Adult Youth Workers

The language used by both adults and youth in youth programs in many ways reflects the relative power of conflicting ways of representing youth in contemporary U.S. society. Nowhere is this more apparent in programs that propose to give youth a greater "voice" and decision-making power within youth organizations. Many youth programs encourage youth to take on responsibilities for planning and implementing their own programs. In this way, these programs encourage a different social language or way of speaking about youth, one that is more attractive and inviting of youth participation. As McLaughlin (1993) noted:

> The youth organizations that attract and sustain young people's involvement give visible and ongoing voice to a conception of youth as a resource to be developed and as persons of value to themselves and to society. (p. 60)

In fact, one can typically find more than one social language at work in most organizations. Few youth organizations are without their champions of youth empowerment and voice, and none can escape the powerful social languages of society that position youth as potential threats to society and drains on its resources. These two social languages, the latter of which I call "Unilateral Youth Worker Language" (emphasizing youth as problems and as needing adult supervision and control) and the first "Empowering Youth Worker Language," can be heard at the Peer Institute, often during heated debates among the staff. I describe each of these languages in some detail here and how they are used to solve a particular conflict that arose at the Peer Institute that the staff met to discuss and attempt to solve. Examining these languages in use to solve an actual conflict conforms to Bakhtin's requirement that language be analyzed in concrete speech situations, and that social languages be understood not simply in terms of their independent power and authority, but through the way they shape ongoing communication and dialogue.

The problem. Two young people come to the staff to complain that they are being treated unfairly by both youth and adult staff at the Institute. They state that flashlights have been shone repeatedly in their faces while walking back to the dorms at night, that staff members have banged on their doors late at night demanding that they be let in to determine if participants were in their room, and that some staff have even rifled through personal items of participants. Such behavior poses a particular problem for the Peer Institute because the Peer Institute is supposedly dedicated to such values as power sharing and respect. Although staff do need to ensure the safety of participants and make sure that they get enough rest, it is unlikely that any staff member would explicitly endorse the idea of banging on people's doors or of rifling through personal items.

A staff meeting is called in which these two young people addressed the entire staff. The two youth then leave, and the staff discuss what is to be done about the situation. The examples of utterances used here are taken from that discussion.

Uses of unilateral youth worker language. This language is so named because it assumes a highly directive role of adults in promoting youth development. It charges adults with the task of unilaterally directing youth toward certain developmental goals. The term is borrowed from Selman (1980) and describes a style of interpersonal negotiation that is characterized by one party or person making demands on or directing the behavior of another without consideration of the other's perspective. If there is any consideration of youth in this language, it considers youth as objects rather than subjects with desires, plans, and competencies.

One of the organizing themes of this social language is control. Situations, problems, or even youth themselves are seen as being either "under control" or "out of control." Most youth programs at one point or another encounter such problems as chaotic structure, erratic participation, high staff turnover, and sometimes open conflict among participants and staff. These problems are often attributed to individuals (rather than to systems or patterns of relating) within unilateral youth worker language to be controlled or kept under control at all costs. There is emphasis also on self-control in this language, on controlling one's own impulses and desires. In this connection, responsibility is defined individualistically as personal accountability and as the ability to control oneself. Most often, this demand is made not on adults, but on youth, who must learn self-control and responsibility.

One illustration of a speaker who uses a unilateral youth worker language to address the problems raised by the two youth is found in Fred's utterance. Fred appears to ignore many of the claims of the youth about unfair treatment and to locate responsibility for breaking rules and for obedience to rules squarely on the shoulders of participants. In addition, he assumes that youth need to exercise personal self-control in order to be invited back again, placing the burden for correcting negative views of young people not on the adults who hold those views, but on the youth themselves:

Fred:

Stanza 46 (Personal Responsibility)

46a TODAY in my family group / I made it a POINT / to address TO THE GROUP that / what their PURPOSE was here /

46b and that THEY needed to be responsible for their own actions and TO MONITOR THEMSELVES / THEIR FRIENDS / and ASSOCI-ATES /

46c that we weren't HERE / to come and POLICE them / to act like their MOTHERS / their TEACHERS / you know to BAD MOUTH them / to take responsibility for their OWN actions

46d SHARE to try / and promote WITH THEM during this family meeting / which is NEXT I believe / um and make them feel COM-FORTABLE / about their own personal level of RESPONSIBILITY /

Coda (Why This Is Important)

47a So that we can BE INVITED back again / not say don't want these YOUNG folks back again / because they MESS up the place / or weren't RESPECTABLE / et cetera, et cetera

Although Fred does emphasize that he did not want to act as a police officer or teacher, the implication here is that he might have to if the young people do not take responsibility for their own actions. The issue of how the staff treat participants is left out of the picture altogether. The facilitator's subsequent comment, perhaps in keeping with the main values and objectives of the Peer Institute, appears to move on without addressing Fred's perspective at all.

Use of empowering youth worker language. A few turns later, another adult staff member, Tom, uses a different social language to put forth a different type of proposal. He uses what I call here a more "empowering youth worker language" in his proposed solution. Empowering youth worker language is consistent with the programming goals of youth empowerment itself: promoting the active participation of youth, viewing youth as partners rather than problems, and emphasizing adults *doing with* rather than *doing for* youth. The values of sharing, creating safe environments for youth where it is easy to learn and respect, are privileged in this language. Responsibility is recast as social responsibility or keeping in mind the concerns and needs of others. There is oftentimes in the use of this language a conscious shifting of perspectives, a consideration of things from the perspective of the other. Finally, a space for youth themselves to be heard is typically legitimated by this social language.

Tom's turn alludes to many of the implicit ways of seeing embodied in empowering youth worker language. He emphasizes that it is important for staff not to be suspicious or distrustful of other youth, but to make clear why a staff person is there in the first place knocking on doors. In addition, he emphasized that he likes to consider that he, as an adult, may be wrong about a situation rather than the young person.

> Tom: 53a I don't think that you have to uh tell people that you think they're LYING / but that you can STATE why you were there in the first place [
>
> Youth: [I know that's what I did /
>
> Tom:
>
> Stanza 55 (Giving the Benefit of the Doubt)
>
> 55a and yeah yeah so just SAY / "I KNOCKED on your door / because I THOUGHT I heard some noise / and it's after lights out / we really need everyone to be quiet because there are PEOPLE on the floor who are trying / trying to uh to sleep and um you and THANKS" /
>
> 55b and then if it happens a SECOND time / you might go to a different a different LEVEL /

55c BUT THAT'LL let them know being maybe / I always like to think
/ well maybe I was wrong about it /
55d GIVE them the benefit of the doubt
Aside (Assurance to Youth)
56a But you say them / you told them WHY they were there /
56b I think that really HELPS

Tom also gives here assurance to the young staff person who had given the reasons why she was knocking on doors, emphasizing that "that really helps." This validation is one way that empowering youth worker discourse both invites young people and adults to think critically about their role as staff, while at the same time respecting the particular decisions made by individual staff. Later, he refers to participants as "allies" who "want the same thing from the Peer Institute," namely, to have a good time and learn while they are there. This kind of perspective taking is supportive of the goals of youth empowerment insofar as it invites the kind of power sharing valued by the Institute to take hold and legitimizes the perspectives of the participants.

How the languages shape problem solving. Across several turns, adults who speak in the staff meeting argue over what it means to be a member of the "staff." Several adults argue persuasively that the staff have wrongly adopted a unilateral stance in dealing with the participants, whereas others promote the idea that regardless of what has happened, the staff ought to adopt a more empowering language to deal with future problems. The discussion revolves around the symbolic meaning of the T-shirts worn by staff, and adults fought over whether the shirts belonged to the Unilateral or the Empowering Language. Meanwhile, interestingly enough, the youth themselves tell counternarratives in which they argue the "facts" of the problem, suggesting that there was no violation of privacy in the first place. In this connection, it might therefore be more accurate to name empowering youth worker discourse as an adult discourse, one that legitimizes but is not the same as youth voice. Ultimately, the solution revolves more about whether to wear the symbolically charged shirts rather than about what happened, even though the youth were given a space in which to speak.

In this connection, the usefulness of Bakhtin's dialogic approach to analyzing communication is not just in the identification of an array of voices used in particular activity settings. Although this identification does help to articulate the differences among speakers as to their orientation to youth work, what matters most is to understand how these voices shape or fail to shape the ongoing dialogue of youth programs. It would matter little, for example, if several adults used the empowering youth worker language, but they are never heard by the other members of the group. It would matter little, moreover, which language adults used if their use of either the empowering or unilateral language never allowed for youth themselves to speak. In short, it is as important to know who is speaking as it is to know how they are speaking.

OFFERING A SPACE FOR RECOGNIZING THE DIVERSE IDENTITIES OF YOUTH

Having the opportunity to speak and be heard by adults is a key aspect of identity formation for young people today. This point has been made recently by a number of scholars in cultural studies and political theory (e.g., Calhoun, 1994), who have emphasized the centrality of recognition in the process of forming a healthy identity. This is particularly true for members of groups who have been historically marginalized by dominant institutions and exclusive social practices. As Taylor (1992) noted, equal recognition is a requirement of modern democratic societies, insofar as "the projection of an inferior or demeaning image on another can actually distort or oppress, to the extent that the image is internalized" (pp. 36-37). For many of the youth who attend the Peer Institute, such demeaning images are a part of their everyday lived realities, and the opportunities that the Peer Institute affords them to be recognized for their identities and for adults to become their allies are important. I now turn to the work of Erikson for a set of tools for discussing the social and developmental processes involved in recognizing identities and becoming an effective ally to youth.

Erikson's Psychosocial Approach to Identity

Identity research in psychology has often looked to the work of Erikson (1964, 1968) for defining themes and approaches. His research emphasizes the active role of the individual in shaping his or her development of identity through a sequence of stage-like transformations. Following in the tradition of Piaget (see Cole & Cole, 1989), Erikson conceived of identity as a constructive process of the organism, closely tied to the development of cognition, directed toward making decisions about who one trusts, what one believes, and what one will do for a living. As children grow to be able to reflect on and coordinate the perspectives of others' views of who one is, the problem of identity becomes more and more salient. As the adolescent moves out of the family and into a wider community of peers at college or at work, individuals are faced with an even more complex task of coordinating and evaluating these different perspectives and of choosing a belief system and a career path.

Although many theorists have interpreted Erikson's work rather individualistically (e.g., Marcia, 1966), Erikson's view of identity also includes an appreciation of the fact that youth do not form their identities in a vacuum, but form them using the tools and cultural resources available to them. The historical era in which a youth lives "offers only a limited number of socially meaningful models for workable combinations of identification fragments" (Erikson, 1968, p. 53). To form an identity, youth must base their choices of values, career, political commitments, and religious beliefs "on ideological alternatives vitally related to the existing range of alternatives for identity formation" (p. 190). In this connection, Erikson places a strong emphasis on communities for providing the necessary cultural resources for youth to be able to recognize themselves and be recognized as vital contributors to their culture.

At this point in Erikson's work, recognition comes to play an important role. For him, the identity choices of individual choices are not enough; an individual's identity is fundamentally dependent on the means by which a community confirms and recognizes those choices (Erikson, 1968). Recognition, for Erikson, and identity formation go hand in hand, and it is the responsibility of adults to assist young people in the formation of healthy identity by providing them with meaningful and useful resources for making decisions about who they are. These tools may come in the form of coherent ideologies, or they may be apprenticeships into a career path; regardless, it is up to adults to both guide youth to understand their options and to respect and support them in the decisions they make.

Diversity in Motion: An Opportunity for Recognition and Identity Formation

One activity at the Peer Institute that is structured to provide young people with an opportunity to be recognized and for adults to support them in their identity claims is called "Diversity in Motion." It is an activity that has been widely used in settings to promote multicultural understanding among participants in various groups, organizations, and projects in which cultural diversity is a focus.

In this activity, participants all begin by sitting at one end of a room. A facilitator then reads the instructions and guidelines to the group. The facilitator explains that the purpose of the activity is "to help create awareness about our feelings about our own cultural identity and their relationships with people from other cultures and groups." The facilitator then explains that she will be naming several groups, and if participants wish to identify as part of that group, they are to move together to the other side of the room. Once they are there, the facilitator will ask the group three questions:

- What do you want us to know about you?
- What do you never want to hear again?
- What can we do to support you and your group?

The group responds one at a time, "popcorn style," until there is a long enough pause that signals to the facilitator to move on. The responsibility of those who are seated is to listen to the others as those on the other side of the room respond to the questions. They may not speak or clap when responses are given; their silence confers their respect for those who move.

The activity provides participants with an opportunity to identify as members of and represent social groups. The social identities include: gender, place of residence (whether in the city, suburbs, or country), age (whether teen or adult), culture (such as African American, Latino, European American), sexual orientation, ability, and life experience (such as living in a family with an addiction). These categories are given by the facilitator, and they are structured so that similar types of categories are grouped together. Women are called, and then men. Teens are called, and then adults. The "culture" groups are called in sequence.

The exercise is first and foremost an opportunity for individuals to voice a self-defined viewpoint and to be heard in a public forum. The activity provides a structured opportunity for individuals to "articulate a self-defined standpoint" (Collins, 1990, p. 96) and to be heard by others in the public sphere (Sampson, 1993). The audience for every utterance is heterogeneous, consisting of people who are not identified with the group that has moved; therefore, each utterance is addressed both to members of one's own group and to people outside of it. In the actual process of the activity it becomes, moreover, an opportunity for members of groups to deflect the "demeaning image[s]" and representations that Taylor (1992) discusses.

From the facilitator's point of view, recognition of the participants' utterances about their identity is conferred ideally by respectful silence, by not interrupting or responding directly to what has been said. During the activity, the best way to honor other persons and to listen to what they have to say about themselves and their group is to be silent and to give those speaking a chance to voice their own self-defined viewpoint. There is no sanctioned time to respond directly to anything that is said in the activity. When, during the course of the activity, someone does speak out of turn, the facilitator interrupts this talk and reminds participants of the need to be quiet.

From a close examination of the utterances of the activity (for the other accounts of study, see Penuel, 1995; Penuel & Wertsch, 1995), it is evident that the stated goals and activity structure designed to meet those goals match only imperfectly. Respectful recognition of others' identity claims, even when people are seated and quiet, are not only evident in the activity of listening. There is far more dialogue, an active responding to other voices (whether or not immediately present) than is sanctioned by the activity's structure. A closer examination of what people say in response to the questions suggests that claims made about one's own identity may be read productively, not so much as independent statements that reflect inner states, beliefs, or attributes of individuals as part of an ongoing dialogue with others about who one is.

As the facilitators have suspected, utterances are made that express pride or gladness in who one is or that demand directly for recognition of one's own group's power and authority in society, for which the activity is designed (i.e., one of many types of utterances formulated by participants). Just as often, however, participants use the opportunity to answer the question: "What do you want us to know about you and your group?" Specifically, most of the utterances are used by speakers to deflect or resist demeaning images and representations of their group and to respond directly or indirectly to the other groups' previous statements or imputed beliefs.

In one session, almost half the responses (46% of 140 total responses) to the first question of Diversity in Motion include explicit forms of negation. In other words, people respond almost as much to this question by stating who they were not as who they were. Most of these negations, moreover, involve a deflection of a demeaning image of one's own group, an image believed to be either widely held or known by other participants in the activity. For example one woman says, "We don't need to be protected"; whereas another followed her in asserting, "We don't want to be exploited for your pleasure."

What is significant about these two claims is not, I would argue, their faithfulness to the reality of these women's own lived realities, but that in uttering these statements, a widely held understanding of women's identity (as needing protection, as a sex object) is invoked and rejected. In order for the listeners to make sense of the claims, it is necessary for them (or us) to recognize that a cultural image or representation is being invoked and explicitly rejected as well. Without that recognition, both these claims make little sense. Why bother to assert, for example, that "we don't need to be protected" unless there is someone or a group of people who maintain and spread that view? Likewise, why bother to assert that "we don't want to be exploited for your pleasure" unless that view is recognized by both men and women as one that has been held in the past by many individuals, institutions, and societies?

Using Bakhtin's terminology, each speech, action, or identity claim may be interpreted as an active response to previous utterances or to a set of cultural voices about one's group. It is not only a statement that expresses some view or perspective of the speaker; it is spoken with a particular audience and context in mind. Each speaker's identity claims are dialogic in that they are the "answering words" of speakers to representations of their life-context or social identity (such as being European American or living in the country) and to the context of the activity (e.g., who is present, how the questions are structured). In producing an utterance, furthermore, individual speakers are both making a claim about who they are and constructing their life-context and audience as contexts or people to whom such utterances can be meaningfully addressed. In addition to being a function of listeners, "recognition," then, is constructed within speakers' own identity claims, in what they "recognize" as their own significant life contexts; in what they assume others "recognize" as commonly held beliefs about the speaker's social identity, and in how they "recognize" and assume the identities of their audience in what they claim.

CONCLUSION: YOUTH EMPOWERMENT AND ADULT DEVELOPMENT

Although youth empowerment poses difficult questions to adults who hope to guide youth toward healthy futures and toward being effective change agents in their communities, these questions are not without their own developmental value for the adults who pose them. By asking the difficult questions about what our role as adults is, as a facilitator rather than as a director of development and as a listener as much as speaker, we open ourselves as adults to new ways of learning from young people.

The different activities of planning, problem solving, and recognizing all afford both adult and youth participants an important opportunity to identify how they want others to support them and how these others can act as allies to them in their struggles. In many ways, the adults are the ones who have learned much from engaging in this process, as they themselves shift from using a "unilateral" language of youth development to using a more "empowering" language that seeks to include youth as partners and teachers of community change. Adults can learn from youth how to listen, how to have the courage to speak the truth of their convictions, and how to maintain hope in the face of adversity.

In this connection, youth empowerment programs might be better understood as a developmental partnership between adults and youth, a partnership that might be informed by the concepts of Vygotsky, Bakhtin, and Erikson. The sociocultural approach and cultural-historical psychology of Vygotsky emphasizes the importance of the specific tools and mediational devices that might be important for young people and adults to practice together as partners in change in their communities. Bakhtin's dialogic approach reminds youth workers of the importance of developing their skills as listeners of their own speech and of developing as speakers of a more empowering, progressive language of youth. Finally, Erikson's approach to identity illuminates the importance of providing opportunities to recognize the diverse identities of youth in the context of youth programming.

Putting these concepts into broader practice and use in our communities, however, requires more than adequate theoretical frameworks. Youth workers in the field of primary prevention are not recognized as a professional body of workers with an identifiable path to training and career advancement (see McLaughlin, Langman, & Irby, 1994). Likewise, federal, state, and local budget cuts constantly threaten either to eliminate successful programs or to pit programs and agencies against one another for an ever-shrinking portion of funding. Perhaps one of the more important uses of these frameworks for youth development in the coming years will be to convince educators and policy makers of the importance, value, and meanings of youth empowerment in the context of making healthier communities.

REFERENCES

Bakhtin, M. M. (1981). *The dialogic imagination.* Austin: University of Texas Press.

Bakhtin, M. M. (1984). *Problems of Dosteovsky's poetics.* Minneapolis: University of Minnesota Press.

Bakhtin, M. M. (1986). *Speech genres and other late essays.* Austin: University of Texas Press.

Calhoun, C. (1994). Social theory and the politics of identity. In C. Calhoun (Ed.), *Social theory and the politics of identity* (pp. 9-36). Cambridge, MA: Blackwell.

Clark, K., & Holquist, M. (1984). *Mikhail Bakhtin.* Cambridge MA: Harvard University Press.

Cole, M., & Cole, S. R. (1989). *The development of children.* New York: Scientific American.

Collins, P. H. (1990). *Black feminist thought: Knowledge, consciousness, and the politics of empowerment.* New York: Routledge.

Erikson, E. H. (1964). *Insight and responsibility.* New York: Norton.

Erikson, E. H. (1968). *Identity: Youth and crisis.* New York: Norton.

Florin, P., & Chavis, D. M. (1990). *Community development and substance abuse prevention.* Santa Clara, CA: Prevention Office, Bureau of Drug Abuse Services, Department of Health.

Holquist, M. (1981). The politics of representation. In S. Greenblatt (Ed.), *Allegory in representation: Selected papers from the English Institute* (pp. 163-183). Baltimore: Johns Hopkins University Press.

Johnson, C. A., Pentz, M. A., Weber, M. D., Dwyer, J. H., Baer, N., MacKinnon, D. P., & Hansen, W. B. (1990). Relative effectiveness of comprehensive community programming for drug abuse prevention with high-risk and low-risk adolescents. *Journal of Consulting and Clinical Psychology, 58,* 447-456.

Lave, J., & Wenger, E. (1991). *Situated learning: Legitimate peripheral participation.* New York: Cambridge University Press.

Marcia, J. E. (1966). Development and validation of ego identity status. *Journal of Personality and Social Psychology, 3,* 551-558.

McLaughlin, M. (1993). Embedded identities: Enabling balance in urban contexts. In S. B. Heath & M. W. McLaughlin (Eds.), *Identity and inner-city youth: Beyond ethnicity and gender* (pp. 36-68). New York: Teachers College Press.

McLaughlin, M., Irby, M., & Langman, J. (1994). *Urban sanctuaries.* San Francisco: Jossey-Bass.

Morson, G. W., & Emerson, C. (1990). *Mikhail Bakhtin: Creation of a prosaics.* Stanford, CA: Stanford University Press.

Palincsar, A. S., & Brown, A. L. (1988). Teaching and practicing thinking to promote thinking in the context of group problem solving. *RASE, 9,* 53-59.

Penuel, W. R. (1995). *Communication processes in cultural identity formation: A mediated action approach.* Unpublished doctoral dissertation, Clark University, Worcester, MA.

Penuel, W. R., & Wertsch, J. V. (1995). Dynamics of negation in the identity politics of cultural self and cultural other. *Culture and Psychology, 1,* 343-359.

Rogoff, B. (1990). *Apprenticeship in thinking: Cognitive development in social context.* New York: Oxford University Press.

Sampson, E. E. (1993). Identity politics: Challenges to psychology's understanding. *American Psychologist, 48,* 1219-1230.

Selman, R. L. (1980). *The growth of interpersonal understanding.* Orlando, FL: Academic Press.

Taylor, C. (1992). Multiculturalism and the "politics of recognition." In A. Gutman (Ed.), *Multiculturalism: Examining the politics of recognition.* Princeton, NJ: Princeton University Press.

Tharp, R. G., & Gallimore, R. (1988). *Rousing minds to life: Teaching, learning, and schooling in a social context.* New York: Cambridge University Press.

Vygotsky, L. S. (1978). *Mind in society: The development of higher mental processes* (M. Cole, V. John-Steiner, S. Scribner, & E. Souberman, Eds.). Cambridge, MA: Harvard University Press.

Vygotsky, L. W. (1981a). The genesis of higher mental functions. In J. V. Wertsch (Ed.), *The concept of activity in Soviet psychology.* Armonk, NY: M. E. Sharpe.

Vygotsky, L. S. (1981b). The instrumental method in psychology. In J. V. Wertsch (Ed.), *The concept of activity in Soviet psychology.* Armonk, NY: M. E. Sharpe.

Vygotsky, L. S. (1987). *Thought and language* (N. Minick Trans. & Ed.). New York: Plenum.

Wertsch, J. V. (1979). From social interaction to higher psychological processes: A clarification and application of Vygotsky's theory. *Human Development, 22,* 1-22.

Wertsch, J. V. (1985). *Vygotsky and the social formation of mind.* Cambridge, MA: Harvard University Press.

Wertsch, J. V. (1991). *Voices of the mind: A sociocultural approach to mediated action.* Cambridge, MA: Harvard University Press.

10 CURRICULAR AND LEADERSHIP ROLES FOR EDUCATING LINGUISTICALLY AND CULTURALLY DIVERSE STUDENTS

Angela L. Carrasquillo
Fordham University

The United States is a country of great linguistic and cultural diversity. This ethnic, racial, and linguistic diversification is evidenced most vividly among young and school-aged children. The diversity of language, customs, traditions, values, and ways of learning that students bring to any learning situation continues to inspire educators to meet greater challenges in their teaching role. At the end of the 20th century and the beginning of the 21st century, educators are critically analyzing the changes or reforms that need to be undertaken in order to prepare themselves to educate all children, including the culturally and linguistically diverse, to meet the challenges imposed by the present society. These new challenges require programmatic and curricular reforms as well as new leadership roles for all educators. Providing quality education to all children not only depends on the expectations and beliefs of educators, but also on the expectations and beliefs of society at large.

This chapter describes the demographic and curricular challenges ahead for educational leaders as they seek to restructure schools and implement programmatic and curricular reforms to meet the academic, cultural, and linguistic needs of linguistically and culturally diverse students.

A DEMOGRAPHIC OVERVIEW

As the nation strives to motivate and engage students of all ages and grades to achieve the maximum of their intellectual and academic potential, educators have become concerned about the ability of schools to educate the increasing numbers of students who are linguistically and culturally diverse. The nation's ability to achieve the national education goals is dependent on its ability to educate students of different languages and cultures, especially the limited English proficient.

The United States Census Bureau data show that Black, Asian, and Hispanic populations are growing faster than the White/Anglo population. The United States Bureau of the Census (1992) projected that an increase in births among women from these groups living in the United Sates, coupled with massive immigration, will add more people to the nation's population during the 1990s and 2000s than any time since the baby boom of the 1950s. By the middle of the 21st century, virtually half the population of the United States will be made up of African Americans, Hispanics, Asians, and Native Americans. In 1992, the United States Bureau of the Census projected the population growth as shown in Table 10.1.

Current population distribution figures indicate that these projections are realistic, and that the linguistically and culturally diverse population in the United States will continue to grow. The African-American group will continue to be a strong group in terms of numbers, followed by the Hispanic,

Table 10.1. Percentage Distribution of the United States Population.

			Year		
Ethnic Group	1995	2000	2020	2030	2050
White	73.6	71.6	63.9	60.2	52.7
Black	12.1	12.3	13.3	13.8	15.0
Hispanic	10.1	11.1	15.2	17.2	21.1
Asian and Pacific Island	3.5	4.2	6.7	7.9	10.1
American Indian	0.7	0.8	0.9	1.0	1.1

Data adapted from information provided in *Population Projections of the United States, by Age, Sex, Race and Hispanic Origin: 1992-2050* (pp. xviii-xx). United States Bureau of the Census, 1992, Washington, DC: Government Printing Office. Copyright © 1992 by United States Bureau of the Census.

the Asian, and the American Indian groups. In addition, other ethnic groups such as Russians and Arabs continue to emigrate to the United States. For example, during the 1980s and early 1990s, there has been a steady increase in immigration from Eastern Europe and the former Soviet Union, especially immigrant Russian Jews. If the current population rate continues, the present terminology of *majority* and *minority* will become meaningless because the United States will not have one majority group, but several ethnic groups that will make up a significant percentage of the U.S. population.

The U.S. demographic changes are the result of fertility (more new-born children, almost two births per woman) and legal and illegal immigration. Thus, the population increase is mainly the result of the foreign born and those children who were born in the United States, but who are raised in a non-English-speaking family environment. The foreign-born population is now more than twice what it was 20 years ago. One of the reasons for the increase in the foreign-born population is family-based immigration, which refers to immigrants who become permanent residents and bring their relatives to the United States. Up to 1994, there were about 1.1 million immigrants (Gonzalez, 1994) entering the United States per year, mostly extended-family relatives. The foreign-born population is concentrated in six states—California, New York, Texas, Florida, New Jersey, and Illinois—and is about 8.5% of the total U.S. population (Gonzalez, 1994; Waggoner, 1991). Illegal immigrants account for 2 to 3 million, who enter each year, about half of them from Mexico. Although language minority students are heavily concentrated in a handful of states, almost every state in the nation has counties that have substantial numbers of culturally and linguistically diverse students.

Linguistically and culturally diverse students' enrollment growth has impacted enormously on educational systems that must be able to provide an adequate education for every student. New York City is an example of the challenges ahead for educators in providing sufficient, safe, supportive, and stimulating space appropriately designed for instruction. The number of students registered in New York City public schools has increased during the last decade. By October 1993, enrollment had reached 1,016,000 students. By itself, this increase exceeded the total public school enrollment in such large cities as Atlanta, Boston, or Newark. School enrollment continues to rise at a rate of 20,000 to 25,000 additional students each year. The growth is closely linked to changing demographics, an increase of about 1 million immigrants from over 160 countries (Citizens Commission on Planning for Enrollment Growth, 1995). This immigrant flow has made New York City a highly complex mosaic of diverse populations. One of the main difficulties facing New York City educators is the lack of space available to accommodate the current enrollment growth. Many schools have reached full capacity, and in some school districts virtually all schools are being utilized above capacity. In the most severe cases, classes are held in closets, bathrooms, hallways, and whatever space can be found. More typically, rooms originally designed to serve as offices, cafeterias, gyms, libraries, storage rooms, and other common and specialized spaces have been reassigned for classroom use. Some schools have leased space or built temporary structures on the school grounds, but this has not provided enough space to alleviate overcrowding (Citizens Commission on Planning for Enrollment Growth, 1995).

LANGUAGE DIVERSITY IN THE UNITED STATES

The U.S. educational system has about 100 distinctive languages represented in the classroom. The multilingual nature of U.S. society reflects the rich heritage of its people. Although the United States is primarily an English-speaking country, there are many other languages spoken. Such language diversity is an asset to the nation, especially in its interaction with other nations in the areas of commerce, defense, education, science, and technology. Language diversity in the United States has been maintained primarily because of continuing immigration from non-English-speaking countries.

The maintenance of native languages other than English depends on the efforts of members of the language group through churches and other community activities. There are over 30 languages in everyday use in the United States. In the largest cities, they represent as many as 100 different countries. This diversity is indicative of the multilingual nature of the United States, a result of its multilingual heritage. In 1993, the United States Bureau of the Census reported major demographic trends in racial and ethnic groups as well as changes in the overall population. This number includes over 200 native/Indian American languages. After English, the most commonly used languages in the United States are Spanish, Chinese, Italian, and sign language.

The report of the United States Department of Education (1993), *Descriptive Study of Services of Limited English Proficient Students*, listed the 20 language groups with the most limited English proficient students in the United States. These are:

Spanish	Cambodian	Hmong	Cantonese
Cambodian	Korean	Laotian	Navajo
Tagalog	Russian	Haitian Creole	Arabic
Portuguese	Japanese	Armenian	Chinese
Mandarin	Farsi	Hindi	Polish

Among the English-speaking immigrant students, there are numerous dialects, from Hawaiian pidgin to southern English to Caribbean English. Each language is distinctive, and each is an effective means for communication for those who share its linguistic style. Language differences ultimately reflect basic behavioral differences between groups of people. Physical and social separation inevitably lead to language differences. For example, although among the nation's Mon-Khmer (Cambodian) and Hmong speakers more than 4 in 10 have either limited fluency in English or do not speak English at all, among Chinese, Korean, Vietnamese, Russian, and Thai language populations the proportion is roughly 3 in 10 (United States Bureau of the Census, 1992). Social variables also contribute to language differences with both class and ethnicity reflecting those differences. The greater the social distance between groups, the greater the tendency toward language differences. Census data indicated that more than 31.8 million people reported that they spoke a language other than English at home in 1990, compared to 23.1 million a decade earlier (United States Bureau of the Census, 1993). This is an increase of three percentage points, from 11% of the nation's population aged 5 and over in 1980, to 14% in 1990. Spanish was the second most common language spoken in the United States after English (Carrasquillo, 1991).

THE CHALLENGES

The foregoing information serves to indicate that educators face many challenges today. The school population is very diverse, not only in terms of ethnicity, race, and language, but also in terms of students' socioeconomic, academic, and educational backgrounds. This diversity challenges educators to look at the forces that are inhibiting students from becoming successful learners. When linguistically and culturally diverse students do not show significant gains in academic achievement and overall satisfactory performance in the society in which they are living, then educators need to recognize that there is a failure to educate a greater percentage of the school population. The following list identifies the educational and social challenges that the significant numbers of linguistically and culturally diverse students pose to educators.

Academic Achievement

No matter what criterion is used (grades, test scores, dropout rates, college acceptance rates), linguistically and culturally diverse students in general do not perform as well as their majority group counterparts in school. With regard to schooling, high school completion rates for linguistically and culturally diverse students are low. For example, data for 1990 indicated that Hispanic students' rate for high school completion in all age groups was only 60% (Waggoner, 1991), whereas the completion rate for Whites was over 80% for all age groups. School failure persists among a disproportionate number of language-minority students. With the exception of some Asian groups (especially Chinese, Koreans, and Japanese), a disproportionate number of linguistically and culturally diverse students do not reach acceptable achievement levels in English literacy, mathematics, or science. For example, Hispanics have the lowest levels of educational attainment of any major population group. Only about half the Hispanic adults are high school graduates. Less than 1 in 10 Hispanics graduate from college (Carrasquillo, 1991).

Data published by the National Education Goals Panel in 1994 gathered by the National Center for Education Statistics on high school completion rate in 1993 indicate lower rates for Hispanic students. Table 10.2 reports the percentage of young adults 16 to 10 years old with a high school diploma.

The reported data revealed that, in general, most U.S. students did not attain the expected high school completion rate of 90%, and more disappointedly, that Hispanic youngsters' completion rate was extremely low.

Will the previous low completion rate and overall low academic performance of students improve in the near future? Infants born in 1995 will enter the first grade in the year 2001. Will the nation be able to say that language minority students are the most ready to learn if compared with any other group of 6-year-olds? Available data (National Educational Goals Panel, 1994) on prenatal care, birth weight, children's health index, children's nutrition, and family-child language and learning activities tend to indicate limited learning opportunities and preschool participation for U.S. school children.

Table 10.2. Percentage of Young Adults with a High School Credential.

	Year	
	1992	1993
All	87	86
Black	81	80
Hispanics	65	66
White	91	90

Data adapted from information provided in *The National Education Goals Report* (p. 40). National Educational Goals Panel, 1994, Washington, DC: Author. Copyright © 1994 by Author.

Additional data reported by the National Education Goals Panel also indicate that in 1992, few U.S. students demonstrated competency in challenging subject matter content and skills (e.g.,mathematics, reading, science, and foreign languages). Table 10.3 reports the percentage of students who met the Goals Panel's performance standard in mathematics in 1992.

Data on school retention are also alarming. In 1993, the dropout rate was 11% for all groups, 8% for Whites, 14% for Blacks, and an alarming 28% for Hispanic students (National Educational Goals Panel, 1994). Reasons for dropping out varied; an alarming number of youths cited pregnancy and conflicts with jobs as reasons for dropping out. In addition to this alarming data, case studies such as Hodgkinson (1991) and Wong-Fillmore (1991) have indicated stories of various factors (e.g.,poverty, family disruptions) as causes for the low academic achievement of a significant number of linguistically and culturally diverse students.

Another reason for the lack of linguistically and culturally diverse students' low academic performance is that their education is not part of a large mission plan from the start of the educational system. Many of these students tend to be enrolled in educational "tracks" that prepare students for neither college nor stable employment. Large numbers of these students continue to receive instruction that is substandard to what mainstream student English speakers receive. In many instances, these students are not expected to meet the same high standards as "mainstream" children. For

Table 10.3. Percentage of 4th, 8th, and 12th Graders Who Met the Performance Standard[a] in Mathematics (Proficient and Above), 1992.

	Grade 4	Grade 8	Grade 12
White	23	32	19
Asian/Pacific Islander	30	44	31
Black	3	3	3
Hispanic	6	8	6
American Indian	10	9	4

[a]The Goals Panel performance standard is a mastery over challenging subject matter as indicated by performance at the proficient or advanced levels on the National Assessment of Educational Progress (NAAEP). These levels were established by the National Assessment Governing Board and reported by the National Center for Education Statistics (NCES).

Data adapted from information provided in *The National Education Goals Report* (pp. 50-54). National Educational Goals Panel, 1994, Washington, DC: Author. Copyright © 1994 by Author.

example, a high percentage of Hispanic youth are in nonacademic tracks that do not offer the required courses, especially in mathematics and science, to enter college. In addition, there is no coordination among programs designed for students who need special educational services. For example, federal programs such as Bilingual Education, Title 1, and Migrant Education offer fragmented services to students; thus, their academic needs are only partially met.

National data on Asian educational achievement indicate that this ethnic group is performing above any other ethnic group in the United States. However, not all Asian-American students are performing above average in U.S. schools. Asian-American students differ significantly in family socioeconomic status, achievement, educational aspirations, and learning environments at home. Asian subgroups differ significantly among themselves. Although the achievement scores of Chinese, Japanese, and Koreans are above the national average, the scores of Southeast Asians (Vietnamese, Laotians, Cambodians) and Pacific Islanders are low. Peng (1995) provided data that indicated that, in 1988, Pacific Islanders had the lowest scores in reading of all racial/ethnic groups.

Poverty

More children live in poverty today than in any year since 1965. Many parents of linguistically and culturally diverse students are likely to live in poor housing and to work at poorly paid jobs. The Children's Defense Fund (1994) summarized United States Bureau of the Census data that reported that the child poverty rate rose to 14.6% in 1992, despite the end of the 1990–1991 recession and restoration of modest economic growth for the nation as a whole. The total number of children living in poverty jumped from 14.3 million in 1991 to 14.6 million in 1992—2 million higher than when the recession began.

Children in female-headed households with no other adult present are especially likely to live in poverty. Of the 14.8 million children in such households in 1992, 54% were poor. The National Center for Children in Poverty (1990) indicated that of the 21.9 million children under 6 years of age, 5 million (23%) were living in poverty. Garcia (1993) indicated that although less than 30% of all children under 6 years of age were non-White and Hispanic, over 50% of the children living in poverty were non-White Hispanic. Hispanic children in the United States are three times more likely to be poor than children in comparable non-Hispanic families. Poverty translates into poor housing, isolated neighborhoods, poor nutrition, and lack of health insurance. In general, the parents of language minority students have a hard time getting access to health care. For example, Hispanics suffer from a high incidence of asthma, diabetes, tuberculosis, certain cancers, and AIDS; yet they are less likely than other U.S. citizens to report a regular source of medical care, largely because they work in industries and occupations that are less likely to provide health care benefits.

Youth Violence

Violence permeates the lives of children and youth. Parents and children are concerned about being victims of violent crime. These crimes can happen in the neighborhood, in school, or at home. In 1991, there were 5,356 reported children and youth who were killed by guns in suicides, homicides, and firearm accidents (Children's Defense Fund, 1994). Gunshot injuries accounted for the leading cause of deaths in children aged 1 to 14. Among teenagers and young adults up to age 25, one in every four deaths was caused by a firearm.

Guns take their highest toll among young African-American and Hispanic males. The risk of being murdered by a gun has increased for all young people, but especially young Black and Hispanic males. Perhaps even more alarming is the fact that teens are killing at younger ages. For every child killed by a gun, several are injured with estimates ranging between 30 and 67 each day (Children's Defense Fund, 1994). The most consistent and most powerful predictor of criminal activity among youths is economic hardship.

Although between 1990 and 1993, the percentage of White 12th-grade students who reported using alcohol, marijuana, and cocaine at school decreased, the number stayed the same or increased for linguistically and culturally diverse students. Violence and disruptive classrooms are frequently found in schools attended by linguistically and culturally diverse students. For example, gang violence among Hispanics and Asian communities is escalating. Children as young as 7 are now joining gangs, and more young women are participating in gang activities.

Contreras-Polk (1994) mentioned that these statistics point to a changing nature among children. Today's child seems to be bolder and more aggressive than those of prior generations. Teachers comment that each year they seem to get more and more children filled with rage. Such children act like walking time bombs ready to explode at the highest provocation, often exploding at the teacher. Many teachers feel unsafe in their classrooms; many of them have experienced youth violence themselves or have heard of other teachers or students who have been attacked.

Children who grow up in poverty confront myriad barriers to their full and healthy development, running higher risks of inadequate nutrition, having developmental delays in early life, and generally attending substandard schools with little access to cultural, recreational, or educational enrichment opportunities as they grow older. The Children's Defense Fund concluded that all these disadvantages contribute to a lack of hope among millions of young people. This results in leaving increasing numbers with feelings of rage who feel that they have no stake in the values and norms of the larger society, including regard for human life. All schools play a significant role in the teaching of discipline and values. Schools need to team up with parents and the community to fight social ills such as drug abuse and crime.

Cultural Value System Conflicts

There are many psychological implications involved in children and youth adapting to the language and habits of a new culture. Immigrant families and their children, who often feel like strangers in a new country, have a hard time trying to get accustomed to U.S. ways. Students' culturally based differences in values have educational repercussions in the school-related behaviors of linguistically and culturally diverse students in terms of teacher–student interactions, parent–child understandings, communication patterns, and school rules and tasks (Cordasco & Bucchioni, 1982). Other values such as aggressiveness and competitiveness, which are endemic to the U.S. value system and into which U.S. students are socialized in classrooms across the country, run contrary to the interactional style of many linguistically and culturally diverse students (e.g., as is the case of Hispanics) who are socialized into more self-effacing, more cooperative types of behaviors. These value conflicts come into play in classrooms when students are compelled to compete for grades, for adult attention in terms of who raise their hands to participate in discussions, give answers to questions, or receive other kinds of rewards for more expansive and visible types of behaviors that are customarily sanctioned by the school culture (Cordasco & Bucchioni, 1982).

The school has a major role in the socialization and education of the student to gain acceptance of what he or she is and to provide an appropriate degree of comfort in establishing his or her ethnic and individual identity. The school should help linguistically and culturally diverse students to feel proud about their ethnic and linguistic backgrounds and to appreciate and value the cultural values of their ethnic backgrounds (Sleeter & Grant, 1993). When the school does not comply with the previously mentioned objective and tends to inculcate only the dominant cultural values and beliefs, students may feel confused and disoriented. This confusion may also create conflicts with their parents. For example, it may reinforce the children questioning the authority of their parents. It may also make parents dependent on their children, especially in contacts with mainstream society, including the school and other institutions. This shift in attitudes may be threatening to parents' roles and values in that the new cultural mores may be alien to their culturally sanctioned behaviors and traditions in which respect for adults and submission to the will of parents are emphasized.

Variety of Language Backgrounds and English Proficiency

Linguistically and culturally diverse students in the United States reflect a variety of language backgrounds and language proficiencies. Although some students are bilingual in English and their native language, others either do not speak English at all or have limited English-speaking skills. There are three broad linguistic groups:

1. *Proficient bilinguals.* These are students whose competencies in their native and English language are well developed (Baker, 1993; Fishman, 1971) and who have attained an approximately equal level of proficiency in the two languages. It is assumed that these individuals are able to understand the communications of others and to communicate and achieve goals in English and their native language.

2. *Partial bilinguals.* These are students who have one dominant language or show a higher level of proficiency in one language or in some aspects of one language (Fishman, 1971). They usually attain native-like proficiency in the full range of understanding, speaking, reading, and writing in one language, usually a language other than English, but they achieve less than native-like skills in some or all of the skill areas in English.

3. *Limited bilinguals.* These students either show deficits or are at an early stage of development in both languages, especially in vocabulary, language usage and functions, and in the processing and using of both languages creatively (Hamayan, 1990).

Linguistically and culturally diverse students have varied language characteristics, as evidenced in their English and native language proficiencies, and show various degrees of bilingualism. Some speak both languages well, others speak limited English, some speak a nonstandard dialect, and some use sign language. Many language minority students have neither the experience nor the opportunity to be able to function in all-English classrooms. However, because they were born in the United States or because they show some level of oral English communicative skills, they are placed in classrooms in which they are required to use more abstract academic

English that they have not yet mastered. Their limited proficiency in this more abstract English, coupled with a curriculum that is often nonstimulating, results in a lack of success for students.

There are a significant number of linguistically and culturally diverse students who are limited English proficient (LEP). The LEP school population in the United States continues to be linguistically heterogeneous with over 100 distinct language groups identified (Garcia, 1993; Waggoner, 1991). Although the number of monolingual English speakers increased by 6% in the 1980s, the number of home speakers of languages other than English increased by 38%. The United States is currently experiencing an increasing representation of LEP students in schools, placing unprecedented demands on teachers, administrators, and educational policy makers. Particularly striking has been the rate of growth of Hispanic and Asian LEP students. On the national level, identified LEP students' enrollment population increased by 56% between 1985 and 1992 (United States Department of Education, 1993). There were 2.31 million identified LEP students in public (elementary and secondary) schools in the 1991–1992 school year (United States Department of Education, 1993). Observers believe that this figure underestimates the actual number of LEP students enrolled in the public schools, and they suggest the number is between 3 million and 3.5 million, depending on the definition of *limited English proficient* (Lara, 1994).

LEADERSHIP ROLES FOR EDUCATORS

Federal, state, and local educational initiatives have established a variety of mechanisms to ensure that a wide range of groups, operating at the national, state, and local levels, play leadership roles in implementing broad and balanced education to prepare learners to become individuals whose values, ideals, and choices will make a positive impact on themselves, on their community, and on society at large (Marsh & Willis, 1995). Historically, every decade has provided a new vision for educational reform. For example, in the 1970s, many pressures mounted on schools for what then became known as "accountability." Accountability asked that teachers assume responsibility for what they did. Essentially, accountability was a popular but flawed way in which U.S. society attempted to force schools to become more efficient. Furthermore, when, at the end of the decade, students did not seem to learn more, skepticism deepened further. Thus, in the 1980s, national efforts were pushed to reform school curricula. In that decade, hundreds of national reports by various governmental and private organizations were issued on the state of U.S. education. In 1983, the National Commission on Excellence in Education released a report, *A Nation at Risk: The Imperative for Educational*

Reform, portraying a crisis in the educational system and proposing the reform of the curricula of U.S. schools, especially the secondary schools. However, students' academic achievement did not improve.

The 1990s brought to the national forum other recommendations for educational reform with the purpose of looking at the social and economic factors contributing to the nation's educational problems. These problems are sufficiently connected with the nation's overall social problems to necessitate systemic educational reform. The message is for schools to look at children's readiness to learn, the content and emphasis in school curricula, the role and competencies of teachers, and the involvement of parents in their children's education performance. This philosophical view provided the foundation for reforms included in *Goals 2000*.

The National Education Goals is a political and educational movement to build a nation of learners. On March 31, 1994, President Clinton signed into law *Goals 2000: Educate America Act*. *Goals 2000* attempts to provide a partnership among educators, parents, politicians, and other interested community parties to help all U.S. children reach their full learning potential. It is a law of standards based on the changes that provides resources to states and communities to implement educational reforms to improve the academic achievement of all students. As the National Educational Goals Panel (1994) said: "These goals are a rallying cry that focuses attention on where we stand, how far we have come, and how far we have to go to guarantee world-class education for all" (p. 3). These goals also emphasize seven general objectives for students completing high school: (a) ready to learn; (b) school completion; (c) students' achievement; (d) teacher education and professional development; (e) adult literacy and lifelong learning; (f) safe, disciplined, and alcohol-free schools; and (g) parental participation.

Every national educational reform has entailed a redefinition of roles and responsibilities at all levels. All people, including parents, must participate in the development of a common vision for the nation's children and youth. Those responsible for instruction in schools must have the authority and competency necessary to make that vision a reality. This will include eliciting public and professional participation, creating state plans, developing content and performance standards, and providing guidance to school districts in meeting defined goals. It is imperative that in structuring schools and specific programs, assurance is provided that curricula, instruction, and assessment will be appropriate for these standards developed, and that it ensures that teachers are prepared to help each student meet those standards. The next section provides specific curricular and instructional recommendations for educators working with linguistically and culturally diverse students.

CURRICULAR AND INSTRUCTIONAL RECOMMENDATIONS

Addressing linguistic and culturally diverse populations calls for a deeper understanding of the interaction of students' home culture and language. This understanding will lead educators to provide curricula and classroom settings appropriate to students' discourse patterns, nonverbal communication, socialization, cultural traits, and learning styles (Garcia, 1993). At the same time, instructional programs must ensure appropriate applications of general effective principles of teaching and learning. Combining these two general principles—students' linguistic, cultural, and cognitive characteristics and the appropriate application of generally effective principles of teaching and learning—is necessary for academic and intellectual success. The areas of first-class curriculum; good teaching; instructing students according to their needs, characteristics, and strengths; and providing necessary specialized services call for a combination of these two general principles.

Using Assessment Data for Instruction

There are several reasons to assess students' learning in the classroom: to place students in classes, to measure students' progress and achievement, to guide and improve instruction, and to diagnose and evaluate students' knowledge on a topic before it is taught. The assessment of culturally and linguistically diverse students is necessary to gain knowledge as to their level of school achievement. If the culturally and linguistically diverse student is not assessed, no one can really be held accountable for what these students know and what they can do in the different subject areas and in their overall educational performance. However, this assessment has to be appropriate to measure the academic, linguistic, and cognitive progress of these students. Identifying these areas in individual students' profiles can provide a sound basis for making instructional decisions about students.

Instruction must also be evaluated on an ongoing basis to determine whether there are sufficient opportunities for students to practice skills or content to reach desired levels of independent performance. Students are sometimes allowed to engage in independent practice before they have demonstrated adequate understanding of the processes and content involved. It is important to remember that independent functioning requires mastery of material at the cognitive level of the students.

Current assessment instruments in English are inappropriate because they actually assess both content concepts and language ability, particularly reading comprehension and writing. Because language and content are intricately intertwined, it is difficult to isolate one feature from the other in the assessment process. Thus, educators may not be sure whether students are simply unable to demonstrate knowledge because of a language barrier or whether, indeed, the student does not know the process, the skills, or the content material assessed. Often these assessments simply become measures of students' English language proficiency rather than measures of content knowledge. One of my recommendations is for states to develop performance objective assessments that are appropriate for these students and are based on students' actual educational experiences.

Linguistically and culturally diverse students' assessment should begin as soon as they arrive in school; written records should begin to be created in the form of cumulative files, observation notes, anecdotal information, test scores, and grades. It is also recommended that a portfolio of the students' work be immediately organized. This is kept in school and provides information on the student's progress toward mastery of important content knowledge, thinking skills, language, as well as the development of reading and writing proficiency. Once assessment information has begun to be compiled, the next necessary step is to use that information for instructional purposes. Also, if linguistically and culturally diverse students are instructed in their native language, they should be assessed and evaluated in that language. The native language assessment should parallel content assessment and performance standards in English.

A First-Class Curriculum

Curriculum is the outcome of deliberate decisions about appropriate provisions for the learner for the purpose of making positive impacts in his or her academic/cognitive development (Marsh & Willis, 1995; Tyler, 1992). In other words, curriculum is the interrelated set of plans and experiences that students undertake under the guidance of the school. All educators are directly involved in making decisions about curriculum, content, and teaching by constantly monitoring and adjusting ends and means. The most fundamental aspect in this process is that all members of the school, the school district, and the community understand that, although not every student in the educational setting is proficient in English, the educational experiences provided to all students emphasize a first-class curriculum—with emphasis on history, civics, democracy, common values, and curriculum standards for all subject areas.

The linguistic and culturally diverse school population must be provided with the opportunity to learn the same challenging content and high-level skills that school reform movements advocate for all students. Programs must be designed and administered differently to provide opportunities for the implementation of language and culturally enriching curricula, challenging content with high expectations for all students, and extracurricular support systems. Linguistically and culturally diverse students can greatly benefit from the movement toward higher standards for all. All students need to be skillful in areas such as mathematics, reading, writing, science, language arts, history, music, and art. All classrooms should adopt the best curriculum frameworks available with the purpose of developing a community of learners and problem solvers. School principals, content area supervisors, as well as teachers need to plan and develop approaches for different alternatives in the classroom. Most of the time, for linguistically and culturally diverse students, the emphasis is on English acquisition basic skills to the exclusion of lesser emphasis on other subjects and skills. These students should be provided access to challenging content while they are acquiring English. The curriculum should be tailored to students' needs and strengths.

What are the characteristics of a first-class curriculum? First, it should provide rich opportunities for literacy development (thinking, discourse, reading, and writing) across the curriculum. It should involve comprehension (an active and goal-oriented construction of coherent mental representation based on newly acquired information and prior knowledge), critical thinking, problem solving, and writing skill development.

Second, it should feature a variety of subject areas with the objective of moving students to the most challenging processes and skills. For example, students at the high school level should have the opportunity to take not only algebra and geometry, but also calculus and trigonometry.

Third, it should involve students in learning experiences or activities related to their aspirations and problems. :earning experiences should be provided that are actually activities that may be written into the curriculum plan and that offer opportunities for students to reach the objectives specified. Tyler (1992) asserted that learning experiences must be selected so that students have sufficient opportunity to experience and complete the tasks required of them successfully. He also asserted that learning experiences must enable students to gain satisfaction from exhibiting particular kinds of behavior.

Fourth, it should encourage the active participation of learners in their own learning and work, thus providing them with opportunities to internalize the criteria for making decisions and judgments they develop with others. According to Tyler (1992), "learning experiences of the curriculum should be on the activities that involve the children's aspirations and problems" (p. 126).

Fifth, it should draw on the thinking process to become the content of curriculum. Development of the intellect, learning to learn, decision making, creativity, and problem solving become the subject matter of instruction. The multicultural content selected thus becomes a vehicle to practice the thinking processes and skills.

Sixth, it should emphasize problem-situated learning. Real-world problems provide authentic content for thinking; these problems require judgment and thinking, organizing, and collaboration. As the personal experiences of students, these problems may not have good solutions or may not lend themselves to more than one solution, but they are worth thinking about and exploring. They should also typically involve more than one content area, reflecting the interdisciplinary nature of learning in the real world.

Finally, it should provide a multicultural curriculum that is integrated throughout the curriculum rather than taught in isolated, fragmented units on special occasions. The concept of culture is seen in a continuum with people demonstrating characteristics ranging from traditional roles to more contemporary ones. The curriculum thus would include content that looks at the customs, folklore, values, and language of the diversity of people and cultures that make up the United States, and not only of groups that are represented in the classroom.

Teaching for understanding will not happen in classrooms where students sit in silent passivity. Classrooms that have linguistically and culturally diverse students reflect a broader variety of linguistic and cultural differences. Teachers have to be aware of these linguistic and cultural differences and plan accordingly to provide instructional experiences that take into consideration students' linguistic levels and cultures (Faltis, 1993). What approaches seem to provoke students' understanding, challenging and involving them in their learning? The literature mentions:

whole class teaching	team teaching	cooperative learning
problem solving	discussion seminars	literacy activities
integrated themes	content integration	science/math projects

Educators encourage and contribute to linguistically and culturally diverse academic success by providing learning experiences and extracurricular tasks that enable students to feel productive, challenged, and successful (Faltis, 1993; Garcia, 1993; Hamayan, 1990; Marsh & Willis, 1995; Tyler, 1992). Emphasis on collaborative learning, problem-solving activities, and activities that combine reading, speaking, and a variety of topics and content areas are the most highly recommended ones.

Good Teaching

Teachers have many factors to consider when planning and delivering instruction. They must consider their own philosophy of education (child-centered, teacher-centered, constructivist); they have to decide the content to be taught, how this content will be organized and presented, the strategies they will use, and the materials needed to present the content. Teachers must have background knowledge in how students learn, how to motivate them, the subject matter they teach, and how to promote critical thinking. They must be able to reflect on the learning process going on in the classroom and the goals and objectives they have set up for their students. Teachers must be knowledgeable about classroom management and how to integrate everyone into the process of learning. Stanz (1994) defined successful teachers as those with a "deep personal commitment to their subject area, having clear instructional objectives and goals and establishing an environment which encourages interaction and activity" (p. 5). Teachers are undoubtedly the major participants in students' learning. It requires both pedagogical knowledge and a deep understanding of the content area one teaches.

Teaching needs to be organized around individual students' work or subgroups within the class. Organizing the school curriculum by subject areas (i.e., the history class, the science class, the French class) has proven to be unsuccessful in challenging language minority students on the basis of effort, ability, and level of development. Perhaps curricula may have to be rethought around integrated themes of subject areas as well as around individual and collaborative experiences. Teaching should be seen as a team effort in which teachers' talents, knowledge, and skills are used to their fullest potential. In this way, all students will have access to at least one teacher who is top notch in each area. If we require curriculum standards, it means that teachers need to improve their own knowledge of content and teaching methodology. In other words, teachers will need to have a stronger grasp of their content and their teaching skills.

Unfortunately, although it is expected that by the year 2000 the U.S. teaching force will have sufficient professional skills to instruct and prepare all U.S. students, the current situation is that teachers, especially those working in districts with large numbers of language minority students, remain unprepared or uncertified. Not only teachers, but the entire school staff as well need training. Teachers, administrators, and related staff are also expected to continue learning. The continuing professional development of school staff was considered by Henry W. Holmes, dean of the Harvard Graduate School of Education in the 1920s, to be a highly significant part of the making of a nation. Local school districts should specifically address the recruitment, training, and development of teachers and aides to provide effective instruction to all students. Staff training should not only revolve around certification requirements; rather, staff training should focus on subject content, instructional methodology, theories of learning, students' diverse learning characteristics, and motivational strategies.

Provision of a Variety of Specialized Services

Services for linguistically and culturally diverse students should represent a continuum of appropriate programs that provide language development support beyond the normal classroom, if necessary. To help these students get on their feet, schools need to offer many extra-specialized services. This is where the social worker, the psychologist, the counselor, and other related staff come together, firmly believing in improving students' academic performance. For example, in order to decrease the number of students dropping out of school, the school may have to provide specialized counseling services and extracurricular activities to motivate these students to attend and stay in school.

Students may need special services related to instruction. Data provided in this chapter reported that linguistically and culturally diverse students are not performing at the expected rate in academic areas, especially in reading and mathematics. Specialized content area classes conducted in small and individualized formats in areas such as reading, English language development, literacy development, and mathematics basic skills may need to be made available to these students. Educators providing these specialized services should have the knowledge and understanding of language minority students' characteristics and individual differences, and they need to be true believers that linguistically and culturally diverse students have the potential and the ability to learn. High school counselors need to stop telling these students not to apply to an "Ivy League university" because "they will never get in." The entire staff needs to put time, energy, and enthusiasm into helping these students become successful learners and achievers.

Using Parents as Partners in Their Children's Learning

This goal calls for the increased involvement and participation of parents in promoting the social, emotional, and academic growth of children. Parents of linguistically and culturally diverse students, although interested in the education of their children, are not participating in their children's education. One reason for this is the failure of the school to involve culturally and linguistically diverse parents. For parents to be participants in their children's education they have to be informed of what their children are learning in school. In turn, parents need to be accountable for that learning with the school. One recommended approach to this end is to organize learning around monthly goals that are sent to parents (in the parents' language) in contract format. Parents read and sign this contract in which they make a commitment to work with their children toward the accomplishment of the respective goals and tasks.

CONCLUSION

Culturally and linguistically diverse students must be provided with an equal opportunity to learn the same challenging content and high-level skills that school reform movements advocate for all students. The U.S. national educational objectives for school students foresees a structured educational system that will hold all students to high common standards of world-class achievement. The idea behind these objectives is the implementation of academic standards to improve teaching, and the provision for more and better learning, which will result in greater and more success for all students. This conceptualization requires that educators carefully find ways of meeting the needs of linguistically and culturally diverse students to achieve the content standards in subject matter areas such as mathematics, science, social studies, and English language and reading skills. Setting high expectations for all children will further the cause of educational equity provided that appropriate, high-quality instruction and other essential resources are available. Educators need to familiarize themselves with students' linguistic levels, cultural diversity, and learning styles and plan and deliver instruction, taking into consideration students' needs and strengths.

Proficiency in two or more languages should be promoted for all U.S. students. Bilingualism enhances cognitive and social growth, competitiveness in a global marketplace, national security, and understanding of diverse peoples and cultures. The students' native language should be seen as a strength in the pursuit of greater competence in foreign languages. The United States needs to begin to recognize that linguistically and culturally diverse students represent an untapped resource that needs to be nurtured and enriched.

REFERENCES

Baker, C. (1993). *Foundations of bilingual education and bilingualism.* Clevedon, England: Multilingual Matters.

Carrasquillo, A. (1991). *Hispanic children and youth in the United States.* New York: Garland.

Children's Defense Fund. (1994). *State of America's children: Yearbook.* Washington, DC: Author.

Citizens' Commission on Planning for Enrollment Growth. (1995). *Bursting at the seams: Report of the Citizens' Commission on Planning for Enrollment Growth.* New York: Board of Education of the City of New York.

Contreras-Polk, C. (1994). Violence in the school: What parents can do. *NABE News, 17*(7), 31-32.

Cordasco, F., & Bucchioni, E. (1982). *The Puerto Rican community and its children on the mainland: A source book for teachers, social workers and other professionals.* Metuchen, NJ: Scarecrow Press.

Faltis, C. (1993). *Joinfostering: Adapting teaching strategies for the multilingual classroom.* New York: Macmillan.

Fishman, J. A. (1971). *Advances in the sociology of language.* The Hague: Mouton.

Garcia, E. E. (1993). Language, culture and education. In L. Darling-Hammond (Ed.), *Review of research in education* (pp. 51-98). Washington, DC: American Educational Research Association.

Gonzalez, C. R. (1994). Immigrants: Understated value, overstated costs— Urban Institute Report, setting the record straight. *NABE News, 17*(7), 17-18.

Hamayan, E. V. (1990). Preparing mainstream classroom teachers to teach potentially English proficient students. In *Proceedings of the first research symposium on limited English proficient students issues* (pp. 1-21). Washington, DC: Office of Bilingual Education and Minority Language Affairs.

Hodgkinson, H. (1991). Reform vs. reality. *Phi Delta Kappan, 73,* 8-16.

Lara, J. (1994). Demographic overview: Changes in student enrollment in American schools. In K. Spangenberg-Urbschat & R. Pritchard (Eds.), *Kids come in all languages: Reading instruction for ESL students* (pp. 9-21). Newark, DE: International Reading Association.

Marsh, C., & Willis, G. (1995). *Curriculum: Alternative approaches, ongoing issues.* Englewood Cliffs, NJ: Prentice-Hall.

National Center for Children in Poverty. (1990). *Five million children: A statistical profile of our poorest young citizens.* New York: Columbia University Press.

National Commission on Excellence in Education. (1983). *A Nation at risk: The imperative for educational reform*. Washington, DC: United States Government Printing Office.

National Educational Goals Panel. (1994). *The national education goals report*. Washington, DC: Author.

Peng, S. S. (1995). Diversity of Asian-American students and its implications for teaching and research. *NABE News, 19*(2), 11-12, 18.

Sleeter, C., & Grant, C. A. (1993). *Making choices for multicultural education*. New York: Macmillan.

Stanz, C. (1994). Classrooms that work: Teaching and learning generic skills. *Centerfocus*, pp. 1-5.

Tyler, R. (1992). The long-term impact of the Dewey school. *The Curriculum Journal, 3*(2), 125-129.

United States Bureau of the Census. (1992). *Population projections of the United States, by age, sex, race, and Hispanic origin: 1992-2050* (Current Population Reports, P25-1092). Washington, DC: Government Printing Office.

United States Bureau of the Census. (1993). *Press release* (CB9318). Washington, DC: Government Printing Office.

United States Department of Education. (1993). *Descriptive study of services to limited English proficient students*. Washington, DC: Planning and Evaluation Service.

Waggoner, D. (1991). *Language minority census newsletter. In Number and needs* (pp. 1-4). Washington, DC: Government Printing Office.

Wong-Fillmore, L. (1991). When learning a second language means losing the first. *Early Childhood Research Quarterly, 6*, 323-346.

11 Challenges to Curriculum Planning in Early Care and Education for All Children

Theresa M. Bologna

Fordham University

Eighteen years after the passage of PL 94-142, the Education for the Handicapped Act (EHA), the special education community continues to examine ways to ensure that children identified in need of special instruction get a free, appropriate, public education (FAPE) under the guidelines and mandates of this landmark legislation. The least-restrictive environment (LRE) as a mandate is described in the United States Code, the record of federal law, to guarantee that

> to the maximum extent appropriate, children with disabilities, including children in public or private institutions or other care facilities, are educated with children who are not disabled, and that special classes, separate schooling, or other removal of children with disabilities from the regular education environment occurs only when the nature or severity of the disability is such that education in regular classes with the use of supplementary aids and services cannot be achieved satisfactorily. (28 U.S.C. section 142(5)(B) and 34 C.F.R. section 300.550)

The breadth of interpretation of this mandate can be observed in practice along with the lengthy list of litigation surrounding the concept of least-restrictive environment (Martin, 1991; Ordover & Boundy, 1991). The most recent attempt to translate this concept into practice is inclusion. In the mid-1980s, Madeline Will encouraged the special education community to reexamine the system she believed had become one of segregating children with disabilities in a separate instructional environment from their typical peers (Will, 1986). Her work led to the beginning of what became known as the "regular education initiative." Regular and special education began to study the existing systems of planning and implementing instruction for children identified in need of special education. The study continues these many years down the road.

Inclusion has taken on a life of its own, although in many shapes and forms. As the special education community became disenchanted with the process and outcomes of mainstreaming, parents and professionals sought new ways to meet the instructional needs of the children considered disabled. For each school system or district that has investigated the use of inclusion, there is a unique case study. The confusion surrounding what is inclusion implies at least two views. For example, as the special education and the regular education communities attempt to realign their forces, the definition of inclusion evolves. It is also possible that inclusion means so many things to so many different people as a reflection of the diversity of the students eligible for special instruction. The philosophy behind EHA, now known as the Individuals with Disabilities Education Act (IDEA), recognized this diversity in the Individualized Education Plan. Each child identified in need of special instruction because of a disability will be taught in such a way that is unique for him or her (i.e., individualized).

The common core in curriculum planning in early care and education as well as early childhood special education is the intent and practice of individualized instruction. The guidelines for Developmentally Appropriate Practice (Bredekamp, 1986) and the Individuals with Disabilities Act (IDEA) both acknowledge and provide definition to individualized instruction.

In many systems, because of the numbers of children identified and taught in special instructional environments, the recognition of an Individualized Education Plan (IEP) and the Individualized Family Service Plan can become lost in labels and classes set up for particular types of children. For example, the numbers of children classified for special instruction can be a barrier in terms of administration. In the New York City public schools, approximately 15,000 children receive special instruction in modified and specialized instructional environments that are unique to children in the special education system. These are essentially self-contained environments for children with special needs. Some school systems have elected computerized IEP systems that allow the selection from prewritten goals to develop a unique list for a particular child. On the one hand, this recognizes the great similarity in the goals written across children. On the other hand, a hazard in such a system is the routine nature of the selection that can blind one from the individual picture of the child. The intent of this chapter is to review some of the challenges that affect curriculum planning for young children (birth through 8 years old), including those at risk for and those already identified as needing special instruction.

CHALLENGE: DEVELOPING A DEFINITION OF "INCLUSION"

Before parents and professionals can assess the validity of inclusion, they must first recognize what it is they are attempting to do or not do. Within five years of the passage of PL 94-142, the original Education for the Handicapped Act of 1975, the number of books and articles written to describe the least-restrictive environment could stagger even the most dedicated doctoral student. Today, the literature overflows with discussions of inclusion. History reminds us that LRE is still broadly defined. Inclusion is one attempt to clarify its meaning. As policy developers recognize this, they have begun to develop operational definitions that suit the needs of their community and the children who live and learn within it.

Some definitions include the following:

> The Board supports the development of the education models that create systematic unity between special and general education, and multiple instructional strategies that include, to the maximum extent appropriate, special needs students in the general education environment. . . . The Board presumes that these goals are best achieved in the school the students would attend if he/she did not have a disability. (Connecticut State Board of Education, 1992, p. 1)

> The term "full inclusion" as used in District 75 is a method of providing special education services in the least restrictive environment and is defined as incorporating the following four elements: (1) students attend, to the greatest extent possible, their neighborhood or home zoned school; (2) students have membership in a general education class, and receive special education services within the context of the general class; (3) the curriculum, activities, materials, and/or schedule, as well as staffing ratios are adapted, modified, and/or enhanced to address the student's individual goals and objectives as specified in the IEP; and (4) students with disabilities participate in activities and classes in numbers which reflect the natural proportions of individuals with disabilities within the community at large. (New York City Public Schools, District 75, 1993, p.2)

IDEA does not use the term "inclusion," consequently, the Department of Education has not defined the term. However, IDEA does require school districts to place students in the LRE. LRE means that, to the maximum extent appropriate, school districts must educate students with disabilities in the regular classroom with appropriate aids and supports, referred to as "supplementary aids and services," along with their nondisabled peers in the school they would attend if not disabled, unless a student's IEP requires some other arrangement. This requires an individualized inquiry into the unique educational needs of each disabled student in determining the possible range of aids supports provided in this area. (United States Department of Education, 1994, p.2).

Inclusion, as a value, supports the right of all children, regardless of their diverse abilities, to participate actively in natural settings within their community. A natural setting is one in which the child would spend time had he or she not had a disability. Such settings include but are not limited to home and family, play groups, child care, nursery schools, Head Start programs, kindergartens, and neighborhood classrooms. (Division for Early Childhood, 1993, p.1)

CHALLENGE: DETERMINING THE MOST APPROPRIATE INSTRUCTIONAL ENVIRONMENT FOR A CHILD ELIGIBLE FOR SPECIAL INSTRUCTION

Developing an Individualized Education Plan or an Individualized Family Service Plan, according to the federal and state mandates, requires the determination of where a child will probably learn what he or she needs to learn during a proposed time frame. According to IDEA, "special education means specially designed instruction, at no cost to parents and guardians, to meet the unique needs of a handicapped child, including classroom instruction, instruction in physical education, home instruction, and instruction in hospitals and institutions" [sec. 602(16)]. The interpretation of this mandate has and continues to occur through due process hearings and court decisions. The interpretation of what constitutes special education in practice covers the breadth of understanding and interpretation of least-restrictive environment.

A number of issues cloud this decision-making process. Once a child is considered eligible for special education, does the team assume that the least-restrictive environment is a self-contained class based on a label such as mentally retarded or severely learning disabled? The issue focuses on making decisions about instruction and the appropriate instructional environment based on the child's current level of functioning and the judgments that such information supports. The intent is to provide the child with the support system that will enable him or her to learn. Special education is not a place but a means to provide the support system for learning to take place.

The special education community in general believes in the importance of a continuum of services. Because of the diversity of the population that receives special instruction, the concept and practice of a continuum of services provides a breadth of opportunities. A problem rests in decision making that eliminates the general education classroom as an option for many children. "Mainstreaming is typically not encouraged because failure to fill special classes can result in the loss of funded units" (Dempsey & Fuchs, 1993, p. 434). Along with funding issues, attitudes of regular and special education personnel about including children with disabilities in general education classrooms for instruction are generally exclusionary. The presumption is that children with special needs learn more or at least are better contained in special classrooms (Eiserman, Shisler, & Healey, 1995; Giangreco, Dennis, Cloninger, Edelman, & Schattman, 1993).

The notion of inclusion proposes the following. The team assesses the child's ability to learn effectively. This information is used to determine if it is at all possible for the child to learn within the environment he or she would be in if the latter had not been considered eligible for special education. Such a presumption moves the perspective to examining the feasibility of instruction along with age mates as the first line of investigated possibilities. When this option proves unacceptable, then the decision-making process moves to the next level on the continuum. Such a problem-solving process proposes that the child is innocent as opposed to labeled "guilty."

In a brief discussion of New York State's approach to developing instructional environments for children eligible for special education, Commissioner Sobel ("NYS Education Commissioner Sobel says," 1993) reminds the education community that inclusion is not a mandate:

> The Board of Regents and State Education Department are not mandating inclusion in the general classrooms as the required placement for all students with disabilities. The emphasis will be on expanding current options for students with disabilities to be educated in the general education environment, where appropriate . . . the State will maintain, as part of its least restrictive environment, the requirement for a continuum of services to be available based on the individual needs of students with disabilities. (p. 1)

Present practice, as reported in the Fourteenth Annual Report to Congress on the Implementation of the Education of the Handicapped Act (1994), describes the extent to which the special education community selects placements in the continuum. For children 3 to 11 years old who are determined eligible for special education, approximately 40% of the instructional environments selected are in general education. The remainder of this age group receives special instruction in a resource room (14% for 3 to 5-year-olds, 35% for 6 to 11-year-olds), separate class (28% for 2 to 5-year-olds, 21% for 6 to 11-year-olds), separate school (15% for 3 to 5-year-olds, 3% for 6 to 11-year-olds), residential facility (0.5% for 3 to 5-year-olds, 0.4% for 6 to 11-year-olds), and home or hospital (2% for 3 to 5-year-olds, 0.3% for 6 to 11-year-olds).

The figures reported in the annual report to Congress represent averages. The averages reported do indicate that the majority of young children receive special instruction in separate environments from their typical age mates. If, indeed, a minority of the children eligible for special education in this age range are significantly compromised in their ability to learn because of a disability, there is a discrepancy between the numbers who could be considered eligible for instruction along with their typical age mates and those who are.

A survey of 893 early care and education programs randomly selected from preschools and kindergartens in the United States indicated that 75% of the programs reported including at least one child with an identified disability in their program (Wolery et al., 1993). The variance in this figure is readily apparent when viewing one of the extremes. In New York City, 95% of the children identified for special education as preschoolers attend segregated early childhood special education programs (Fruchter, Berne, Marcus, Alter, & Gottlieb, 1995).

CHALLENGE: INDIVIDUALIZED INSTRUCTION IS MANDATED BY IDEA. THE PRACTICE OF INDIVIDUALIZED INSTRUCTION REPRESENTS THE CORE OF DEVELOPMENTALLY APPROPRIATE PRACTICE IN EARLY CARE AND EDUCATION

All children are entitled to a free appropriate public education. This is the premise upon which the United States Department of Education and each state and local education agency operates. How this right to an education is operationalized varies. Goodlad (1984), Sizer (1984), and, more recently, Kozol (1991) propose that the instructional environments in which most children learn (regular and special education) are ineffective and often boring for the children coming to school each day. In response to this, Katz and Chard (1991) describe an approach that enhances the interactive nature of instruction as it is simultaneously individualized:

That all children should have the disposition to be readers requires heterogeneous treatments. In other words, to achieve the same objectives with diverse children different teaching strategies and curriculum elements are called for. . . . If homogeneous outcomes are best achieved in heterogeneous treatments, it follows that when a single teaching method is used for a diverse group, a significant portion is likely to fail. (p. 45)

Ensminger and Dangael (1993) portray a similarly bleak picture of the instructional environment in special education. Keogh (1990), in her analysis of a series of research projects investigating the impact of including children with disabilities in general education instructional environments, commented that, despite the growing body of research, there is much to learn. The variable that appears to continue to drive practice is instruction. Instruction is designed by the teacher, whether in a regular or special education environment. Keogh proposes that the regular and special educators share the responsibility for designing effective environments that individualize instruction for the diverse populations entering the classroom today.

Baker and Zigmond (1990), sharing the research on Project Meld, suggest that the instructional models presently used in special education and regular education are not meeting the needs of the children considered eligible for special instruction. They suggest that "business as usual" cannot continue to meet the needs of the children, regardless of the environment, either mainstreamed or self-contained.

Individualizing instruction is not a new approach in education. The history of education, and particularly early care and education, abounds in efforts to describe and actualize individualization. The National Association for the Education of Young Children (NAEYC) has developed an evolving document that presents the guidelines for developmentally appropriate practice for children birth to 8 years old (Bredekamp, 1986). An integral component of Developmentally Appropriate Practice (DAP) is individualization of instruction. The special education literature overflows with research and theory to facilitate the development and implementation of individualized instruction for the categories of children receiving special instruction. Katz and Chard's (1991) recommendation to use heterogeneous approaches to meet the diverse needs of students goes beyond the implications of individualizing instruction. Through their analysis and description of "the project approach," they provide educators with concrete methods to facilitate and achieve heterogeneity in instruction and outcome.

McClean and Odom (1993) described their analysis of the alignment between the NAEYC's (1994) curriculum guidelines (Bredekamp, 1986) and the Division for Early Childhood (DEC, 1993) recommended practices related to intervention. McClean and Odom (1993) highlight the similarities in these frameworks, noting that "considerable similarity and agreement exist in virtually every area discussed" (p. 289). The specificity of descriptions and the role of families and related service personnel in the early childhood special education framework provide the focus of differentiation in approach. This analysis supports the strong relationship between early care and education and early childhood special education. The latter, representing a specific expertise in early childhood education, further differentiates expertise with its knowledge base concerning young children with disabilities and their families.

Although the methods are not new to education, the practice of them apparently is not common. Dewey (1917) spoke and wrote of the errors of an educational system built on rote learning and the singular use of didactic instruction. Bruner (1966), another leader in developing the theory upon which educators operate, elaborated on the theory of instruction:

> The fact of individual differences argues for pluralism and for an enlightened opportunism in the materials and methods of instruction. . . . It is not possible to put together a curriculum that would satisfy a group of children or a cross section of children. . . . If a curriculum is to be effective in the classroom it must contain different ways of activating children, different ways of presenting sequences, different opportunities for some children to "skip" parts while others work their way through, different ways of putting things. (p. 71)

CHALLENGE: THE CHILD'S NEEDS MUST STAND AS THE DRIVING FORCE BEHIND DECISION MAKING AND PLANNING

As child study teams plan instruction that includes placement in typical early care and education programs, multiple problems arise. These include staff patterns and assignments, developing collaborative relationships between staff that are used to functioning independent of each other, providing staff the time to collaborate and plan, meeting the needs of all the students in the typical setting, and recognizing and respecting the attitudes of parents, staff, and the community. The author examined these issues in relation to experiences shared by teachers, parents, and administrators. These experiences were shared in a number of ways: consultation, masters' and doctoral student observations, and review of written documents prepared by school system representatives. The problem-solving process used in the situations described occurred after a conscious decision to plan instruction based on the child's needs. System needs were addressed after this decision was made.

Developing Staff Patterns and Assignments

The issue of who should or could teach a class that includes a child eligible for special education brings up administrative, union, and funding concerns. One option is to develop mixed-aged group classrooms that include a small proportion of children considered for special education. A recommended proportion is one that matches the makeup of the local community. Staffing includes a collaboration of regular and special education, sometimes in someone dually certified, other times as team teachers or in consultative roles. An assistant, instructional aide, or paraprofessional often joins this group. Selection and training of paraprofessionals vary dramatically. The NAEYC (1995) recognized this concern with the development of standards for professional development. The Council for Exceptional Children (CEC) and the Division for early Childhood of CEC are in the process of developing standards (CEC, DEC, personal communication, 1996).

Developing Collaborative Relationships Between Staff that Are Used to Function Independently of Each Other

Educators, regular and special, generally work within a contained environment that is uniquely their domain. The classroom becomes Mrs. Harris's room, Mr. Johnson's reading lab, Ms. Jacobs's gym. Attempting collaboration can start by involving many captains and no crew. Teachers and related service personnel are trained to teach or provide treatment; they are not trained to collaborate (Bruder & Bologna, 1993). In the case studies used to develop this discussion, attempts at collaboration that began to click grew based on mutual trust and respect for the expertise of each member of the team. These characteristics are prized when present but they require continuous time to develop.

One method that lays the groundwork for collaboration is the selection of staff who are interested in working in such a model and who have already begun to develop working relationships across the disciplines involved. Recognition of what one can bring to a collaborative effort is as important as the recognition that one needs support and further information to design an effective learning environment. One system wrote into its teacher union contracts that prior to placing a child in need of special instruction in a placement alongside his or her age mates, the teacher must participate in staff development to learn about the implications of inclusion on classroom instruction for the identified child, the whole class, and the team made up of parents and professionals.

Providing Staff the Time to Collaborate and Plan

Teachers' time is already stretched to its limit. The recognition of the need for time to discuss and plan is evident. Some teams have even chosen to write such time into the IEP. Even when this happens, finding this time in an already crammed day is difficult. Solutions have included using time during staff development or hiring a floating assistant or teacher within a school to take over classes to provide release time for collaboration. The advantage to this latter approach is that the children know this person as a familiar part of their school community who has already earned their respect. Providing staff time translates to additional funding. This remains a barrier in relation to a number of issues. This issue of the allocation of funds earmarked for special education and regular education is one of the concerns before the present Congress as it struggles through the reauthorization process of IDEA.

Meeting the Needs of All the Students in the Regular Education Classroom

The intent of including children with special education needs in the mainstream should never be at the expense of any other child. Few would argue this point. The reality is that many children have extensive instructional needs. These can draw significantly on the time and energy of a teacher. Team teaching, cooperative learning environments, and mixed age groupings are some of the strategies employed to deal with this issue. An initially unexpected outcome that many teachers have reported is the opportunity to provide specialized instruction for children not considered eligible for special education. The apparent "luxury" of collaboration provided support for a large number of children in the general education classroom.

Recognizing and Respecting the Attitudes of Parents, Staff, and the Community

Change is rarely easy. Sarason (1982) reminds us of the journey we undertake in our attempts to examine what works and what does not work in our schools. He proposed that our judgments are encumbered with "images, expectations, and implicit and explicit attitudes. We come to the task after a long process of socialization and acculturation from which in countless ways, witting and unwitting, we have absorbed conceptions of and attitudes toward school settings" (p. 14). The acknowledgment of the differences between these preconceived attitudes and what appear to be new ideas produces conflict. Conflict turned to reflection can lead to growth. Conflict turned to confusion and fear leads to more confusion and fear and often inertia, withdrawal, or combativeness.

Respecting the attitudes of others in our community requires the ability to perceive these attitudes. Attitudes are ingrained. Often knowledge does not change attitudes, but experience often can. One method for dealing with this issue is to provide knowledge and experience simultaneously. For example, telling children or parents about a child with a disability who is going to join the regular education class group can generate more questions and concerns than answers. Introducing the children to each other as the information about the child is shared by the child at the children's level of understanding vitalizes the information and the experience.

CHALLENGE: IMPLICATIONS FOR EARLY CARE AND EDUCATION FOR ALL CHILDREN

What inclusion could and should look like will remain the focus of discussion and research until the education system as a whole does one of two things: comes to a consensus concerning its operationalization, or replaces this discussion with the newest "hot issue." The former could lead to a resolution of the conflicts raised as one plans for children with special education needs. The larger issue that confronts the community of educators represents the vast area of reform that writers such as Goodlad, Sizer, Kozol, and Boyer address. The bottom line for all of this is already legislated: All children are entitled to a free appropriate public education. The job of educators is to get on with the task of insuring that the instructional environments designed for all children match the breadth of diversity and developmental experiences of the children we call our students.

REFERENCES

Baker, J. M., & Zigmond, N. (1990). Are regular education classes equipped to accommodate students with learning disabilities? *Exceptional Children, 56*(6), 515-526.

Bredekamp, S. (1986). *Developmentally appropriate practice in early childhood programs serving from birth through 8.* Washington, DC: National Association for the Education of Young Children.

Bruder, M. D., & Bologna, T. M. (1993). Collaboration and service coordination in effective early intervention. In W. Brown, S. K. Thurman, & L. Pearl (Eds.), *Family-centered early intervention with infants and toddlers* (pp. 103-127). Baltimore: Paul H. Brookes.

Bruner, J. S. (1966). *Toward a theory of instruction.* Cambridge, MA: Belknap Press.

Connecticut State Board of Education. (1992). *Position statement on the education of students with disabilities.* Hartford, CT: Author

Dempsey, S., & Fuchs, D. (1993). "Flat" versus "weighted" reimbursement formulas: A longitudinal analysis of special education funding practice. *Exceptional Children, 59*(5), 433-443.

Dewey, J. (1917). *Democracy and education.* Carbondale: Southwestern Illinois Press.

Division for Early Childhood of the Council for Exceptional Children. (1993). *Position on inclusion.* Reston, VA: Author.

Eiserman, W. D., Shisler, L., & Healey, S. (1995). A community assessment of preschool providers' attitudes toward inclusion. *Journal of Early Intervention, 19*(2), 149-167.

Ensminger, E. E., & Dangael, H. L. (1993). The Foxfire pedagogy: A confluence of best practices for special education. *Focus on Exceptional Children, 24*(7), 1-16.

Fruchter, N., Berne, R., Marcus, A., Alter, M., & Gottlieb, J. (1995). *Focus on learning: A report on reorganizing general and special education in New York City.* New York: New York University, Institute for Education and Social Policy.

Giangreco, M. F., Dennis, R., Cloninger, C., Edelman, S., & Schattman, R. (1993). "I've counted Jon": Transformational experiences of teachers educating students with disabilities. *Exceptional Children, 59*(4), 359-372.

Goodlad, J. I. (1984). *A place called school: Prospects for the future.* New York: McGraw-Hill.

Katz, L. G., & Chard, S. C. (1991). *Engaging children's minds: The project approach.* Norwood, NJ: Ablex.

Keogh, B. K. (1990). Narrowing the gap between policy and practice. *Exceptional Children, 57*(2), 186-190.

Kozol, J. (1991). *Savage inequalities.* New York: Crown.

Martin, R. (1991). *Extraordinary children: Ordinary lives.* Champaign, IL: Research Press.

McClean, M. E., & Odom, S. L. (1993). Practices for young children with and without disabilities: A comparison of DEC and NAEYC identified practices. *Topics in Early Childhood Special Education, 13*(3), 274-292.

New York City Public Schools. (1993). *Final report, 1993: The District 75 Office of Inclusive Education.* New York: Author.

NYS Education Commissioner Sobol says "inclusion" is not a mandate. (1993). *New York Teacher, 25*(7), p. 1.

Ordover, E. L., & Boundy, K. B. (1991). *Educational rights of children with disabilities.* Cambridge, MA: Center for Law and Education.

Sarason, S. B. (1982). *The culture of the school and the problem of change* (2nd ed.). Boston: Allyn & Bacon.

Sizer, T. R. (1984). *Horace's compromise: The dilemma of American high school.* Boston: Houghton Mifflin.

Will, M. (1986). *Educating students with learning problems: A shared responsibility.* Washington, DC: Office of Special Education and Rehabilitation Services, U.S. Department of Education.

Wolery, M., Holcombe-Login, A., Brookfield, J., Huffman, K., Schroeder, C., Martin, C., Venn, M., Werts, M., & Fleming, L. (1993). The extent and nature of preschool mainstreaming: A survey of general educators. *Journal of Special Education, 27,* 222-234.

12 DATA-BASED STAFF DEVELOPMENT FOR INCLUSION EDUCATION

Terry Cicchelli
Fordham University

An explosive issue in schooling today is that of inclusion education. The working definition of *inclusion* offered by the National Center on Educational Restructuring and Inclusion (NCERI, 1991) stated:

> Providing to all students, including those with significant disabilities, equitable opportunities to receive effective educational services, with the needed supplementary aids and support services, in age-appropriate classes in their neighborhood schools, in order to prepare students for productive lives as full members of society.

On the one hand, the attitudes and concerns of teachers toward the inclusion of disabled students have been influenced by our nation's obsession with individual differences (Prawatt, 1992). For Prawatt (1992), the focus on individual differences has shifted away from sorting students into ability groups, tracks, and special education programs to an emphasis on learning, which requires meaningful, shared activity within a community of learners. On the other hand, this shift requires a fundamental change in the philosophy and practice of teaching—no easy task—because teachers find it difficult to change, particularly because they are influenced mostly by the way they were taught (Kennedy, 1991).

Regular and special education teachers especially find pullout programs for disabled students to be satisfactory despite the issue of isolation relative to special students (Semmel, Abernathy, Butera, & Lesar, 1991). Although teachers are conscientious and care about children, their mindset is conformity, not accommodation, which produces little success for students who cannot perform academically or behaviorally (Baker & Zigmond, 1990). Not surprisingly, inclusion education produces skepticism among regular and special educators alike (Davis, 1989).

Although Lieberman (1985) and Messinger (1985) claim special and regular teachers are inherently different in their views and practices of education, Stainback and Stainback (1989) attribute these differences to training. In extension, training usually leads to actual teaching. This point is of special interest because in coordinating and even collaborating for inclusion, special and regular teachers may be teamed in some configuration. No doubt these changes in teaching have to be dealt with in professional development activities. In fact, research reports both regular and special teachers indicate the necessity for staff development in inclusion, but teachers also cite little confidence in the kinds of development activities usually implemented along with the sense that the "idea" of teaching in an inclusion setting is not necessarily their responsibility (Lembo & Adams, 1995).

Collectively, these observations reinforce the difficulty of the change process for inclusion teaching. The Lembo and Adams (1995) research should be especially noted with regard to the nature of the staff development that is typically implemented. However, change is a complex process, entailing variables such as nostalgia for what schools used to be like (Meier, 1992) or a school's organizational structure (Stainback & Stainback, 1989), and an important and unique variable that is not always considered is that of resistance of teachers to change (House, 1975).

Hall (1978) verified that one of the critical variables in any change effort remains the individual teacher. Furthermore, he stated that a major reason for our failure to implement innovations (in this case inclusion) has been the inattention accorded the individual first in the change process. His work with the Concerns Based Adoption Model (CBAM) and its three dimensions (Stages of Concern, Levels of Use, and Innovation Configuration) provides a discussion for change from the point of view that change is a process, not an event, made by individuals first, then institutions, through highly personal, developmental experiences in feelings and skills. In combination, the three dimensions of CBAM create a framework to support data-based staff development for regular and special teachers.

The first dimension is the Stages of Concern (SoC), a conceptual framework used to provide insight into seven suggested Stages of Concern that teachers manifest in any educational change effort. The Stages of Concern include: Stage 0—Awareness; Stage 1—Informational; Stage 2—Personal; Stage 3—Management; Stage 4—Consequence; Stage 5—Collaboration; and Stage 6—Refocusing (see Table 12.1).

Table 12.1. Stages of Concern About the Innovation[a].

0	AWARENESS	Little concern about or involvement with the innovation is indicated.
1	INFORMATIONAL	A general awareness of the innovation; an interest in learning more detail about it is indicated. The person seems to be unworried about him- or herself in relation to the innovation. He or she is interested in substantive aspects of the innovation in a selfless manner such as general characteristics, effects, and requirements for use.
2	PERSONAL	Individual is uncertain about the demands of the innovation, his or her inadequacy to meet those demands, and his or her role with the innovation. This includes analysis of his or her role in relation to the reward structure of the organization, decision making, and consideration of potential conflicts with existing structures of personal commitment. Financial or status implications of the program for self and for colleagues may also be reflected.
3	MANAGEMENT	Attention is focused on the processes and tasks of using the innovation and the best use of information and resources. Issues related to efficiency, organizing, managing, scheduling, and time demands are utmost.
4	CONSEQUENCE	Attention focuses on the impact of the innovation on students in their immediate sphere of influence. The focus is on relevance of the innovation for students, evaluation of student outcomes, including performance and competencies, changes needed to

Table 12.1. Stages of Concern About the Innovation[a] (con't).

5	COLLABORATION	The focus is on coordination and cooperation
6	REFOCUSING	The focus is on exploration of more universal benefits from the innovation, including the possibility of major changes or replacement with a more powerful alternative. Individual has definite ideas about alternatives to the proposed or existing form of the innovation.

From *Measuring Stages of Concern About the Innovation: A Manual for Use of the SoC Questionnaire.* Austin: Research and Development Center for Teacher Education, The University of Texas, Copyright © 1979.

[a]Original concept from *A Developmental Conceptualization of the Adoption Process Within Educational Institutions.* Austin: Research and Development Center for Teacher Education, The University of Texas, Copyright © 1973.

Hall (1978) successfully operationalized the Stages of Concern using a 35-item instrument referred to as the Stages of Concern Questionnaire (SoCQ), thereby verifying the usefulness of these constructs. Furthermore, he found that the SoCQ revealed several important principles about the arousal and decline of concerns for nonusers. Initially, Stages 0, 1, and 2 concerns about self are likely to be high. However, during the early phases of implementation, Stage 3 or Management concerns about the task are likely to increase in intensity, whereas Stages 0, 1, and 2 concerns generally decrease. Over a period of time, Stages 4, 5, and 6 or impact concerns can become more intense. Thus, teacher concerns in idealized situations are typically developmental, moving to higher stages over time as earlier stages are resolved.

This survey instrument, taking approximately 15 to 20 minutes to administer in a group setting, yields valid and reliable information about the developmental Stages of Concern of teachers involved in a planned change effort for inclusion. A reliability study of SoCQ has indicated raw score, test–retest correlations ranging from 0.65 to 0.96 on the seven SoCQ factors and an internal consistency (alphas) from 0.80 to 0.93. A series of validity studies has been conducted, providing confidence that the SoCQ measures the hypothesized Stages of Concern.

By means of the SoCQ, the variable concerns of teachers can be systematically explored in order to determine one piece of data to be used to design a differentiated series of staff development activities that will assist in the decrease of early teacher concerns about the implementation of inclusion on self and task, increase subsequent concerns about the impact of inclusion, and eventually support a level of comfort in teaching in inclusion classrooms.

The second dimension is the Levels of Use (LoU), a concept that accounts for individual variation in the use of an innovation. It is proposed that there are eight discrete levels of use of an innovation that an individual may demonstrate. These levels range from lack of knowing that the innovation exists to an active and highly effective use of it to an active searching for a superseding innovation. Furthermore, it is hypothesized that growth in quality of use of an innovation (movement toward higher levels) by most individuals is developmental. Individuals do not typically use an innovation for the first or even the second time as effectively and efficiently as they do after their fourth or fifth use.

The Levels of Use dimension portrays the various behaviors the innovation user displays through the various stages—from spending most efforts in orienting, to managing, and finally to integrating use of the innovation. The individual becomes familiar with and increasingly knowledgeable about the innovation before actually using the innovation. The first use is generally disjointed, especially common with management problems. Management becomes routine with further use, and the user (teacher) is able to direct more effort toward increased effectiveness for the learner while integrating what he or she is doing with what others are doing. Obviously, these advanced levels of use are not attained merely by using the innovation. Although experience is essential, it is not sufficient to insure that a given individual will develop high-quality use of an innovation (Hall, Loucks, Rutherford, & Newlove, 1975).

The LoU dimension contains typical behavioral indices of the eight discrete levels of use of an innovation (see Table 12.2). In viewing the LoU table, it is important to note that in addition to defining the eight Levels of Use, each level is further defined in terms of seven subparts of categories. These categories represent the primary functions that users carry out when they are using an innovation. At each level, the category descriptions represent the usual behaviors that users at that level are engaged in.

The focused interview is the method used to assess a teacher's LoU. The focused interview is used rather than a highly structured one requiring standardized questions in order to respond to the complexities of the LoU concept. Furthermore, less rigidity in asking questions encourages more natural, authentic responses, allowing teachers to follow a spontaneous train of thought. The amount of freely provided information obtained through over 1,680 LoU interviews (Hall et al., 1975) supports the belief that the focused interview provided appropriate data for staff development.

Table 12.2. Levels of Use of the Innovation: Typical Behaviors[a].

Level of Use		Behavioral Indices of Level
VI	Renewal	The user is seeking more effective alternatives to the established use of the innovation.
V	Integration	The user is making deliberate efforts to coordinate with others in using the innovation.
IVB	Refinement	The user is making changes to increase outcomes.
IVA	Routine	The user is making few or no changes and has an established pattern of use.
III	Mechanical Use	The user is using the innovation in a poorly coordinated manner and is making user-oriented changes.
II	Preparation	The user is preparing to use the innovation.
I	Orientation	The user is seeking out information about the innovation.
0	Nonuse	No action is being taken with respect to the innovation.

[a]CBAM Project: Research and Development for Teacher Education. The University of Texas at Austin.

Table 12.3 offers an example of interview questions and procedures that can be used in assessing a teacher's LoU. With some practice, staff developers can rather quickly separate out information to assess a teacher's level of use, especially with differentiating a "user" from a "nonuser."

The third dimension is Innovation Configuration. Simply stated, Innovation Configuration means the logical analysis of the curriculum content components of an innovation. Curriculum content and related questions emphasizing inclusion theories, principles, and practices may be identified in the literature, as well as from actual inclusion models operating in schools. In particular, this content may be organized to match the teacher's stages and level of concern about inclusion. An example of Innovation Configuration, Inclusion, is provided in Table 12.4.

In review, CBAM's three dimensions allow for the collection of a database to be appropriately matched to create a "best-fit" model for designing staff development for regular and special teachers working in inclusion teaching (see Table 12.5). In addition to the curriculum and teaching elements of inclusion, attention should be directed to some notions that may increase the likelihood of teachers accepting this innovation. These notions include:

Table 12.3. Levels of Use Interview Questions.

Question	Purpose
Are you using the innovation? LoU 0-II from LoU III-VI.	To distinguish between users and nonusers; to break
IF YES	
What do you see as the strengths and weaknesses of the innovation in your situation? Have you made any attempt to do anything about the weaknesses?	To probe Assessing and Knowledge categories
Are you currently looking for any information about the innovation? What kind? For what purpose?	To probe Acquiring Information category
Do you ever talk with others about the innovation? What do you tell them?	To probe Sharing category
What do you see as being the effects of the innovation? In what way have you determined this? Are you doing any evaluating, either formally or informally, of your use of the innovation? Have you received any feedback from students? What have you done with the information you get?	To probe Assessing category
Have you made any changes recently in how you use the innovation? What? Why? How recently? Are you considering making any changes?	To distinguish among LoU III (user-oriented changes), LoU IV B (student-oriented changes), and LoU IV A (no or routine changes); to probe Status Reporting and Performing categories
As you look ahead to later this year, what plans do you have in relation to your use of the innovation?	To probe Planning and Status Reporting categories

Table 12.3. Levels of Use Interview Questions (con't.).

Question	Purpose
Do you ever talk to others about the innovation? What do you tell others when you talk with them? Are you working with others (outside of anyone you may have worked with from the beginning) in your use of the innovation? Have you made any changes in your use of the innovation based on this coordination?	To separate LoU from III, IV A, and IV B. If a positive response is given, LoU V Probes (below) are used

LoU V PROBES

How do you work together? How frequently?

What do you see as the strengths and weaknesses of this collaboration?

Are you looking for any particular kind of information in relation to this collaboration?

When you talk to others about your collaboration, what do you share with them?

Have you done any formal or informal evaluation of how your collaboration is working?

What plans do you have for this collaborative effort in the future?

PAST USERS

Why did you stop using the innovation?

Can you describe for me how you organized your use of the innovation, what problems you found, what its effects appeared to be on students?

Table 12.3. Levels of Use Interview Questions (con't.).

Question	Purpose
When you assess the innovation at this point in time, what do you see as the strengths and weaknesses for you?	
IF NO	
Have you ever made a decision to use the innovation in the future? If so, when?	To separate LoU 0 from I; to probe Status Reporting, Planning, and Performing categories
Can you describe the innovation for me as you see it?	To probe Knowledge category
Are you currently looking for any information about the innovation? What kinds? For what purposes?	To probe Acquiring Information category
What do you see as the strengths and weaknesses of the innovation for your situation?	To probe Assessing category
At this point in time, what kinds of questions are you asking about the innovation? Give examples if possible.	To probe Assessing, Sharing, and Status Reporting categories
Do you ever talk with others and share information about the innovation? What do you share?	To probe Sharing Category
What are you planning with respect to the innovation? Can you tell me about any preparation or plans you have been making for the use of the innovation?	To probe Planning category
Can you summarize for me where you see yourself in relation to the use of the innovation? (Optional Question)	To get a concise picture of the user's perception of his or her use or nonuse

Table 12.4. Innovation Configuration: Inclusion.

Stages 0-2	<u>Self-Concerns (What Does This Mean to Me?)</u> * Knowledge Regarding Theories, Research, and Best Practices * Cultural Nature of Schools * Restructuring for Unitary System of Schooling, Issues of Access, and Equity * Self-Fulfilling Prophecy and Philosophical Issues—Principle of Normalization * Economic Issues * Fitting In? * **Changing?**
Stage 3	<u>Task Concerns (What Do I Do?)</u> * Planning and Implementing Instruction * Interdisciplinary Teaching * Leaner Profiles (i.e., Learning Styles) * Most Enabling Environment * Collaborative Learning Models * Peer-Mediated Learning * CAI * Different Time Schedules * **Changing?**
Stages 4-6	<u>Impact Concerns (How Does This Affect Me and My Students?)</u> * Giving Up Control? * Alternative Assessment Modes? * Reflective Learning Logs for Me and My Students? How Do I Use the DATA? * What About Detracking? * What About Retention? * Who Else Can I Work With? * How Can We Expand This Concept? * Should We Test More Than One Model? * **Changing?**

* Operating CBAM dimensions simultaneously in order to support the concept of "best fit"
* Developing teams of regular and special teachers, each offering a kind of expertise
* Valuing both academic and social aspects of inclusion
* Viewing change as a necessary aspect of a teacher's professional growth

Table 12.5. "Best Fit" Model for Staff Development: Inclusion.

Innovation Configuration Inclusion Content	"Best-Fit" Combination of SoCQ and LoU	Implementation Strategy
Module I		
• Culture of Schools	Set A	Large and small group discussion, content-specific, attitude inventory, Reflection Journal, creating a Learning Community
• Restructuring		
• Philosophical Issues: Equity, Access, Principle of Normalization	SoCQ 0, 1, 2 + LoU 0, I, II	
• Economic Issues		
• **Change**		
Module II		
• Creating Different Teaching Schedules	Set B	Demonstrations, role playing, simulations, small groups, Reflection Journal
• Team Teaching	SoCQ 3	
• Team Planning	LOU III	
• Creating Learning Environments that FIT KIDS		
• **Change**		
Module III		
• Most Enabling Environment	Set C	Large and small group session simulations, consultants in classroom, case studies, Reflection Journal
• Data-Based Learner Profiles	SoCQ 3	
• Planning and Implementing Teaching Strategies	LoU IVA	
• **Change**		

Table 12.5. "Best Fit" Model for Staff Development: Inclusion (con't).

Innovation Configuration Inclusion Content	"Best-Fit" Combination of SoCQ and LoU	Implementation Strategy
Module IV • Alternative Assessment Modes • Reflective Learning Logs • Issues Related to Inclusion (Retention—Detracking) • Creating New Models • Creating New Learning Communities • **Change**	Set D SoCQ 4, 5, 6+ LoU IVB. V. VI	Some of the previous strategies, peer tutoring, analysis of data, gathering activities from field-based programs, creating new models, analysis of Reflection Journal, creating a learning community

In conclusion, this change model assumes a person-level team, data-based approach to staff development for inclusion. It fosters collegiality, reflection, and a strong interdependence between regular and special teachers regarding the change process.

REFERENCES

Baker, J., & Zigmond, N. (1990). Are regular education classes equipped to accommodate students with learning disabilities? *Exceptional Children, 56*, 515-526.

Davis, W. (1989). The regular education initiative debate: Its promise and problems. *Exceptional Children, 55*, 440-446.

Hall, G. (1978). Teacher concerns as a basis for facilitating and personalizing staff development. *Teachers College Record, 80*, 36-53.

Hall, G., Loucks, S., Rutherford, W., & Newlove, B. (1975). *Measuring levels of use of the innovation: A manual for the LoU.* Austin: University of Texas.

House, E. (1975). *The politics of educational innovation.* Berkeley, CA: McCutchan.

Kennedy, M. (1991). Some surprising findings on how teachers learn to teach. *Educational Leadership, 49*(3), 14-17.

Lembo, M., & Adams, D. (1995). *Inclusion educational practices: Teacher perceptions of academic and social learning.* Paper presented at the annual conference of the New England Educational Research Organization, Portsmouth, NH.

Lieberman, L. (1985). Special and regular education: A merger made in heaven? *Exceptional Children, 51*, 513-517.

Meier, D. (1992). Reinventing teacher. *Teachers College Record, 93*, 594-609.

Messinger, J. (1985). A commentary on a rationale for the merger of special and regular education. *Exceptional Children, 51*, 510-524.

Prawatt, R. S. (1992). From individual differences to learning communities—our changing focus. *Educational Leadership, 49*(7), 9-13.

Semmel, M. I., Abernathy, T. V., Butera, G., & Lesar, S. (1991). Teacher perception of the regular education initiative. *Exceptional Children, 58*, 9-24.

Stainback, S., & Stainback, W. (1989). *Educating all students in the mainstream of regular education.* Baltimore: Brookes.

CONTEXTS AND STRATEGIES FOR LEARNING: THE HOW-TO FOR CONSTRUCTIVIST CURRICULA

13 TEACHING THINKING: HOW CAN WE AND WHY SHOULD WE?

Cathy Collins Block
Cathleen M. Cavanagh
Texas Christian University

The principal goal of education is to create [people] who are capable of doing new things, not simply of repeating what other generations have done—(people) who are creative, inventive discoverers. The second goal of education is to form minds which can be critical, can verify, and not accept everything they are offered. (Piaget, 1963, p. 62)

Many U.S. students exert little or no effort to learn because our schools are not addressing their cognitive and affective needs. "The old theory that 'We can make 'em work; all we have to do is get tough' has never produced intellectual effort in the history of the world," said William Glasser as interviewed in *Phi Delta Kappan* (in Gough, 1987, p. 605). Instead we need to enable students to satisfy their needs for power, caring, sharing, creating, and cooperating as they reach goals they set for themselves. As educators, we know students can easily repeat what you tell them, guess at answers to comprehensive questions, memorize information, move their eyes across text as their minds wander, copy from the board, and think what you want them to think.

Teachers are also probably aware that most of their students do their highest levels of thinking outside the classroom. As they conduct the inescapable personal affairs of everyday life, students are forced, and often flounder as they try, to think. Unassisted, trial-and-error thinking is unnecessary. By teaching thinking strategies, students can learn how to initiate their own higher level thinking strategies, enact their own initiatives, speak up, listen actively, read purposefully, write originally, and modify strategic processes as they construct ideas.

Lessons that teach thinking should promote students' positive attitudes toward reading, writing, and thinking. Students develop higher levels of self-esteem using the following instructional methods that provide:

- multiple opportunities for teacher/student selection of material and activities
- flexibility in the difficulty of lesson content
- rewards for partially correct answers
- encouragement to ask questions
- adequate pupil response time

These lessons should explicitly model and instruct "sense making," metacognition, higher level comprehension and thinking, decision making, problem solving, group work skills, and reflectivity (Block, 1993a; Porter & Brophy, 1988). Students complete authentic, intrinsically motivating activities. Students become engaged in real-life experiences and are more likely to retain the lessons they learn (W. Paul, 1989). Assessments occur during, rather than after, instruction to document students' achievement and thought while they are involved in the processes.

WHY DO WE NEED TO BUILD THINKING ABILITIES DURING INSTRUCTION?

Students must reach responsible decisions earlier in contemporary society than in the past. Today's youth, often by the ages of 10 to 15, "have their last best chance to choose a path toward productive and fulfilled lives" (Carnegie Council, 1989, p. 20). Many students live in neighborhoods where they are afraid to walk to school. Many students are tempted or pressured to experiment with drugs and alcohol at a young age. Without sound thinking strategies, they are surrounded by equally confused peers, who use destructive means to fulfill a need for power and importance. Research demonstrates that without instruction, the patterns of thinking developed during childhood will not change in adulthood (Eichhorn, 1989).

Furthermore, students in North America do not perform as well on measures of higher level thinking as students in other countries (Kutscher, 1989). We contend that if our students are to continue to rise to contemporary international concerns, we must begin to teach them how to (a) use thinking strategies, (b) employ fair-minded flexibility in groups, (c) create ideas cooperatively, (d) encourage multiple options, and (e) select among equally attractive alternatives. To help students develop these abilities, we need to devote more time during instruction to the development of critical thinking about print materials, which is the goal of programs for teaching thinking. As Beck (1989) stated:

> Reading and language arts are the perfect vehicle for developing higher-order thinking because literature—perhaps more than any other source of information—provides powerful models of problem-solving processes. It is full of characters who engage in effective and ineffective attempts at solving problems, who use incisive or fuzzy reasoning, and who rely on adequate or inadequate evidence. . . . What is needed is to move the activities that involve higher-order thinking into the mainstream of instruction. (pp. 680, 682)

In addition, educators realize that language abilities and thinking competencies shape each other, and that both are of equal intensity in fostering learning. For example, through the power of academic development, the quantity and quality of student thought improve. Likewise, by improving thinking strategies, the transitory thoughts that occur in the process of reading, writing, and interacting with others can be transformed into lasting principles. These transformations occur when new ideas enter the mind as cognitive entries, and readers use cognitive strategies to bond these ideas with previously collected categories of thought. In turn, combinations of categorical thought fostered by strategic processes are stored as dense cognitive structures (schema), those collections of learning, experiences, emotions, and values one has about a topic. Subsequently, the nerve endings, or dendrites, in schema expand in length and breadth as students discuss and learn new thinking strategies and concepts. This depth and breadth force more and more dendrites to intertwine, increasing students' reflection and thoughtfulness (Rosenblatt, 1978; Smith, 1978). As students learn the thinking strategies, they will regularly and continuously develop concept attainment and strengthen or modify the understandings that already exist.

The popularity of television and the increasingly busy pace of contemporary society has also greatly decreased the oral interaction between children and adults. Prior to the 20th century, after-school apprenticeships performed the role of developing strategic processes and higher level thinking abilities. Every day children worked with adults. They observed and questioned mentors about work skills and world events. In addition, students enjoyed the stories their parents and grandparents told and often read in common rooms at the end of the day. Elders would explain the strategies and thinking processes they used in their lives. Through the instruction, however, teachers can create these thinking and communication opportunities for students.

Knowledge in a contemporary society is also increasing at a rate of more than 15% per year. Many jobs that students will hold in the 21st century have not yet been invented. Today's required technological competencies are only 10% of what present kindergarten students will need when they become adults (Duffy, 1992). Contemporary literacy requires that students independently validate spoken and written statements and solve problems using incomplete data. They must also discern thought patterns among disparate sources of information. Therefore, although much of the content and informational instruction students receive will become obsolete by the time they become adults, the thinking competencies that teachers assist them to develop today will retain their value.

Furthermore, lessons that teach higher level thought promote students' creativity. Creativity will not develop to its fullest extent without instruction. In a longitudinal study of kindergarten students, 84% ranked high in aptitude for creative thinking. By the end of second grade, without instruction only 10% sustained even a significant level of inventive capacity (Block, 1993a). Without assistance, most students will stop their exploratory thinking processes when they state their first convergent answer to a teacher's question. Through their school experiences, learners will come to erroneously accept that *there is only one right answer, and that it is very easy to be wrong.*

Creativity instruction enhances students' abilities to resolve conflicts and solve complex problems. Unless teachers assist students to recognize the complexities and relationships between seemingly disparate ideas, forces outside of school will suggest that answers to problems are simple, and that problems do not demand deep, creative reflection. On television, students see that "all you need is one grand shoot-out at the O.K. Corral at high noon and all this complex fuss that they have watched for three hours will be over" (Stuart & Graves, 1987, p. 23). In the same way, all problems in their lives will be instantly and simply solved. Developing students' creativity strengthens qualities that lead to student success outside of school. Specifically, research indicates that creative people maintain high standards, accept confusing uncertainties, and view the higher risks of failure as part of a process for great accomplishments. Such creative and reflective individuals approach what they perceive to be important aspects of their work with considerably more intensity than students who use fewer creative critical thinking strategies. Creative people also exhibit an internalized license to challenge the conventional and to express their own insights frequently and fervently (Stuart & Graves, 1987).

RESEARCH: LESSONS THAT TEACH THINKING

Research on a Teaching Thinking program was carried out by the authors. A rigorous Teaching Thinking program was developed using the underlying premises that higher level thinking can be taught. The theoretical constructs used to develop content area lessons with students, along with directions and descriptions for teaching thinking were developed, including the four parts of each lesson for students' creative and critical thinking and learning. Teaching Thinking lessons were implemented in three studies by the researchers and their findings and conclusions are presented in this section.

Four premises underlie the notion that teaching thinking is feasible. First, research has demonstrated that if students use strategic processes consistently and reflectively as they read, they comprehend more. Second, students who have trouble comprehending have shown a need for new reading or thinking strategies before they can be successful readers because these students' thinking processes appear to be underdeveloped, leaving them without strategic knowledge to effectively and simultaneously decode and comprehend. As lessons in teaching thinking strengthen students' thinking processes, their learning problems are reduced.

Third, students who become confused about important concepts, inferences, and relationships in text appear to experience these difficulties because past experiences have not exposed them to the inductive or deductive reasoning patterns the author used to create that text. Learners do not understand the connections between pieces of information. However, students who learned the inductive and deductive thinking strategies in the program Teaching Thinking comprehended authors' thought patterns better. Finally, students can learn to solve their own decoding and comprehension problems independently if they use a variety of thinking and problem-solving processes.

Description of Lessons for Higher Level Thought

Each lesson for teaching thinking is divided into four parts. Part 1 provides an introduction to a strategy. Teachers begin by describing the strategy to students, the goals for the day's work, methods students will use to apply the strategy, and ways to know that they have learned to use the strategy effectively. Teachers may dispel misconceptions students may hold about a particular strategy, eliminate their inaccurate prior knowledge, and discuss students' successful or unsuccessful attempts to think strategically in the past as part of this discussion. Immediately following this introduction, students are given a thinking guide, a one-page diagram of the a strategic process. Thinking guides are designed to make the information vivid and memorable for students.

Prior to the first use of a strategy, several examples are provided so students can use the strategy during the subsequent study. In essence, Part 1 contains the following components that can be instructed in one class period:

- a statement of student objectives
- a listing of the reading and language competencies addressed in the lesson
- an explanation and model of the thinking strategy
- an opportunity for students to view and use a one-page graphic depiction of the strategy for thinking
- an activity in which students use the thinking guide while reading from a selection
- a list of assessment options

Part 2 of the lesson enables students to choose an activity in which they can employ the thinking strategy as they read. Such choices enable students to regulate the depth of their thinking while they read and establish their own purposes for reading. When students select a strategy and goal before reading, their lessons simulate the means for thinking and reading in real-world situations. This simulation makes transfer of instruction easier (J. Mangieri, personal communication, August 30, 1991). Part 2 begins when students engage in a reading activity of their choice that can be completed alone, with a friend, or in a small group. Students place their thinking guides on their desks beside the material they choose to read, allowing for easy reference, reflection, and application of the strategy. After completing their reading, students can self-assess or the teacher can evaluate how much students have learned through several options, such as (a) answering the question, "What have I learned from this lesson that I will use away from school?"; (b) generating and reporting new uses of the strategy; (c) discussing what they have learned with a peer and preparing a report of their joint work; and (d) presenting a summary to the class.

Part 2 can be completed more rapidly by increasing the time students read their content selection. Students can set their own objectives, select their reading material, and begin reading and applying the strategy introduced on the previous day in Part 1 of the lesson. Students complete their readings and plan their self-assessments and demonstrations based on what they have learned. Finally, students write about their work and/or perform their demonstrations.

In essence, Part 2 of each lesson contains:

- A review of the thinking guide and description of literature that students may wish to consider as they use the strategy
- Student selections from several activities or designs of their own in which they apply the strategy to an area of their interest (activities provide opportunities for students to elect to work alone, with a friend, in a small group, or with the teacher)
- Student self-assessments and teacher assessments in which several evaluation options are suggested.

Part 3 of each lesson for thinking enables students to use the strategy across several curriculum areas. Activities are designed for all areas of the curriculum, including fine arts, physical education, social studies, history, mathematics, and science. Part 3 is designed to build students' automaticity. The goal is for students to use thinking strategies without being prompted.

Part 4 of the lesson for teaching thinking facilitates the ability to meet individual students' needs and gives students extended opportunities to apply the strategy to their lives. Activities in this part of the lesson are designed to provide opportunities in the following ways:

- Less able readers may elect to meet with their teacher
- Gifted readers learn advanced applications of the strategy
- Students of multicultural backgrounds interpret their understandings through avenues that reflect their respective cultures
- Individual students develop reflectivity as they work alone to apply the strategy to a personal incidence in their lives
- Groups of students develop a deeper understanding of themselves and others as they use the strategy to solve difficult situations that frequently occur in their lives. The goal in Part 4 is to provide new methods of learning the strategy and to extend the strategy to new situations in life situations.

There are eight domains of thinking strategies that are amenable to instruction (Baron & Sternberg, 1987; Beyer, 1987; Collins & Mangieri, 1992; DeBono, 1970). These strategies affect the quality of students' reading and thinking abilities. Two strategies from each of Domains 1-6 and three strategies from Domains 7 and 8 were included in our study (see Table 13.1 later in chapter).

The definition and description of each domain included in these lessons are as follows:

Domain 1: basic cognitive operations, including the ability to clarify ideas, examine relationships, see errors, summarize, and remember.

Domain 2: thinking processes that call on more than one mental operation, including inferencing, interpreting, thinking like experts, and making multiple comparisons. In Domain 2, concepts, literal elaborations, and connections are formed.

Domain 3: decision-making abilities with which one must select from competing alternatives that may or may not be obvious to the decision maker, using decision-making tools, and recognizing critical points when making a decision to eliminate problems before beginning.

Domain 4: ability to solve problems, including resolving perplexing situations, assessing the quality of ideas, eliminating biases, establishing criteria, and judging the credibility of sources.

Domain 5: metacognitive thinking, involving control of self; assessing one's current knowledge relative of individual tasks; and identifying barriers that interfere with one's talents, projects, and goals.

Domain 6: creative and innovative thinking, includes shifting frames of reference and using models, metaphors, substitutions, humor, risk taking, and curiosity, as well as forecasting, to create new thoughts and products.

Domain 7: thinking effectively in groups, understanding the nature and quality of thinking in a group setting, exercising power/authority/influence appropriately, using talents interactively, and developing analytical listening abilities.

Domain 8: ability to think effectively when alone, set goals, establish redirection, take action, and elicit self-motivation to increase productivity.

Table 13.1. Thinking Domains Amenable to Instruction.

Domain 1: Basic thinking skills

Domain 2: Fundamental thinking processes

Domain 3: Decision-making tools

Domain 4: Problem-solving strategies

Domain 5: Metacognitive strategies

Domain 6: Creative and innovative thinking process

Domain 7: Thinking effectively when working in groups

Domain 8: Thinking effectively when working alone

EFFECTS OF TEACHING THINKING ON STUDENT'S COMPREHENSION AND THINKING DEVELOPMENT

Research Bases, Data Analysis, Findings, and Conclusions

> My problems seem less complicated now that I know problem-solving techniques. I did not expect to list my problems on paper and figure out an answer, but I do. Because of you [the reading teacher], I make decisions now instead of beating around the bush. Thank you very much! Thank you for teaching me how to think. (Jason, a seventh-grader's unsolicited note to a teacher using Teaching Thinking)

The purpose of this section is to report data from studies of the effects of *Teaching Thinking*. We began our research with four premises. First, if teaching thinking can assist students to think consistently and reflectively as they read, they will improve their comprehension and use more information from printed sources in their daily lives. Second, students who have trouble comprehending may need more than improved schema and decoding competencies. In *Teaching Thinking*, the program develops a capacity to strengthen thinking processes and helps reduce learning difficulties. Third, when students become confused about important concepts, inferences, and relationships in reading, their repertoire of thinking abilities may be so limited that they have never encountered (nor can they replicate) an author's reasoning and problem-solving processes. Because *Teaching Thinking* expands students' repertoires, they should become less confused. Fourth, if we want students to address their decoding and comprehension problems independently, we need to provide extensive opportunities for them to practice problem solving and to self-select from a repertoire of thinking guides. To develop these guidelines we reviewed taxonomies and descriptions of thinking competencies. Thinking abilities that are amenable to instruction were categorized into eight dimensions (Baron & Sternberg, 1987; Beyer, 1987; Collins, 1989b, 1990b; DeBono, 1970; Marzano, Jones, & Brandt, 1988; R. Paul, 1990).

Several research studies involving Teaching Thinking have been completed by the authors. The first took place from 1989-1990, the second from January-April 1990, and the third began in 1991 and continues to the present.

The first study field-tested lesson formats in kindergarten through 11th-grade classrooms. These field tests involved 32 teachers in nine schools and 643 Anglo, African-American, and Latino students. Several important findings from this study guided construction of the present lesson plan format. First, we asked students what skills they felt they needed in order to think better. The attributes most frequently expressed were stimulation of intellect through cognitive challenges, advanced information on topics, positive thinking models and instruction, decision-making tools, and a classroom environment that offered autonomy (Collins, 1990b).

The students in the field test described our best lessons as those that included student self-selection of reading material; contained dense but sequential information; allowed high-level, small-group discussions; and incorporated individual goal-setting activities and personal assessments that pushed them to exceed their past performances. Students also reported the best teachers praised them specifically for their thinking and modeled, through think-alouds, the "hard-won" thinking habits they had developed. They believed these lessons gave them the direction, autonomy, and courage to think through their own problems (Collins, 1989a).

When the lessons that resulted from our first study were incorporated into the curriculum in our second study, experimental participants significantly outperformed untrained participants in many ways. First, experimental participants scored significantly higher on the posttest for reading comprehension (RCOMP) of the Iowa Test of Basic Skills, $F = 91.49$, $p < .001$. The experimental group also scored significantly higher than the control group on vocabulary (VOCAB), and total battery scores (TOTAL), $F = 42.47$, $p < .001$, and $F = 12.65$, $p > .001$, respectively (see Table 13.2).

Another effect of teaching thinking was demonstrated in postexperimental writing samples. Without being told that their responses were a part of a study, participants were asked to "Describe some important things you learned this year." Experimental participants used all domains of thinking in their writing; control participants used only the lowest two domains. A statistically significant association existed between thought categories used in writing and experimental control groups ($F = 258.52$, $p < .0001$). The following are the categorizations we used for this analysis:

Table 13.2. Middle School Students' Mean Scores and Standard Deviations on the Iowa Test of Basic Skills After Lessons in Eight Domains of Thinking Skills.

	Subscales of the ITBS			
Student Group	RCOMP	VOCAB	LANGTOT[a]	Total
Control	27.52	15.71	75.23	255.91
	(8.1)	(7.3)	(24.0)	(65.24)
Experimental	51.08*	29.62*	81.39	328.23*
	(4.8)	(3.3)	(14.0)	(42.90)

[a]Tests of spelling, capitalization, punctuation, and usage.
*$p < .001$.

Noting facts
Content elaborations
Personal elaborations
Evaluative thinking
Metacognition
Expressing a lack of understanding
Asking questions
Confirming beliefs
Transferring content learned
Expressing attitudes/values about content learned
Expressing attitudes about instruction received
Changing classroom practices
Evaluating one's own thinking
Drawing analogies and making abstract comparisons

To analyze whether students transferred their reasoning skills to life, all subjects were asked to respond to the question, "Have you used anything you learned at school this month to help you with problems outside of school?" While 0% of the control participants answered affirmatively, 92% of the experimental group used their new thinking tools outside of school and related specific incidents:

When I get home the first thing I do is plan or sketch out the next day so that I will be prepared.

My older brother lost his license and I helped him find it by asking him what he was doing the last time he saw it and together we used backward reasoning.

I recently used the backward reasoning accomplished that day. I organize my things to do that day better.

I used backward reasoning when I lost a grooming brush at the stables. Prediction skills I've been using, and I've been getting into less trouble.

Because of my reading teacher, I make decisions now instead of beating around the bush.

I feel more confident to ask someone something in a strange environment without feeling like a nerd.

The fact that experimental participants self-selected all levels of thought is educationally significant. The differences in slopes between groups was also statistically significant (see Figure 13.1).

In the third measure of this study, the self-esteem scores of the experimental subjects in social competence, behavior in groups, appearance, and physical competence (as measured by the Harter Self-Perception Profile for Children, 1985) were compared to self-esteem scores in control groups. Although there were no significant differences between groups on pretest measures, experimental subjects scored significantly above control subjects on posttests of their self-perception of social competence, behavior in groups, appearance, and physical competence (Block, 1993b).

Finally, five raters viewed tapes of the last lesson taught in experimental and control classes. All raters ranked subjects in experimental classes as better thinkers than subjects in control classes. These raters also identified 12 differences between interactions that occurred in experimental versus control groups. For example, experimental subjects:

- did not interrupt the person talking
- asked each other questions
- made fewer random comments during discussion
- built on each others' answers
- volunteered ideas, evidence, and rationale to help classmates' thinking
- gave each other sufficient time to answer questions
- were more interested in the class and their tasks until the end of the period
- used terms to describe their thinking
- used jargon less frequently
- had lower noise levels
- had teachers who engaged a greater number of students in discussions.

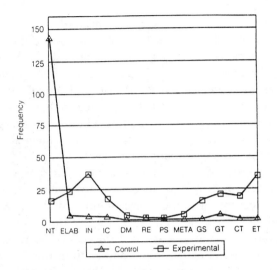

Figure 13.1. Dimensions of thinking reflected in free recall

These very positive results emanated after only 33 days of instruction in only one curriculum area. Their success would justify incorporating thinking intervention lessons into the curriculum.

The third study began in September 1991 and has continued for five years. This study involves 1,704 participants.

In this study, after 11 weeks of instruction with teaching thinking, we assessed experimental participants' ability to generate ideas and to think with reflectivity. Experimental participants significantly increased their ability to generate plausible solutions to problems. (For example, six ideas in a 7-minute period were gathered in four-member groups prior to instruction, and 15 ideas per group were generated following instruction.) Likewise, experimental participants significantly increased their reflectivity. The test of reflectivity was to read a first-person narrative in which the narrator was identified only as "I."

Students were to determine the identity of the narrator using one to six clues. On the pretest, 88% of the experimental and control participants could not identify the narrator. These participants' reflection time (time from point of beginning to read until selection of narrator) was 1-minute and 14-seconds. Of the 12% who eventually identified the narrator, all made at least one inaccurate identity within the same 1-minute and 14-second reflection time. On the posttest, 96% of the experimental participants identified the narrator of a first-person narrative (with Forms A and B being counterbalanced in pretesting and posttesting). The participants identified this narrator on their first attempt and increased their reflective time. They averaged 3 minutes and 46 seconds before stating an answer.

In the present study, we have also analyzed data concerning 433 middle school students' abilities to solve problems, think critically, and generate alternatives using an assessment instrument designed by Irving Sigel (1996). Students' problem-solving abilities were analyzed by three criteria: number of thinking strategies stated, precision of thought in statements made, and number of alternative solutions stated. A significant effect was found between groups concerning the number of thinking strategies used to solve a problem ($t = -11.15$, $p < .0001$). The experimental groups also included significantly more thinking strategies to solve the problem than control subjects ($M = 2$, $SD = 1.40$ for experimental and $M = .5$, $SD = .69$ for control subjects). Similarly, a significant effect was found between groups concerning the precision of thought and number of alternative solutions cited ($x_2 = 14.61$, $df = 2$, $p < .001$; and $t = -7.69$, $p < .0001$, respectively).

The ability to reason was assessed through comparison of student answers to two questions of reasoning ability from the California State Department of Education Statewide Assessment Test. A significant relationship was found between groups and their selection of the most valid reason for a stated judgment ($x_2 = 361.98$, $df = 4$, $p < .0001$). Experimental participants significantly outscored the control group.

SUMMARY AND CONCLUSION

Through our studies we are more convinced that thinking abilities can be increased, and that teaching thinking lessons are a valuable section of the curriculum in which they are developed. Comprehension abilities increase through *Teaching Thinking* lessons. We also know that teacher direction and student selection interact to expand thinking. We have evidence that teacher scaffolding and thinking guides provide the support and opportunities for increased student thinking and positive self-esteem. Moreover, data were produced to support the hypotheses that teaching thinking develops reasoning abilities, reflectivity, and problem-solving skills. Two types of thinking/reading objectives interact to produce greater gains than instruction to build one at a time. Furthermore, activities that purposely integrate reading/thinking objectives with listening, writing, and speaking have a positive effect on thinking/reading development. Authentic instruction, as we have described it in this study, enhances students' reasoning and problem-solving abilities. As Sternberg (1985) stated:

> Nature enjoys playing an occasional trick on humans, and one of her favorite tricks is to make an important discovery or principle too simple to be recognized as important. However, a growing body of educational research seems to have caught nature at this game. It suggests that one

of the most important lessons teachers can impart to students is simple: "Be extremely thorough and careful in your thinking." For years we urged students not to count on their fingers, not to move their lips when they read, and to try to read faster. Research has now shown that there are engineers who count on their fingers, lawyers who move their lips while reading, and literary figures like William Buckley who admit they read "painfully slowly." What we have not done is stressed emphatically to students that the core of academic success is systematic, accurate thought. Newton modestly observed: "If I have succeeded in my inquiries more than others, I owe it less to any superior strength of mind, than to a habit of patient thinking." (p. 310).

Although we are unable to predict the problems our youth will face in the future, we have learned that teaching young adolescents to think increases their thinking repertoires, helps them gain more control in their lives, and enables them to meet new challenges more successfully. We encourage teachers to take a first step to better prepare our students for the cognitive demands in their future.

REFERENCES

Baron, J., & Sternberg, R. (1987). *Teaching thinking skills: Theory and practice.* New York: Freeman.

Beck, I. (1989). Reading and reasoning. *The Reading Teacher, 42*(9), 676-684.

Beyer, B. (1987). *Practical strategies for the teaching of thinking.* Boston: Allyn & Bacon.

Block, C. (1993a, April). *Effects of strategy instruction upon students of above average, average, and below average reading achievement.* Paper presented at the annual meeting of the American Research Association, Atlanta, GA.

Block, C. (1993b, November). Strategic instruction in a literature-rich classroom. *Elementary School Journal,* pp. 135-153.

Carnegie Council on Adolescent Development. (1989). *Turning points: Preparing American youth for the twenty-first century.* New York: Carnegie Foundation.

Collins, C. (1989a). Administrators hold the key to thinking development. *REACH, 3,* 139-147.

Collins, C. (1989b, December). *A new approach to middle school reading: Expanded thinking.* Paper presented at the annual conference of the National Reading Conference, Austin, TX.

Collins, C. (1990). *Reasoning through reading: Vignettes that produce engagement.* Paper presented at the annual conference of the International Reading Association, Atlanta, GA.

Collins, C., & Mangieri, J. N. (1992). *Teaching thinking: An agenda for the twenty-first century.* Hillsdale, NJ: Erlbaum.

DeBono, E. (1970). *Lateral thinking.* New York: Harper & Row.

Duffy, J. (1992). Business partnerships for a thinking populace. In C. Collins & J. Mangieri (Eds.), *Teaching thinking: An agenda for the twenty-first century* (pp. 139-152). Hillsdale, NJ: Erlbaum.

Eichhorn, D. (1989). *The middle school.* New York: The Center for Applied Research in Education.

Gough, P. (1987). An interview with William Glaser. *Phi Delta Kappan, 69*(7), 593-607.

Harter Self-Perception Profile for Children. (1985). Denver: Colorado Department of Education..

Kutscher, R. E. (1989). Projections, summary and emerging issues. *Monthly Labor Review, 112*(11), 66-74.

Mangieri, J. (1991). *Personal communication.* Fort Worth, TX: Texas Christian University.

Marzano, R., Jones, B., & Brandt, R. (1988). *Dimensions of thinking.* Alexandria, VA: Association for Supervision and Curriculum.

Paul, R. (1990). *Critical thinking: What every person needs to survive in a rapidly changing world.* Rothmert Park, CA: Sonoma State University.

Paul, W. (1989). *How to study in college.* Boston: Houghton Mifflin.

Piaget, J. (1963). *The origins of intelligence in children.* New York: W. W. Norton and Co.

Porter, A., & Brophy, J. (1988). Synthesis of research on good teaching. *Educational Leadership, 45*(8), 74-85.

Rosenblatt, L. M. (1978). *The reader, the text and the poem.* Carbondale: Southern Illinois University Press.

Sigel, I. (1996) *Problem-solving essay assessment test.* Sacramento, CA: State Department of Education.

Smith, F. (1978). *Understanding reading.* New York: Holt, Rinehart, & Winston.

Sternberg, R. (1985). *Beyond IQ.* New York: Cambridge University Press.

Stuart, V., & Graves, D. (1987). *How to teach writing.* Urbana, IL: National Council of Teachers of English.

14 USING MULTIPLE INTELLIGENCES FOR STUDENTS AND FACULTY SUCCESS

Thomas R. Hoerr

New City School

WINNERS AND LOSERS IN SCHOOL

Children come to school at age 5, full of enthusiasm, eager to learn, and feeling good about themselves. Kindergarten is a world of wonder and fun. Children exhibit many talents, love their teachers, and try to please them. However, shortly, for many kids, that changes. All too often, instead of being a place where students grow and find success, schools become places of frustration and failure.

Sometimes this happens in first grade. Occasionally it happens sooner; frequently it occurs later. Children begin to fail and come to see, rightly, school as a place where they do not succeed. They pull back, focusing their energies in areas in which success is possible for them, perhaps on the athletic field or hanging around with their peer group. Before they reach the 12th grade, vast percentages of students drop out of school. Many more kids withdraw psychologically; they become class clowns or reluctant learners. To be fair, there are a myriad of reasons for this kind of failure, not all attributable to schools. Some children come from homes that are unable to provide the kind of support to help kids learn best. Children may be under-

245

nourished or in poor health. In some neighborhoods, physical safety and security is a factor. Although these kinds of conditions are outside the purview of educators, it would be remiss not to note them.

Yet for all kids, those who come from difficult home situations as well as those who come from "good" environments, there is another problem. All too often curriculum, instruction, and assessment fail to take into consideration students' talents and needs. Students who read and write well are successful in school, but those with strengths in other areas are not as fortunate. As a result, some kids find school fun, exciting, and learn well; too many do not. Surely not every child will be an above-average student, and certainly there are some basic understandings and skills that all children must learn. That said, our approach to curriculum, instruction, and assessment creates too many educational losers, students who do not succeed in school.

THE THEORY OF MULTIPLE INTELLIGENCES (MI)

The theory of Multiple Intelligences (MI) offers a different way to look at student achievement and, as a result, curriculum and instruction. As we have used MI at the New City School, it is more than a theory of education. For us, MI is an educational philosophy that says all kids can learn. As educators, the implications are clear: Each child has a set of unique strengths, and our job is to identify and nurture these strengths, to use them to help each child learn.

Howard Gardner first described the theory of Multiple Intelligences in his 1983 book, *Frames of Mind*. Working with patients who had experienced brain damage, Gardner noticed that the particular location of the injury had an effect on which specific abilities and capacities were lost. Depending on where in their brain the injury occurred, patients might lose the ability to recall words, to sing, or even to recognize certain pictures; again, depending on where the injury occurred, other abilities remained intact. Also studying idiot savants and prodigies, Gardner focused on determining what constitutes an intelligence. The more he looked at the nature of intelligence, the more convinced he was that the traditional definitions and measures fell far short of capturing all the intelligence we might possess. Gardner developed a list of criteria to use in determining whether an area of talent qualified as an intelligence (Table 14.1).

Using these criteria, Gardner came to view intelligence not as a single entity, but as an array of potentials. Defining *intelligence* as the ability to solve a problem or fashion a product that is valued in at least one culture, he identified seven different intelligences. At the time, he noted that if there

Table 14.1. Gardner's Criteria for Intelligence.

1. Potential isolation by brain damage
2. Existence of idiot savants, prodigies, and other exceptional individuals
3. An identifiable core set of operations, basic kinds of information-processing operations, or mechanisms that deal with one specific kind of input
4. A distinctive developmental history, along with a definite set of "end-state" performances
5. An evolutionary history and evolutionary plausibility
6. Support from experimental and psychological tasks
7. Support from psychometric findings
8. Susceptibility to encoding from a symbol system

are seven intelligences, there probably are more. (Subsequently, Gardner, 1995, tentatively identified an eighth intelligence, the "naturalist," "an individual who is able readily to recognize flora and fauna, to make other consequential distinctions in the natural world, and to use this ability productively" [p. 206].) The seven intelligences are shown in Table 14.2.

Defining intelligence as "the ability to solve a problem or fashion a product that is valued in at least one culture" is profound in two ways. First, of course, is Gardner's pluralization of the construct of intelligence. Representing intelligence as something more than an unidimensional "g factor" changes how we think about being smart. Fashioning a product greatly expands the kinds of behaviors that indicate intelligence. Rather than defining and identifying intelligence through performance on multiple-choice tests or written essays, as educators have done for decades, this new definition of intelligence includes such different acts as creating a work of art (visual, musical, or bodily-kinesthetic), providing the leadership that turns a group of individuals into a team, or showing insight into understanding oneself.

Second, the phrase, "that is valued in at least one culture," points out both the culture-specificity and pragmatic nature of intelligence. Abilities are not valued the same in all cultures and at all times; Gardner points out that the spatial intelligence of a South Seas islander often proved the difference between life and death while navigating at night, using only the stars to guide the way home. Today that spatial intelligence, thanks to maps and cellular telephones, is far less valuable in our society. Although

Table 14.2. Gardner's Multiple Intelligences.

Linguistic	Sensitivity to the meaning and order of words
Logical-mathematical	The ability to handle chains of reasoning and to recognize patterns and order
Musical	Sensitivity to pitch, melody, rhythm, and tone
Bodily-kinesthetic	The ability to use the body skillfully and handle objects adroitly
Spatial	The ability to perceive the world accurately and to recreate or transform aspects of that world
Interpersonal	The ability to understand people and relationships
Intrapersonal	Access to one's emotional life as a means to understanding oneself and others

the basis of this kind of spatial intelligence has not changed, how our society values it has diminished. Similarly, other than for a relatively few highly paid professional athletes, bodily-kinesthetic intelligence is not as important as it was centuries ago when survival depended on one's ability to hunt, fish, or physically defend oneself from enemies. The fact that it is intelligence has not changed; what has changed is society's valuing of it.

The linguistic and logical-mathematical intelligences are valued in our Western culture today, not because they are inherently more valuable than the other intelligences, but because educators have come to rely on them in their curriculum design, instruction, and assessment. In large part this is because educators have, rather naively, equated the behaviors that cause success in school to be the same as those that cause success in life. Indeed, although the scholastic skills of reading, writing, and calculating are important, they are only the beginning of what is necessary to succeed in life. Yet they are the intelligences around which most curriculum and instruction are designed.

Gardner's definition breaks away from the intelligence quotient (IQ) dominated model of intelligence that we have used for so long. Conceived by Alfred Binet near the turn of the century in Paris, the concept of IQ was developed in order to identify students who were not likely to do well in school. Binet decided that "normal" would be those abilities that were held in common to 65% to 75% of the children, and he designed tests to yield a distribution that would support his model. However, as James Fallows (1988) said in *More Like Us*, there is no reason to assume that intelligence is distributed according to this pattern any more than is hair color. Yet an entire psychometric industry has evolved around creating and supporting aptitude and achievement tests that yield bell-shaped results. Educators use scores on these tests to determine student placement and progress.

Relying on the traditional definition of academic success, linguistically and logically mathematically based, is not without its cost. As noted earlier, many children have strengths other than linguistic and logical-mathematical intelligences. Unless curriculum, instruction, and assessment are modified to give these children opportunities to capitalize on their talents, too often they wind up experiencing failure. This does not mean that reading, writing, and calculating are unimportant. No one can reasonably question their importance. People who cannot read, write, or calculate are at a decided disadvantage. Similarly, this does *not* mean that standardized tests are unimportant. Standardized tests remain education's "gatekeepers," and it is important that students are able to perform well on them.

However, more and more evidence points to the fact that traditional scholastic performances, whether in the classroom or on standardized tests, only capture a portion of what determines success in the real world. Writing in the September 10, 1995 *New York Times,* Daniel Goleman says:

> A recent study done at Bell Laboratories . . . found that the most valued and productive engineers—at least among electrical engineers working in teams of up to 150 people—were not those with the highest IQs, the highest academic credentials or the best scores on achievement tests.
>
> Instead, the stars were those whose congeniality put them at the heart of the informal communications networks that would spring up during times of crisis or innovation.
>
> When these likeable engineers hit a snag and E-mailed for help, they got an answer instantly; when others less gifted in interpersonal realms sent similar messages, they sometimes waited days or weeks for a reply. The standouts excelled in rapport, empathy, cooperation, persuasion, and the ability to build consensus among people.
>
> To predict the success of a financial analyst or geophysicist, IQ is still crucial. But within a pool of high-IQ people, those with high emotional intelligence will have an extra competitive edge.

Goleman's notion of "emotional intelligence" is comparable to Gardner's personal intelligences. It includes the ability to read one's own feelings, to control one's own impulses and anger, to calm oneself down, and to maintain resolve and hope in the face of setbacks. Goleman's work supports Gardner's theory that the ability to understand others and to understand oneself are kinds of intelligences.

THE NEW CITY SCHOOL APPROACH

Because Gardner's model of MI is a theory of intelligence, not an educational theory, there is no single "right" way to go about implementing it. This means that the approaches to MI are as varied as are the educational settings in which they are used. MI is brought to life differently in the Fuller School in Gloucester, MA than it is in the Key School in Indianapolis, IN. And the New City School implementation in St. Louis, MO is different still. All these approaches should share a respect for individual differences and an integration of intelligences throughout the day, but other than that, there may be few strategies and procedures that they have in common. How MI is used to help kids learn reflects the institutional values and norms of each setting. This means it is up to each teacher—or, preferably, faculty—to determine how to approach MI in a way that supports their school's unique culture.

History

We first became involved in studying MI after I read *Frames Of Mind* (Gardner, 1983). Gardner's theory seemed to reinforce the values of our school, so I invited faculty members to meet with me after school and over the summer to read and discuss the book, consciously seeking to determine whether it was applicable to the New City School. Almost one third of our faculty volunteered to join what was called the Talent Committee. Because we believe in experiential learning, teachers worked as teams, presenting the content of a chapter to the rest of us so that we could learn by actually using the intelligences being studied. As a result, the two teachers who taught the bodily-kinesthetic chapter did so with the aid of small- and large-motor games and activities. Similarly, the teachers who introduced us to spatial intelligence used puzzles, mazes, and graphics.

   Aside from helping us learn about the seven intelligences, this approach helped us learn about ourselves and also made the relevance of MI very clear to us. As we worked through understanding by using the various intelligences, some of us found using a particular intelligence liberating and exciting, whereas others became frustrated from the same experiences. Which of us was "smart" and which of us was "dumb" varied, in large part, by which intelligence was being used to help us learn. The message to us was powerful: Our students would certainly have the same reactions, the same degrees of success or failure, depending upon the intelligences being used in their classrooms.

   As we worked through Gardner's book, we created a list with three columns: things we were already doing that supported MI, things we would like to do to bring MI more into our school and classrooms, and things we would like to do to bring MI more into our school and classrooms if we had money. We felt that this was a good way to begin looking at the applicability of MI to our school. It enabled us to focus on where and how MI might help our kids, recognizing budgetary limitations; yet it also allowed us to cite the areas in which we were already addressing different intelligences. (Indeed, many good teachers are already bringing different intelligences into their classrooms, without even having knowledge of MI. Although it is necessary to focus on where you want to go and how you want to change, it is also important to identify those areas in which you are already successful.)

New City has always been a school that valued the arts and put a strong emphasis on affective development. We have always worked at helping our students develop their strengths and engage in joyful learning experiences. As a result, seeing how MI could help us help our students was easy. Structuring instruction through an MI lens gave us a tool to fashion curriculum in a way that supported our values.

Diversity

Another reason why we pursued MI was that it supported our thrust for respecting and appreciating student diversity. Racial and economic diversity are integral to New City's success. We believe that children learn best when they learn with students who are both similar to, and different from, themselves. We incorporate a respect for and knowledge of multicultural and diversity issues throughout our curriculum. At New City, for example, we do not celebrate "Black History Month"; doing so would imply that we ignore Black history the remaining 11 months of the year. The contributions and perspectives of all people need to be recognized and honored throughout the year. A faculty Diversity Committee works on helping teachers incorporate diversity and multiculturalism into the curriculum. As we talked about MI, it became obvious that this was another way to look at the diversity within our student population. Our students vary by race, ethnic group, and socioeconomic background, but they also vary by the intelligences with which they are most likely to succeed and those in which they are the weakest. Looking at MI through a diversity lens allowed us to help our students see still another way in which they are different and similar, to reinforce the belief that what matters most is who one is.

Curriculum and Instruction

As noted earlier, an MI orientation does not mean that traditional learning outcomes are unimportant. Using MI means that curriculum and instruction are fashioned so that children can use different intelligences in learning whatever curriculum is to be covered. Teachers who bring MI to their classrooms think about how curriculum will be delivered and how instruction will take place in a different way than those who teach within the traditional intelligences. Rather than focusing planning solely on what is to be covered, planning with an MI approach includes recognizing the students' different intelligences and finding ways to let them use their strengths to learn.

MI is typically brought into the classroom either through integrating the intelligences into lessons or units, or by using centers and letting students choose where they will put their efforts. (Students may also be required to cycle through each of the centers so that all intelligences are addressed.) At New City, both approaches are used, integrating MI and using centers. This enables all children to be exposed to all intelligences, yet also allows students to choose those areas in which they have the most interest and, possibly, the most potential.

Starting with the objectives of the lesson or goals of the unit, New City teachers refer to all the intelligences as they plan. They look for opportunities to use the "other" intelligences (other than linguistic or logical-mathematical) to present information with their students. They also look for ways for students to use the other intelligences to show what they have learned. As teachers work with MI, incorporating various intelligences and approaches to understanding in their curriculum and instruction, they become curriculum designers and evaluators. The focus becomes students' understanding and actually using the knowledge and skills that they have learned, not just giving it back to the teachers in the form in which they received it. This "genuine understanding" (described in Gardner, 1991) should be the goal of all educators. Some examples of how MI is brought into classrooms at New City School follow.

A teacher might give students different options, corresponding to the different intelligences, to learn their spelling words. Students could choose among memorizing them linguistically, learning them spatially through drawing pictures or making fancy decorations on the words or letters, or by using their fingers to drum letters or syllables, creating a "tune" with their musical intelligence. Others might use their bodily-kinesthetic intelligence to make letters in sand or salt, tracing the words on their desktop.

Teaching the concept of "cause and effect," a teacher determines the students' understanding by reading an unfamiliar story and stopping before the end. Students are asked to show their understanding of cause and effect by drawing a cartoon with several cells or by creating a brief dramatic presentation that explains what happened next in the story and why.

Venn diagrams, capitalizing on the logical-mathematical intelligence, can be used to help students report their understanding. Students can create a Venn diagram to look at characteristics of the protagonists in books that they have read and compare them to themselves and their classmates. Venn diagrams can also be used at the conclusion of units to determine understanding. For example, at the conclusion of a unit on the Revolutionary War, students might be given a set of terms (land, equality, voting, taxation with representation, food, royalty, freedom of religion) and asked to use a Venn diagram to classify whether these terms represent colonists' needs, wants, or values.

In a unit on the 50 states, a teacher might create a bulletin board with a variety of activities categorized under the seven intelligences. Students would complete all the activities, so that all their intelligences would be used. They would create a hand-clap jingle to recognize the spelling of state names; they would also work at this task through completion of a crossword puzzle. Students would work in teams, using their bodies to form the shapes of the 50 states, being photographed as they complete each state (with photos put in their student portfolios). They would illustrate a journal showing their imaginary journey through the states, make fact flash cards, and create computer games for other students to use in learning about the states. The activities are designed so that the students work both individually and in groups.

Teachers let students share their understanding of books they have read by creating a "T-shirt book report." There must be at least 10 sentences written on character, setting, and plot. The T-shirt design may include hand-drawn pictures, photos, pictures cut from magazines, or computer-generated art.

What these examples share is a realization that children have many different intelligences. Curriculum and instruction are modified so that students can learn through their strengths. The different approaches to learning do not indicate a lack of intellectual rigor; rather, they allow students to learn best through their different intelligences.

Assessment

Assessment drives curriculum; just as an MI approach broadens the instructional approaches that are used, so, too, it will expand assessment techniques that a teacher uses in the classroom. Rather than relying on short-answer, paper and pencil, exercises (which are primarily linguistic or logical-mathematical), teachers who use MI will need to find ways for students to use other intelligences in demonstrating their understanding. Again, this does not mean that students do not need to be able to write cogent paragraphs or calculate three-digit numbers; those skills are important. It means, though, that if knowing what students understand about a concept is our goal, then letting students use all their intelligences increases their ability to show that they understand.

"Intelligence fair" assessments (Krechevsky, Hoerr, & Gardner, 1994) should be used as much as possible. In these, students demonstrate their knowledge and understanding through the intelligence being tested, rather than filtering their comprehension by writing their answers linguistically. There are many ways, using different intelligences, by which a student could demonstrate an understanding of Native American cultures. Students could create dioramas, posters, chants, or dances: they could use graphs or keep journals to show their understanding of Native Americans. Limiting students to using their linguistic intelligence to show their understanding means, in effect, that students are being assessed as much—if not more—on how well they write. Similarly, students who are asked to show the evolution of Anne Frank's feelings during the time while she was hidden in the attic should have their entire repertoire of intelligences available to show their understanding, not just linguistic intelligence.

Demonstrating the understanding of complex concepts usually requires more than the use of just one intelligence. This is best done through the use of projects, exhibitions, and presentations. Working over time with peers to complete a project or offering an exhibition or presentation to an audience requires that students utilize several of their intelligences.

"What we measure is what we value" is a short-hand way of saying that if we value all the intelligences, this needs to be reflected in what we measure and what we share with our students' parents. In addition to our September Open Houses, we also have a Fall Specialists' Open House. This evening is devoted to the intelligences that are often given less attention at that regular open house: spatial, bodily-kinesthetic, and musical. Educators decry the attention given to standardized tests, but we often do nothing to help our students' parents understand that there are other, more valid, ways of looking at their children's progress. Although the attendance is not as large as the Specialists' Open House and the September back-to-school Open Houses, it is a successful night for all involved. We also have a Portfolio Night each spring. Parents and children are invited to school to review the contents of the children's portfolios. This is a very salient way of seeing the child's growth in all the intelligences.

Our report card is framed around the intelligences. Not only do we use titles such as "linguistic intelligence" and "bodily-kinesthetic intelligence," our entire first page is devoted to reporting on student progress in the personal intelligences. All too often progress in these intelligences is reported in a small box, on the last page (generally through the use of innocuous statements such as "works with best effort" and "gets along well with peers"). Because we believe that *who you are is more important than what you know,* we feel that we have a responsibility to begin parent–teacher conferences by discussing student growth in these areas. A copy of the first page is shown in Figure 14.1.

The Personal Intelligences

We give a great deal of attention to the personal intelligences because we believe that they are the most important intelligences. In any arena, people who excel do not do so because they read and write better than their peers. These people succeed because of their inter- and intrapersonal intelligences. Success with the personal intelligences, as Goleman (1995) points out in *Emotional Intelligence,* is the best predictor of success in life. It is important, then, that we help our students develop these intelligences.

We have our students work together in groups and as part of teams because they will be doing this as adults. It is important that students learn how to negotiate, how to compromise, how to play both the leader and follower roles. Being in the group, alone, is not sufficient for this kind of growth. It is important that students reflect on their experiences so that they can learn from them. Many times, after students have worked collaboratively, teachers will say, "Think for a moment about what you did that helped the effort. Were there ways in which you were productive? Were there things you did that weren't positive? What actions moved the group forward?" At the end of written tests teachers will sometimes allocate space for students to respond to "What did you do that helped you learn this information?" and "If you could prepare for this test again, what would you do differently?" Helping children reflect on their performance, gain intrapersonal intelligence, is the goal.

Similarly, some times, after working as part of a team, students are given a sheet to complete with the sentence stems shown in Table 14.3. These, and similar other efforts, help children reflect on their behavior, their role as part of the team. Helping our students gain self-knowledge, intrapersonal intelligence, is one of the more important things we can teach them. For if they truly understand themselves, know their strengths and weaknesses, they can make accommodations for what they do not do well and put themselves in a position to capitalize on the areas in which they are the strongest.

Communicating with Parents

Parents must understand what educators are doing and why they are doing it. Although this is always a good rule to follow, it is even more important

NEW CITY SCHOOL • 5209 Waterman Avenue • St. Louis, MO 63108

4th Grade PROGRESS REPORT

Name _____ Date_____
Attendance: Absent _____ _____ Tardy_____
Teachers:

Key: ED = EXCEEDING DEVELOPMENTAL
EXPECTATIONS
DA = DEVELOPING APPROPRIATELY
AC = AREA OF CONCERN
# = NEEDS ADDED ATTENTION

INTRAPERSONAL DEVELOPMENT
Can self-assess; understands and shares own feelings

Reporting Period: 1 2 3

I. CONFIDENCE
· Is comfortable taking a position different from the peer group
· Engages in appropriate risk-taking behaviors
· Is comfortable in both leader and follower roles
· Copes with frustrations and failures
· Demonstrates a positive and accurate self-concept

II. MOTIVATION
· Demonstrates internal motivation
· Is actively involved in the learning process
· Shows curiosity
· Shows tenacity
· Exhibits creativity

III. PROBLEM SOLVING
· Shows good judgment
· Asks for help when needed
· Can generate possible hypotheses and solutions
· Shows perseverance in solving problems
· Accepts and learns from feedback

IV. RESPONSIBILITY
· Accepts responsibility for own actions
· Accepts responsibility for materials and belongings
· Handles transitions and changes well
· Accepts limits in work and play situations
· Uses an appropriate sense of humor

V. EFFORT AND WORK HABITS
· Participates in activities and discussions...
· Works through assignments and activities carefully and thoroughly...........................
· Keeps notebook, desk, and locker/cubby organized...
· Completes homework assignments on time...
· Has age-appropriate attention span...
· Works independently...
· Follows written and oral directions...
· Listens attentively...
· Proofreads carefully...
· Uses time effectively...

INTERPERSONAL DEVELOPMENT
Can successfully interact with others

I. APPRECIATION FOR DIVERSITY
· Makes decisions based on appropriate information, rather than stereotypes
· Understands the perspectives of others, including those of other races and cultures
· Shows concern and empathy for others
· Respects the individuality of others

II. TEAMWORK
· Cooperates with peers and adults
· Works at conflict resolution
· Behaves responsibly in groups
· Demonstrates an ability to compromise
· Expresses feelings and gives feedback constructively and appropriately

O V E R

Figure 14.1. Page 1 of the New City Progress Report

Table 14.3. Reflection Stems.

1. Working with my group was . . . .
2. The role I played in this group activity was . . . .
3. Three ways that I contributed to my group were . . . .
4. A time that it was difficult for my group to work with me was . . . .
5. I found it difficult to work with my group when . . . .
6. If we could do it over again, I would . . . .
7. Other thoughts about the group and my role are . . . .

when educators are doing something that is unfamiliar to their students' parents, such as implementing MI. Because none of the students' parents will have gone to a school that addressed all the intelligences, classrooms that make good use of MI will seem quite different to parents. Educators need to help parents understand the rationale behind using MI so that parents accept and appreciate why their children are receiving a very different kind of education.

In addition to the ways parents are educated that have already been cited—Portfolio Nights, Specialists' Open Houses, formatting report cards around MI—we prominently display the MI model in our halls and in the classrooms. Believing that the halls should educate, we view this as an opportunity to help parents and other visitors learn about MI and why we value it so. A giant poster in the hall near our front door, titled "We All Have Many Intelligences," explains MI theory. Likewise, examples of students using all their intelligences to learn abound. Walking down the hall one passes three-dimensional Adobe villages, self-portraits, bar-graphs likening students' skin color to common foods, Venn diagrams showing what family members like to do on weekends, spelling tests and essays, and book reports that have been done as T-shirt designs. Music greets everyone each morning as they enter the building. Aside from highlighting our students' success, this array guarantees that someone walking in our halls is educated about the merits of MI.

Although all teachers should know what their students do on weekends and in the evenings, we felt it was even more important that we, believing in MI, have this knowledge. After all, this is typically when students work at developing their "other" intelligences (e.g., taking a karate class or musical lesson, joining Scouts, or painting in the basement). As a result, we took our first parent–teacher conference (typically held in

November) and moved it up to the last week in September, intentionally too early in the school year for us to have much knowledge about our students. Calling it an Intake Conference, we asked that parents play the role of experts and do 75% to 80% of the talking; teachers would be the listeners. I sent home some of the questions or issues that parents might want to consider in planning for the conference. Intake Conferences have been an overwhelming success, appreciated by both parents and teachers.

Collegiality

Another way that MI has had a positive impact on us is the way that it has supported the faculty's sense of "collegiality" (Barth, 1990). Barth defines *collegiality* as having four components: teachers talking together about students, teachers developing curriculum together, teachers observing one another teach, and teachers teaching one another. The single most important factor in determining the success of a school, he believes, is the quality of the adult–adult interactions within that school, its sense of "collegiality."

At New City, MI has been the vehicle for our collegiality. Certainly teachers talk about kids and how their various intelligences (their "intelligence profiles") help them learn. Teachers have also worked together to develop and share curriculum that brings MI into the classroom. *Celebrating Multiple Intelligences: Teaching For Success* (Faulty of the New City School, 1994), a book of articles and lesson plans about MI that was written collegially by our faculty, has sold 11,000 copies. Teachers have visited one another's classrooms, seeking out ways that others bring MI to life, and teachers have taught one another as well. In short, MI has not only helped our kids by valuing all their intelligences; it has helped our faculty work more closely in growing together.

SUMMARY

What began with a faculty reading group, going chapter by chapter through *Frames Of Mind* (Gardner, 1983), has become a schoolwide philosophy for us at New City School. We find MI a tool that helps us view kids through their strengths. It has had an impact on how we design our curriculum, present our instruction, assess our students, and communicate with their parents.

MI is not a panacea, of course. Indeed, one of the reasons it works so well for us is that it reinforces the biases we have always had: *who* you are is more important than *what* you know; all children have strengths, and it is the responsibility of educators to identify and nurture those strengths; and the aesthetic arts play an important role in school and in life. Whether these beliefs are held by a school faculty or by an individual teacher, MI can be used to help children develop their many talents. Simply put, using MI in the classroom increases kids' opportunities for success.

Implementing MI does not necessarily cost significantly more money. It does require adequate teacher time for planning, for working collaboratively and developing new teaching strategies and curriculum materials. Teachers will probably work longer and harder, at least initially, in using MI. But teachers will also be far more pleased with their efforts and, consequently, find investing the extra effort well worth it. Teachers succeed with MI too.

Because Gardner's theory is not an educational model, it is up to each teacher, or group of teachers, to bring MI to life in a way that reflects the values and culture of their particular educational setting. In this regard, other important strategies for school reform—teacher empowerment, site-based management, and collegiality—are all supported through using MI.

REFERENCES

Barth, R. (1990). *Improving schools from within.* San Francisco: Jossey-Bass.

Faculty of the New City School. (1994). *Celebrating multiple intelligences: Teaching for success.* St. Louis: New City School.

Fallows, J. (1988). *More like us.* Boston: Houghton Mifflin.

Gardner, H. (1983). *Frames of mind.* New York: Basic Books.

Gardner, H. (1991). *The unschooled mind.* New York: Basic Books.

Gardner, H. (1995). Reflections on multiple intelligences. *Phi Delta Kappan, 77*(3), 200-209.

Goleman, D. (1995). *Emotional intelligence.* New York: Bantam Books.

Goleman, D. (1995, September) *New York Times.*

Krechevsky, M., Hoerr, T., & Gardner, H. (1994). Complimentary energies: Implementing MI theory from the lab and from the field. In J. Oakes & K. H. Quartz (Eds.), *Creating new educational communities: Schools and classrooms where all children are smart: 94th National Society for the Study of Education Yearbook* (pp. 166-186). Chicago: University of Chicago Press.

15 PROBLEM-BASED LEARNING ACROSS THE CURRICULUM

William J. Stepien

Northern Illinois University

Important criticism of current educational practices can be answered directly through problem-based learning (PBL). Educators concerned with superficial treatment of complex issues and the general lack of explicit attention to problem solving in K-12 classrooms should consider designing PBL units that open with students meeting an ill-structured problem, using their reasoning skills to first understand and then resolve that problem, and building sizeable knowledge bases while gaining experience with real-world problem solving. This chapter establishes a connection between the goals of educational reform and problem-based learning, and then presents guidelines for designing and teaching PBL units across the curriculum.

PROBLEM-BASED LEARNING ACROSS THE CURRICULUM

Fifth-grade students are in the midst of a problem. In their role as highway patrol supervisors, they have been called to the site of a traffic accident that has closed the only bridge on the main highway through a small city. At the scene, the students find a monumental traffic jam caused by an overturned truck pouring a liquid onto the road's surface. There is a small sign on the truck with "Corrosive" written on it. The liquid from the truck is running into the creek under the bridge and causing a white cloud to rise from the water. The fifth graders have a problem to solve. What should they do about the leaking liquid? (Coleman et al., 1992).

High school students in the Cherokee Nation's summer program for gifted and talented youth also have a problem to solve. They must select a group of sites to commemorate important people and events in the history of the Cherokee people in eastern Oklahoma. In their role as consultants to their tribe, they will survey their history, identify people and events with special significance, visit the sites associated with each person or event, and design the commemorative plaques that will be erected at the selected sites. The students will also present their recommendations to the tribal council.

Elementary school students in Baltimore will also be making a presentation at the conclusion of their problem unit. They are designers of a new exhibit at a simulated zoo. The zoo will be receiving a panda from China, and the students have been asked to design an appropriate exhibit space. Along with investigating the habitat of pandas in order to decide what elements will be reproduced in the new space, the students have been told that the perimeter of the zoo will need to have a shape that accommodates the greatest number of viewers at one time. They have decided for themselves that each spectator will also want a good "line of sight" from wherever they choose to view the panda. What should be the shape of the perimeter? How much wood will be needed to build a fence along that perimeter? How can they best present their ideas to a real engineer visiting their class at the end of the unit?

High school biology students are engaged with a problem that has far-reaching implications for our global community—an ebola outbreak. They are in the role of United Nations medical advisors called to a small village in central Africa to investigate an affliction that brings high fever, flaming red eyes, and extreme bleeding to those afflicted. These students met their problem in the form of 14 paper "bodies" on the floor of a small hut (an available classroom), and they had to collect symptomatic data from each body, form hypotheses about the origin and nature of the affliction, identify the infectious agent, and come up with a plan to control the outbreak (Stepien & Stepien, 1996).

All around the country, K–12 students are finding more and more problems of the ill-structured variety in their classes and courses. These students are faced with problems that do not have enough information in them when first encountered to know what is going on so they must begin each unit with an inquiry into the issues and key questions in the situation they have been given. Their problems involve complexities that cannot be understood or resolved through simple formulas, but require the application of reasoning if real progress is to take place. As the investigators learn more about their ill-structured problem, the nature of the problem is likely to change, demonstrating the danger of building solutions before adequately defining the problem. Especially perplexing to the novice problem solvers is how to fashion appropriate solutions when important data are unavailable, in conflict, or involve competing value positions; yet actions need to be taken.

Students meeting and resolving ill-structured problems like the previously mentioned are being engaged in problem-based learning. Their teachers are responding to the call for school reform by designing units that help students construct significant knowledge bases consistent with the curriculum responsibilities of typical courses, while providing each student with an opportunity to develop his or her ability to reason.

The Need for Reform

The call for school reform is coming from both inside and outside the educational community. Whatever its origin, its messages are clear. Help young people become more productive thinkers. Prepare students for jobs that require problem solving, especially in small work groups. Develop the skills for self-directed learning so U.S. citizens can constantly "retrain" themselves for changes in the workplace. Prepare all students to recognize and be comfortable using the "habits of mind" of each subject matter discipline. Be sure all students leave school having constructed a foundation of substantive knowledge, organizing that knowledge around concepts and themes that foster deeper understanding and promote transfer, having investigated problems representative of each subject matter discipline (Gallagher, 1996), bringing an end to reliance on "bumper-sticker" thinking (Schriesheim, 1992) by citizens faced with the complex scientific, technological, economic, political, and ethical issues of modern life.

The goals for reform are based on study after study that raise significant doubts about the effectiveness of present school practices. The results from a longitudinal study of U.S. youth show that few young adults have the requisite knowledge to be considered "scientifically literate" (Miller, 1989) and that precollege education has almost no sustained impact on the development of the building blocks for scientific literacy, namely: (a) understanding basic science concepts, (b) understanding the process of science, (c) making decisions using information and skills from the sciences, and (d) understanding the impact of science on society (Miller, 1992). Furthermore, most of our young people leave science classrooms without ever being actually engaged in "doing science," putting concepts and skills into practice (Berryman, 1983; Rutherford & Ahlgren, 1990; Tobias, 1990).

The news is not much better from testing programs measuring achievement in mathematics and history. Scores on national tests indicate that students at virtually all grade levels are unable to apply mathematical concepts to real-world problems. In fact, one third of all 8th graders cannot solve problems that have more than one step, and half of all 12th graders "appear to have an understanding of mathematics that does not extend much beyond simple problem solving with whole numbers" (Mullis, Dossey, Foertsch, Jones, & Gentile, 1991, pp. 7-8).

Recent data from the National Assessment of Educational Progress indicate a similar situation in the teaching of history. About half of the nation's 4th, 8th, and 12th graders can identify important individuals from the United States' past, but only about 11% of the 12th graders tested could use historical examples to defend their opinions ("Few students understand history facts," 1995). Instruction in history has stressed the coverage of numerous historical characters, events, and concepts at a superficial level and paid little attention to engaging students with the complexity of historical issues.

Based on these and equally distressing data from other areas of the National Assessment of Educational Progress (Mullis et al., 1991), coupled with observations regarding the importance of problem solving and higher order thinking as necessary skills for success in the market and workplaces (Paul, 1992; Toffler, 1980) and estimates of the doubling rate of information in our world (Breivik & Jones, 1993), rethinking our instructional delivery system, as well as the subject matter content in our schools, should be included in any discussion of education for the next century.

In preparation for restructuring education for the next century, dependence on instructional methods that cast learners as passive recipients of inert information is under critical review (Resnick & Klopfer, 1989). A principle emerging from that review and the review of instructional practices across the disciplines calls for making students more active participants in the learning process, being responsible for: (a) constructing personal knowledge bases through inquiry and investigation that stress connections between facts, (b) using information to build concepts or organizing ideas, and (c) using information in a meaningful context in order to become more adept at transferring knowledge to new situations and more proficient at thinking and reasoning (Bransford & Vye, 1989; Rabinowitz & Glaser, 1985). Because problem-based learning explicitly asks for students to construct substantial knowledge bases through rigorous inquiry into ill-structured problems, deepen their understanding of important concepts as they hone their reasoning skills on real-world problems, and build their knowledge bases through experiences that foster transfer of information and skills to new settings, an effort has been made to convert this unique approach, used widely in medical education, to precollege classrooms (Stepien & Gallagher, 1993; Stepien, Gallagher, & Workman, 1993).

What Is Problem-Based Learning (PBL)?

Problem-based learning was initially designed for medical education when Barrows (1985) recognized that medical students typically graduated with considerable information but little critical reasoning skill to use it wisely. Three features identify problem-based learning: Learning begins when students meet a situation containing a problem; the problem is always ill-structured; and the teacher using a PBL unit is committed to coaching students, not directing them, through their problem.

Problem-based learning is initiated in a classroom when students meet a situation or scenario containing an undefined problem they must ultimately identify, describe fully, and resolve by way of an appropriate solution. The scenarios presented to students demand problem solving the way we use it in life: making observations, building hypotheses, defining issues, conducting searches to collect data, evaluating earlier hypotheses through critical thinking, developing solutions that fit the conditions of the problem, and justifying solutions based upon their likelihood to produce desired effects by way of ethical means. Students move ahead, hit dead ends, revisit data, revise their thinking, choose new strategies, and move on. In the process, the paths of the students' inquiries criss-cross domains of knowledge that relate to the problem, illuminating interdisciplinary connections between ideas. The apprentice problem solvers build substantial knowledge bases, enter into real collaborations with classmates, and gain experience in solving authentic problems through the application of reason. The steps of the reasoning process used to define and then resolve an ill-structured problem are shown in Figure 15.1.

The description of the steps for designing a problem-based learning unit that follows provides guidelines for constructing each component of a unit and an explanation of the implications each component has for what and how students learn.

Designing Problem-Based Learning Units

Problem-based learning starts when students, in the role of an authentic problem solver, meet a situation containing an ill-structured problem. The opening situation of a unit can be thought of as the tip of an iceberg, with

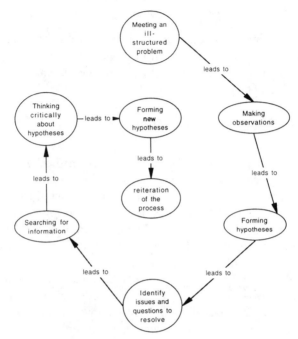

Figure 15.1. Reasoning used for the resolution of an ill-structured problem

the portion under the water's surface made up of significant and appropriate curriculum outcomes waiting to be revealed through investigation and inquiry. A well-crafted opening situation starts students on a hunt for new insights into the topics, concepts, and issues surrounding the ill-structured problem and provides them the opportunity to acquire and practice the skills needed to become more expert problem solvers. Imagine the opportunities for uncovering new information and refining reasoning skills when:

> Kindergarten students, in their role as photographers, are asked to resolve the problem of finding geometric shapes in the environment around their school and capturing those discoveries in photographs to be exhibited at a home-school counsel meeting.

> Fourth-grade students, in their role as biologists, receive a letter from an elementary school student who has found a brown furry "something" hanging under the eaves of the family's garage. The letter writer wants to know if there would be any problem with making the "cool" creature a pet. The picture accompanying the letter is clearly that of a bat.

> Seventh-grade students interrupt their reading of *Lyddie* in language arts to become members of a commission examining child labor in the Massachusetts textile mills in the early 1800s. The text becomes testimony before the commission.

High school students become lawyers for a community receiving an application for a parade permit from a hate group and must determine an appropriate response under the First Amendment; artists wishing to do a still-life in water color; playwrights creating dialogue for a short scene from To Kill a Mockingbird; and mathematicians asked to be expert witnesses at a trial where the issue is whether a trucking company is delivering the right amount of a chemical for an industrial process. Evidence involves the volume of an irregularly shaped storage tank and the consumption of the chemical.

Each of these situations engages students directly with an ill-structured problem selected by the unit's designer because it involves a process, skill, theme, or issue the designer wants students to understand more deeply. In addition to enlarging each student's knowledge base, the designer has crafted the situation so that students must construct their knowledge base through the use of reason to resolve each problem. The necessity to use reason instead of simple formulas to resolve each problem also provides each apprentice investigator with the experience necessary to move toward more expert use of problem-solving skills. Before considering the steps needed to construct an effective problem-based unit, an introduction to the four phases of activity that normally take place during a unit will help explain why the planning steps are necessary (Stepien, 1995).

The First Phase of Problem-based Learning—Meeting the Problem

During the opening class periods of a PBL unit, students explore the situation they have been given, building hypotheses that might help them better understand the problem they face. As hypotheses are built, students identify questions and issues that need to be investigated in order to expand their knowledge of what is at work in the problem. Their list of questions and issues, in response to the teacher's probe—"What do we need to know?"—becomes a blueprint to guide students in search of relevant new information.

A good example of building a blueprint for inquiry comes from the opening of a middle school science unit involving the protection of habitat for northern spotted owls in the Pacific Northwest. In their role as forest rangers at a simulated national park in Oregon, students are faced with trying to determine what might have happened to five pairs of spotted owls that have been nesting in the park for the last few years. This year's owl inventory team is having difficulty finding any trace of the owls. During the first class period of this problem, students look over maps of their park, read the owl inventory team's memo describing their search results, and then begin to form hypotheses that might account for the missing owls. The inferences in each hypothesis are supported with available facts. As students prepare hypotheses, they simultaneously develop a list of questions and issues to be investigated that will lead them to a deeper understanding of the forces at work in their problem.

Phase 2—Inquiry and Investigations

During the inquiry and investigation that follow the opening class period of a PBL unit, students increase their understanding of the issues and concepts in their problem by consulting information resources and receiving some direct instruction from their teacher or other mentors. A well-crafted opening situation requires students to recycle through the reasoning process until they are capable of defining their problem and then constructing and justifying an appropriate solution.

During the investigation of issues in the owl problem, students organized themselves into research teams around questions having to do with the owls' diet, migration patterns, range requirements, predators, nesting site criteria, reproductive habits, and reactions to conditions brought about by lumbering practices in the park. After two days in the school's resource center, where the librarian is ready to mentor the apprentice investigators in the skills needed to uncover and organize relevant information, students prepare briefing sheets for their classmates on each question they investigated, with the sheets becoming an assessment of each research team's progress.

Armed with their new information, the students are ready to reassemble as a large group and begin critically evaluating the hypotheses they prepared on the first day of the unit. During large-group discussion, students present data, revise hypotheses, conduct additional information searches around new questions, and are held to rigorous standards for critical thinking as they zero in on conclusions about the owls' disappearance. As a part of the inquiry phase, their teacher might even insert a laboratory experience around the dissection and analysis of owl pellets to help with the identification of elements of an owl's diet or show students how to mathematically model the life cycle of owls when they inquire about the owls' population stability. Once the components of the problem can be identified, the students' attention turns to considering appropriate solutions.

Phase 3—Solution Building

Each student is responsible for building a solution, complete with rationale or justification, expressed in a fashion that is authentic to the role the student has occupied during the unit. For example, the high school students mentioned earlier examining the First Amendment in the role of lawyers for a community facing a public demonstration by a hate group were asked to advise the mayor on the best course of action to take regarding the group's application for a parade permit. Each student wrote a memo to the mayor summarizing the constitutional and case law basis for his or her recommended action. The solutions were presented as memos because attorneys often use that form of written communication when asked for advice. Solutions to problems can also take the form of dramatic presentations, oral arguments, panel presentations, video productions, posters, or formal papers; but the form of the solution should always be consistent with the type of products created by the real-world problem solver the students emulate during the unit.

The same degree of rigorous reasoning should be used during solution building as was used to diagnose the problem. In the middle school owl problem, students treated possible solutions as hypotheses needing investigation just as they did during the inquiry phase of their unit, and they recycled their reasoning until they could defend solutions based on the feasibility and likelihood ethical consequences would emerge.

Phase 4—Debriefing the Unit

After students have completed building and presenting their solutions, a debriefing is conducted by the teacher to help students deepen and extend their understanding of concepts and skills encountered during the unit. During this phase, teacher and students review complex ideas, discuss insights into the problem-solving process, conduct self-assessments and assessments of small-group work, and focus on metacognitive skills.

The phases of activity during a PBL unit are summarized in Figure 15.2.

Beginning the Design of a Problem-based Learning Unit

The opening situations for problem-based learning units all start as creative flashes or inspirations initiated by a discovery in a textbook, literary source, curriculum guide, newspaper, or other source. Once a hunch surfaces, that some issue, process, event, decision, dilemma, or theme might become the focus of problem-based learning, four steps are used to turn the inspiration into a complete unit. These steps include: (a) mapping the potential concept and skill content for a unit, (b) constructing a role and situation to engage students with an ill-structured problem, (c) mapping the actual content of a

Figure 15.2. Phases of activity during a problem-based learning unit

unit to identify learning outcomes, and (d) visualizing the day-to-day activity of the unit in order to plan authentic assessments and identify resources students will need during their inquiry and investigations.

Designing the opening for a PBL unit begins with finding or constructing a situation containing a problem. In order to maximize learning during problem-based learning, the problem must be ill-structured. By their nature, ill-structured problems offer an ideal environment for students to acquire deeper understanding of concepts and issues and develop the skills to reason effectively, especially the skills of metacognition.

Ill-structured problems stand in bold contrast to the well-structured variety that are most frequently used to bring problem solving to the classroom. Well-structured problems come to students already organized, containing all the information needed for resolution when first encountered. There is little need to form hypotheses, gather information, or think critically. The teacher has already stockpiled all the necessary and relevant information for the students. Using the provided raw materials, students can find a solution through the application of a formula in which there is little doubt regarding the criteria for a right answer. Throughout the process of resolving a well-structured problem, the need and opportunities for reasoning are minimal.

In contrast to well-structured problems that offer students little mystery or complexity, ill-structured problems come to students messy, needing organization, with too little information to know what is going on when first encountered (Mason & Mitroff, 1981, p. 29). Simon (1978) and Barrows (1988) identify three characteristics of ill-structured problems that make them superior to their well-structured counterparts as settings for learning to resolve complex problems.

First, ill-structured problems contain numerous ambiguities and unknowns. Students must conduct investigations and use their powers of reasoning before they can define and then resolve the problem in front of them. Even after careful inquiry, solutions and their implementation may differ from student to student because important data may be in conflict, central issues in the problem may involve strong value positions, or the problem solvers bring different weights to the criteria for an appropriate solution.

Second, ill-structured problems contain so little information when first encountered that they require the problem solver to organize and conduct searches for relevant information in order to illuminate the issues and concepts at work in the situation. Because searches for information must be conducted, students get practice in forming hypotheses, identifying questions that will lead to useful information, and thinking critically about and with the newly discovered data.

Finally, both Simon and Barrows point out the importance of the ill-structured problem for providing students with an opportunity to become self-directed, self-regulated learners. Because ill-structured problems must be organized or "structured" by the problem solver, they offer opportunities for students to think about their thinking: to deliberate, reflect, and revise their reasoning based on the progress of their inquiry. For Barrows (1988), resolving ill-structured problems under the careful coaching of skilled tutors leads students toward more expert use of the reiterative reasoning process, especially in the critical skill of metacognition:

> Steps [in reasoning] may be performed rapidly and almost unconsciously, often with shortcuts, by the problem solver who has accumulated considerable experience and knowledge from the kinds of problems he deals with daily. However, when the experienced expert runs across an unfamiliar, complex, confusing or difficult problem, all these steps become apparent as does the metacognitive effort required. . . . Students must acquire, through practice, well developed metacognitive skills to monitor, critique and direct the development of their reasoning skills as they work with life's ill-structured problems; to critique the adequacy of their knowledge and to direct their own continued learning. (pp. 2, 3)

Table 15.1 summarizes the characteristics of ill-structured problems and the opportunities they provide.

Table 15.1. Characteristics of Ill-Structured Problems and the Opportunities They Offer Through Problem-based Learning.

Ill-Structured Problems	Offer Students Opportunity to
1. Are not tidy but messy when first encountered	Make observations; think creatively; form hypotheses
2. Initially lack the needed information for being defined or resolved	Identify issues and questions needing investigation; search for and organize relevant information; conduct experiments
3. Require elaboration, organization, and analysis through inquiry (reasoning)	Think critically with collected data; evaluation hypotheses; analyze; synthesize; practice the process of scientific or reflective reasoning
4. Are likely to change as more is learned about them through inquiry	Develop persistence and precision as a problem solver; recognize the tentative nature of conclusions based upon incomplete data
5.Require decisions even if data are missing, in conflict, or involve conflicting value; may be resolved through alternative solutions	Recognize implications and consequences of decisions; recognize the role of values in the construction of knowledge; analyze decisions based upon ethical appeals; build solutions that fit the problem's definition; justify solutions by their likelihood to improve a situation

Adapted from *The Tutorial Process* (pp. 28-42), by H.S. Barrows, 1988, Springfield: Southern Illinois University, School of Medicine; and "Problem-Based Learning from Traditional and Interdisciplinary Classrooms" (pp. 341-343), by W.J. Stepien, S.A. Gallagher, & D. Workman, Summer, 1993, 16(4).

Planning Step 1: Mapping the Potential for a Unit

Finding or building a situation containing an ill-structured problem can be frustrating for some designers and a breeze for others. Sometimes the stimulus for a problem jumps out from a source, and sometimes it does not reveal itself until sources have been surveyed with some care. Begin the search for a situation containing an ill-structured problem by examining sources such as those listed here, looking for signs that a problem exists currently, existed in the past, or exists in the fictional setting created by an author. Remember that a problem can be based on a skill or process for students to understand and apply, especially in the areas of mathematics, language arts, or foreign languages, as well as on an issue or controversy to be resolved as might be found in the social sciences, natural sciences, or again, language arts.

Sources to examine:	Things to look for:
Textbook topics and themes	Decision to make or that was made
Newspaper articles	Issue to be resolved
Curriculum guides	Concept to understand or use
Radio commentary	Puzzling situation or problem to solve
Literary works	Dilemma to resolve or was resolved
Mathematical topics or applications	Process or skill to understand and use
Children's stories	Moral or principle to explore
Television programs	Character in a problematic situation
Advertisements	Use of language; chance to analyze claims
Movie plots	Controversy to resolve
Journal articles	Discovery to understand or apply

As you examine sources like these, try to sense the existence of a problem. Ask yourself: Is there a problem to be solved by someone in this situation? Is this skill, process, or concept used in resolving problems? Could my students meet the same problem the character in the article or story met?

When a creative flash strikes during the examination of sources, examine its potential to be at the core of a unit by brainstorming its components with the help of a graphic organizer like the brainstorm map or web diagram. Creating a diagram of the content that might be encountered by students if they work on an ill-structured problem based on your inspiration will help you decide if a complete PBL unit should be designed.

A brainstorming map or web diagram is constructed by placing your inspiration inside a circle in the center of a large sheet of drawing paper or newsprint. Then identify the components of your inspiration, the concepts, issues, and topics that must be understood to gain a deep understanding of the idea in the center of the paper. Build branches of these concepts, issues, and topics radiating away from the circle in the middle of the page. Each branch should begin with a major issue or concept and include increasingly smaller concepts related to the major concept. The completed map will graphically portray the content and skills students are likely to meet if they are given a problem with your inspiration at its core. Figure 15.3 shows the general model of a brainstorming map.

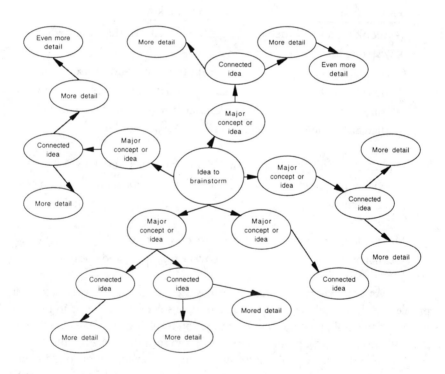

Figure 15.3. Model of a brainstorm map

Planning Step 2: Building the Role and Situation to Open a Unit

The second step in the development of a problem-based learning unit actually involves two tasks. The first is to develop a role for students and a situation through which they will meet their ill-structured problem. As you draft the role and situation, begin the second task, drafting a description or definition of the actual ill-structured problem your students will be responsible for solving.

Creating a role and situation begins with a review of the brainstorm map created during Step 1 of the design process. Looking at the information on the map, ask yourself (a) if the concepts and topics on the map constitute significant learning outcomes for your students, (b) if those outcomes are consistent with your curriculum responsibilities, and (c) if the content is appropriate for your students. If the contents of the brainstorm map do not fit these criteria, put the map away and find another inspiration. However, if you are encouraged by the information on the map, begin brainstorming roles and situations for your students that would put them into contact with desired branches of concepts and topics. Because your map probably contains more content than is possible to be covered through a single problem, you will need to select a role and situation that is likely to involve the concepts you want your students to encounter and steer them away from branches of lesser importance.

The brainstorming map for the problem involving the northern spotted owls is a good example of how important selecting a role and situation are for determining the content students will encounter during a PBL unit. The unit's designer began brainstorming the possibilities for a unit after reading a newspaper article about the impact of logging restrictions in the Pacific Northwest on state economies and families in timber towns. To protect the owl habitat, large sections of old-growth forests have been closed to logging operations. In the center of the map, the designer wrote "Owl controversy" and then began creating branches from concepts such as *habitat, population stability, endangered species, timber harvests, technology, specie characteristics,* and *politics.*

When the map was complete, the designer was excited about the content but undecided about the role and situation for his students. If he put them in a political role, a legislator, for example, the problem would turn out featuring the political content on the map and giving only minimal attention to the problem's science concepts. Because he intended to use the unit in a science course, he turned his attention to more science-related roles and situations. With this perspective in mind, the role of park rangers and the situation of missing owls emerged within a short time. After a number of attempts at composing the actual situation for the unit, the designer arrived at the concrete situation shown in Table 15.2, and then wrote the accompanying memo from the owl inventory team to help initiate the process of inquiry.

An important bit of advice must be given here. Care should always be taken to construct a situation that is concrete enough to be managed within available class time. Problems that are too big, too abstract, or impossible to be resolved within the time set aside for them are not effective settings for problem-based learning. For example, putting fifth-grade students, or older students for that matter, in the role and situation of planning a political candidate's campaign is a virtually impossible situation to use because it is so immense and complex, calling for information, skill, and time that are unavailable to students at almost any grade level. An issue of this magnitude can only result in superficial treatment by students and frustration at not being able to "get a hold" on anything concrete.

Table 15.2. Opening Role and Situation for the Owl Problem.

You are the chief park ranger at Spy Mountain National Forest. You find the attached memo on your desk when you arrive at work

SPY MOUNTAIN NATIONAL FOREST

Spy Mountain, Oregon

TO: Chief Park Ranger

FROM: Owl Inventory Team

We have visited each of the owl nests a number of times this week. When we get near each nest, we make our owl calls and play the owl calls on the tape recorder. There are no answers from the northern spotted owls. When we turn on the radio telemetry equipment, there are no signs of the five owl pairs we put radios on four years ago. We haven't spotted owl signs along any of the paths or logging roads.

When we started counting spotted owls seven years ago, we found six pairs and two single owls in the park. Three years ago we could locate only the five pairs we put radios on. Last year, we could find only three pairs with radios and a new single owl. What's happening to our owls? What do you want us to do next?

Smaller, more concrete problems involving political campaigns might make wonderful PBL units, however, and introduce students effectively to issues also found in the broader problem mentioned above. For example, putting students in the role of a political advisor faced with the problem of organizing a presidential candidate's last month of campaign appearances before the national election could introduce students to many important concepts regarding candidates and campaigns, but in a concrete enough fashion to insure an effective problem-based experience. For fifth graders, the problem might center on organizing the last month's campaign stops, taking into consideration each state's electoral votes, the popularity of the candidates in each state, and how many miles can be reasonably covered each day, even by jet.

When designing a role and situation, remember to match the situation and its complexity with the students who will meet the problem and the amount of time they will have to work on it. As a general rule, units always grow longer when handed over to students. PBL units seem to have a "yeast factor" in them.

As the role and situation take shape, begin to consider the second task in this step—building your own definition of the problem your students will face. Start by visualizing the role your students will take in the problem. Ask yourself: What is the central issue this problem solver would have to resolve, given the situation? In the political campaign situation, the central issue facing a political consultant would be how to schedule the candidate's time so that he or she would appear most often in the states with the largest number of electoral votes, recognizing that the need to visit each place is in part the product of the candidate's popularity compared to that of the rival. Notice that the problem definition is made up of a central issue ("Where should the candidate appear?") and a set of criteria that are necessary to accommodate through the solution. In this example, popularity ratings, number of electoral votes, and geographical separation are criteria or conditions that need to be taken into account if a solution is to be considered appropriate.

Some adjustments to both the role and situation and problem definition will probably result from completing these two tasks. As a role and situation begin to take shape, start defining the problem your students will need to resolve. If the problem is not the one you want for your students, adjust your design of the role and/or situation until it produces a problem appropriate for your students and your curriculum responsibilities.

Planning Step 3: Mapping the Unit's Actual Content

As you become comfortable with the role and situation you are creating, construct another map or web of the unit's content. Use the same technique described earlier, but this time concentrate on mapping the actual content your students will find in the problem. In contrast to the brainstorming you did at the beginning of the design process, the purpose of this step is to produce a diagram of the actual concepts and skills that will make up the learning outcomes for the unit. When you have completed the new map, examine it to be sure the role and situation you have designed will produce outcomes of significance that fit your curriculum responsibilities and are appropriate for your students. If you are not satisfied with the map, adjust the role and situation until it produces the map you want.

By adding a branch to the map for skills, you will have completed identifying the learning outcomes for your unit. Every two connected ideas (circles) are actually a knowledge outcome that could be worded beginning with: "Students will _____." Outcomes from the skills branch could be worded: "Students will be able to _____."

Planning Step 4: Visualizing the Day-to-Day Activity During the Unit

With the development of the role and situation, the content for the unit has been established. It is illustrated for you on your second map. Now consider how the unit will unfold, day to day. Do this by using another large sheet of paper and numbering each class session down the left side of the sheet. Then label the first class session "opening the unit" and describe the way that session will unfold, as you visualize it. Write only to the center of the sheet, saving the area from the center to the right margin for a second task.

After the first class session, some number of sessions should be labeled "inquiry and investigation." As you describe the activity during these class periods, the actual length of the unit will become more obvious.

At the end of the investigation and inquiry class phase of the unit, create and label a period of time for "solution building." This represents class time needed by students to craft their solutions, complete with rationale or justification. Describe the activity that will take place in class during the solution-building phase of the unit.

Time at the close of the unit will be needed for debriefing. Make a list of the issues that will probably need to be reviewed with students. Be sure to include examination of the subject matter, if necessary, and the students' performance as problem solvers. Probe student understanding of major concepts and their implications. Be sure to include issues pertaining to small-group performance, insights into problem solving in the real world, critique of resources used during inquiry, self-appraisals of problem-solving efforts, and evaluations of the unit and your performance as the student's coach.

When your visualization and writing is finished, check the number of days the unit will require and the activity taking place on each day. Ask yourself if this is a satisfactory unit, evolving over an appropriate amount of time. Adjustment should be made in the role, situation, and activity if necessary.

Now go back to the top of the sheet and begin a second examination of each day's activity. In the space remaining on the right side of the sheet, list the resources students will need for the activity on each day. This list will help you anticipate or prepare resources students need during the unit. As you list resources, also note class periods that might require some direct instruction on a topic or skill. Be sure to hold these sessions to a minimum; the problem should not become a disguise for routine discussion or lecture.

The last planning task to complete on this sheet of paper is to identify places at which assessments should be carried out. In problem-based learning, assessment is designed to gather evidence regarding student understanding of the issues in the problem and proficiency with the reasoning process. All the assessment tasks completed during the unit should be authentic, of a nature similar to those tasks naturally performed by the problem solver the students are emulating. Therefore, authentic assessment tasks should be designed that:

- Look and feel like real-world work, not like tests
- Involve higher-order thinking and reasoning skills, including metacognition
- Involve the use of rubrics to guide student performance; developed jointly by the students and coach
- Identify learner strengths, as well as areas that need improvement, and encourage self-assessment.

All the assessment information assembled during a unit is collectively referred to as the student's problem portfolio. Each student's solution to the problem, accompanied by appropriate justification and supporting information, functions as the unit's summative assessment.

To illustrate the variety of authentic tasks that can be included in a portfolio, consider these samples from the unit on the spotted owl. As the unit opened, students were asked to create hypotheses that might explain the owls' whereabouts. At the end of the first class session, the teacher handed students a list of the "hypotheses" collected from the chalkboard during discussion and asked them to find any statements that were not hypotheses. Those statements that were not hypotheses were to be labeled, more accurately—statements of solutions, facts, or pure speculation without any evidence to support them. He also asked each student to decide which two hypotheses seemed to have the greatest amount of evidence to support them this early in the investigation. Before class ended and the students left to complete the assessment task, the teacher and students decided on a rubric to aid in the assessment.

A second assessment was collected at the close of the visit to the resource center. Each student had to list five of the most important items discovered during his or her search for information and describe their relevance to the issue each was investigating. At the middle of the unit, a third assessment was used. Each student had to define the problem facing the park rangers complete with essential conditions or criteria to be considered during solution building. The rubric for an acceptable definition included (a) a clear description of the issue to be resolved, and (b) at least two sentences of explanation to accompany each important condition, of which there needed to be at least three.

An intermediate grade teacher adapted the owl problem for her students and developed an intriguing way to assess and display the information students were finding about their owl issues. She had her students create a diorama of an ancient-growth forest in the back of her room and place the information from their searches in the display. What was truly unique about this setting was that the display was almost life-size. Trees, shrubs, brambles, and downed trees, along with the snags that owls use for nesting sites, were built from scrap cardboard and assembled into a model owl habitat. When students talked about altering the habitat, they could actually move the elements around or remove them completely. Assessment of information being offered for inclusion in the model was completed by the teacher and class before it was allowed to be added to the diorama.

Teacher as Cognitive Coach

Two elements are critical for problem-based learning to be effective. A well-designed unit is the first. Use of *coaching* as the teaching style during a unit is the second. In the setting of problem-based learning, coaching should be thought of as teaching behavior that stresses direct involvement of students in the construction of knowledge and solving of problems. Coaching employs direct instruction as one tool for improving performance, but it relies more heavily on giving students practice in the use of reasoning skills so they can demonstrate strengths and weaknesses that become prompts for possible interventions on the part of the teacher. Most often, the interventions are in the form of questions that probe student understanding or ask for reflection on their practice. To explore coaching more fully, consider the following analogy of the athletic coach interested in improving the performance of his or her players. Which of the coaching styles described is most likely to better prepare players for their upcoming game?

The first coach greets the players as they enter the gym and tells them to sit quietly in the bleachers with their note pads and pens ready. Practice opens with the coach holding up a basketball and asking the players to describe what they see. The players are then asked to diagram the ball and label all its parts. They are next asked to watch the coach dribble the basketball, first with the left hand and then with the right. After repeated demonstrations of dribbling, the coach asks for questions. Because just a few hands are raised, the coach reminds the players that "dribbling" will be an important part of the quiz at next practice, and they should be more interested. Too many poor quiz scores could result in a poor grade, keeping those players on the bench. Participation is not much better as the coach shows transparencies of the plays to be used in the next game, so the players are given extra reading assignments that night to make up for their poor performance at practice. How is this team going to do in their next game?

Now consider the second coach's approach to preparing for the game. Practice begins with a review of what needs to be accomplished, and then the players are given the ball to practice plays they will use in the game. As the players run through the plays, the coach fades to the sidelines, watching each player and the entire group simultaneously. Everything seems to be going well, but wait, the players on this side of the floor seem to be having trouble with the newest play. Do they see the trouble? Will they correct themselves? A few more attempts produce the same results. The coach blows the whistle. With the team gathered around, the coach asks: "What should be happening on this side?" A player offers an observation. The coach probes deeper and then demonstrates a way to improve performance. The ball goes back to the team, and they continue practicing, building on the observations from the coach. Based on each team's preparation, which is likely to do better in the game?

Coaching students to be better problem solvers is very similar to improving athletic performance. Only so much can be accomplished by telling students what to do. When improvement of performance is important, students must "come down from the bleachers" and be given an opportunity to join the activity, experience the contest, practice appropriate skills, and learn how to adjust to game conditions. With this type of involvement, students are more likely to perform well at the complex task of resolving ill-structured problems during an athletic contest or when faced with them in the real world. Good coaching involves:

1. *Guiding metacognitive development*—calling attention to and helping students monitor, assess, and grow in the development of their reasoning skills
2. *Monitoring the progress of the unit*—being sure the phases of the unit and steps in the reasoning process are given appropriate attention
3. *Probing students' knowledge*—asking appropriate questions to be sure students are developing more than a superficial understanding of the issues
4. *Facilitating student involvement*—managing student participation when necessary to be sure everyone is engaged and learning
5. *Adjusting the unit's effect*—being sure students remain appropriately challenged, interested, and guided by the problem; adjusting the situation when necessary

The second basketball coach demonstrated behaviors that would also be appropriate for metacognitive coaching. The coach opened practice by reviewing the goals for the session. The players then began working on their problem (practicing the plays) while the coach faded to the sidelines, observing performance and letting the players gain experience with the plays. When a particular play began to break down, the coach intervened, probing the situation with the players, and then modeling appropriate behavior. As the players engaged again with their problem (went back to practicing), the coach faded once more. As practice continued, it is not unrealistic to imagine this coach managing each player's involvement in the session as necessary, continuing to intervene through modeling or even some direct instruction when needed, and adjusting the segments of the practice to match the player's needs. The essence of good metacognitive coaching, like good coaching in the athletic sense, is to use the context of the problem to help students deepen their understanding of the issues confronting them while helping them gain experience in resolving real-world-like problems.

Teachers and administrators searching for ways to meet the challenges of reform identified at the beginning of this chapter can choose among several different instructional options. However, only problem-based learning provides a system for curriculum organization and instructional design that gives simultaneous attention to both the acquisition of knowledge and provision of an apprenticeship in real-world problem solving.

SUMMARY

In problem-based learning, students meet an ill-structured problem head on at the very beginning of a unit of study. During their quest to better understand the issues that make up the problem and then build appropriate solutions, students construct new knowledge, develop their ability to reason, and gain experience in resolving real-world problems. As they wrestle with their problems, students learn skills and gain experience needed for self-directed, productive problem solving.

Planning an effective PBL unit begins with the identification of an ill-structured problem that (a) contains significant content, (b) fits curriculum outcomes for a specific course or program, (c) is appropriate for the targeted students, and (d) can be managed effectively by students in the time available to them. After locating an appropriate problem, curriculum designers need to create the role and situation through which students will meet the problem they need to resolve. As the role and situation are being crafted, a problem map is constructed to identify the concepts and skills students will work with during the unit. The problem map helps the designer identify the principal learning outcomes for the unit and visualize the flow of activity during engagement, investigation and inquiry, solution building, and debriefing.

Visualizing the flow of activity during the unit helps the designer anticipate information resources students will need to use. Being able to anticipate the activity that will take place during the unit is important preparation for effective coaching of the students during the process of making observations, forming hypotheses, raising issues, collecting data, thinking with the data, and acquiring metacognitive skills. With the help of the map and after visualizing the flow of the unit, authentic assessments are created, and the unit's time schedule is formalized. The unit is now ready to be used by students as an apprenticeship in real-life problem solving.

REFERENCES

Barrows, H. S. (1985). *How to design a problem-based curriculum for the preclinical years.* New York: Springer.

Barrows, H. S. (1988). *The tutorial process.* Springfield: Southern Illinois University School of Medicine.

Berryman, S. E. (1983). *Who will do science?* New York: Rockefeller Foundation.

Bransford, J. D., & Vye, N. J. (1989). A perspective on cognitive research and its implication for instruction. In L. B. Resnick & L. E. Klopfer (Eds.), *Toward the thinking curriculum: Current cognitive research* (pp. 173-206). Alexandria, VA: Association for Supervision and Curriculum Development.

Breivik, P. S., & Jones, D. L. (1993). Information literacy: Liberal education for the information age. *Liberal Education, 79*(1), 24-29.

Coleman, S. B., Gallagher, S. A., Bailey, J. M., Sher, B. T., Crouch, M. F., & Fettig, M. (1992). *Acid, acid everywhere: The interacting systems in an acid spill.* Williamsburg, VA: College of William and Mary, School of Education, Center for Gifted Education.

Few students understand history facts. (1995, November 2). *The New York Times*, p. 1A.

Gallagher, J. J. (1996). A critique of critiques of gifted programs. *Journal for the Education of the Gifted, 19*(2), 234-249.

Mason, R. O., & Mitroff, I. I. (1981). *Challenging strategic planning assumptions.* New York: John Wiley.

Miller, J. D. (1989, January). *Scientific literacy.* Paper presented at the annual meeting of the American Association for the Advancement of Science, San Francisco.

Miller, J. D. (1992). *The public understanding of science and technology in the United States, 1990* (Report to the National Science Foundation). Washington, DC: Division of Science Resource Studies, NSF.

Mullis, I. V., Dossey, J. A., Foertsch, M. A., Jones, L. R., & Gentile, C. A. (1991). *Trends in academic programs: Achievement of US students in science, 1969-1990; mathematics, 1973-1990; reading, 1971 to 1990; and writing, 1984-1990.* Washington, DC: U.S. Department of Education.

Paul, R. (1992). *Critical thinking: What every person needs to survive in a rapidly changing world.* Sonoma, CA: Foundation for Critical Thinking and Moral Critique.

Rabinowitz, M., & Glaser, R. (1985). Cognitive structure and process in highly competent performance. In F. D. Horowitz & M. O'Brien (Eds.), *The gifted and talented: Developmental perspectives* (pp. 75-98). Washington, DC: American Psychological Association.

Resnick, L. B., & Klopfer, L. E. (1989). Toward the thinking curriculum. In L. B. Resnick & L. E. Klopfer (Eds.), *Toward the thinking curriculum: Current cognitive research* (pp. 8-29). Alexandria, VA: Association for Supervision and Curriculum Development.

Rutherford, F. J., & Ahlgren, A. (1990). *Science for all Americans.* New York: Basic Books.

Schriesheim, A. (1992, September 29). Science is not "bumper-sticker" simple [Editorial]. *Chicago Tribune.*

Simon, H. A. (1978). Information-processing theory of human problem solving. In W. K. Estes (Eds.), *Handbook of learning and cognitive processes: Vol. 5. Human information processing*. Hillsdale, NJ: Erlbaum.

Stepien, W. J. (1995). *Designing problem-based instructional materials*. DeKalb: Northern Illinois University, Center for Governmental Studies.

Stepien, W. J., & Gallagher, S. A. (1993). Problem-based learning: As authentic as it gets. *Educational Leadership, 50*(7), 25-29.

Stepien, W. J., Gallagher, S. A., & Workman, D. (1993). Problem-based learning in traditional and interdisciplinary classrooms. *Journal for the Education of the Gifted, 16*(4), 5-17.

Stepien, W. J., & Stepien, B. W. (1996). *The affliction*. DeKalb: Northern Illinois University, Center for Governmental Studies.

Tobias, S. (1990). *They're not dumb, they're different: Stalking the second tier*. Tucson, AZ: Research Corporation.

Toffler, A. (1980). *The third wave*. New York: Bantam.

Author Index

Subject Index